In Your Greenhouse with Percy Thrower

In Your Greenhouse with Percy Thrower

Line drawings by Norman Barber

Hamlyn: London · New York · Sydney · Toronto

Contents

Published by
The Hamlyn Publishing Group Limited,
Bridge House, 69 London Road,
Twickenham, Middlesex, England

Filmset in Great Britain by
Filmtype Services Limited, Scarborough
Printed in The Canary Islands by
Litografia A. Romero, S.A. Santa Cruz
de Tenerife DLTF 27-74

First Published by W.H. and L. Collingridge
Limited in 1963
Revised edition published in 1972
Seventeenth impression, 1987
© Percy Thrower and The Hamlyn Publishing
Group Limited, 1963, 1972

ISBN 0 600 34839 3

Colour Illustrations

ACKNOWLEDGEMENTS
The Editor would like to thank
Amateur Gardening, Robert Corbin, Anthony
Huxley, Elsa Megson, Sheila Orme and
Harry Smith for the photographs used in
this book.

Introduction

The cultivation of plants in a greenhouse is one of the most fascinating branches of gardening and there can be few gardeners who have not, at some time or another, had the desire to grow plants under glass. In this new edition of my book, greatly enlarged and completely re-illustrated, I have endeavoured to show what greenhouse gardening can offer and the wide range of beautiful plants which can be grown.

To be successful, however, one must create conditions within the greenhouse which are as near the normal for any particular plant as possible, bearing in mind that even on the warmest day a plant growing out of doors has its roots in the cool earth, with moisture rising up round its leaves, stems and flowers, and the maximum amount of light available. We should aim to create a similar situation in the greenhouse by providing a moist atmosphere, moisture in the pots (according to the particular plant's needs) and the correct amount of light and fresh air.

This may sound a tall order, for if one grows a fairly wide range of plants they are bound to have differing needs. Obviously everything we do must, to some extent, be a compromise, but the point is that it works if one follows a reasonable code of practice, as generations of gardeners have found.

With modern aids, such as those described in this book, it is becoming easier all the time to provide the correct conditions. Nevertheless, gardening under glass requires more skill than growing plants in the open. One has to control the climate by means of the heating system, ventilation and damping down, and there is much to learn about potting and watering plants and pricking out seedlings. All this may seem a little frightening at first but with practice and good instruction it is surprising how soon one can master the art of greenhouse cultivation. That it is immensely satisfying and exciting goes without saying.

Percy Thrower

Types of Greenhouse

It would be a very demanding gardener indeed who would not be able to find a greenhouse completely to his liking from the wide range that are now available. Between the cheapest and the most expensive models there is almost an embarrassing richness of choice.

I have something to say on this matter of choice on p. 14, but before considering this important decision (for even the smallest, most modestly equipped greenhouse will mean quite a bit of expense) it is necessary to discuss the different types of greenhouse that are on the market and the purposes for which these are most suited.

The Span-roof Greenhouse. The even-sided, free-standing, span-roof greenhouse is perhaps the most popular type for it allows the widest possible range of plants to be grown under the best possible conditions.

There are several variations on the theme but span-roof greenhouses with glass to ground level are, generally speaking, the most suitable for the average gardener. Such structures are ideal for edible crops such as lettuces and tomatoes and for decorative plants like chrysanthemums and carnations which can be grown in beds on the floor of the house. Span-roof greenhouses of this kind are also just as satisfactory for growing pot-grown plants on an ash or gravel base. The great advantage of this type of house is that the plants get the maximum amount of light. It must be said, however, that the plants are less easily attended to when grown at floor level rather than on staging. Also, the heat loss from a completely glass greenhouse is greater than when the sides of the house consist of a low brick or wooden wall.

If the intention is to grow plants on staging, then the span-roof house with low walls such as I have just described is more suitable. This type is the standard span-roof house with a door at one end and staging on both sides at the height where the walls end and the glass begins. A useful compromise between the two types already referred to is the design which allows for glass to ground level on one side, so allowing plants to be grown in beds, and a low wall and staging on the other side which allows plants to be grown in pots.

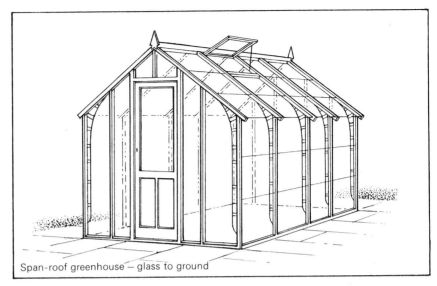
Span-roof greenhouse — glass to ground

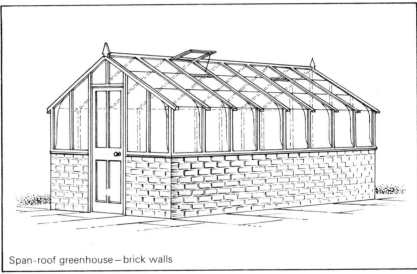
Span-roof greenhouse — brick walls

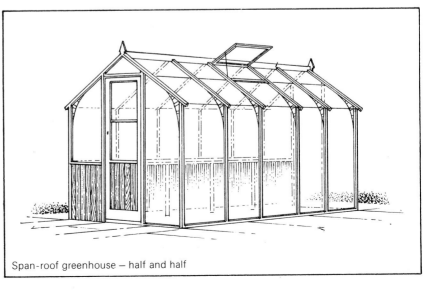
Span-roof greenhouse — half and half

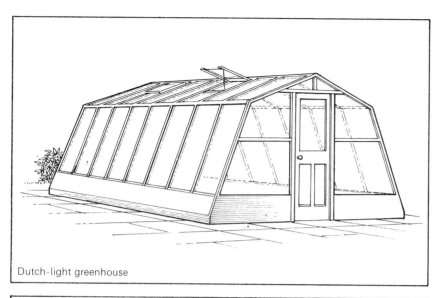

Dutch-light greenhouse

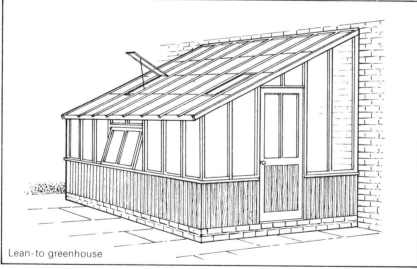

Lean-to greenhouse

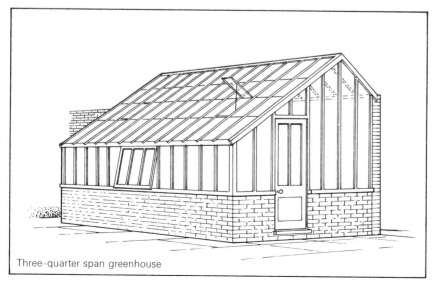

Three-quarter span greenhouse

The Dutch-light Greenhouse. This type of greenhouse is less costly to buy than others as it consists basically of standard Dutch-light panels which are fixed together to make a greenhouse. Such a structure is notable for the amount of light which is able to reach the plants through the large areas of unobstructed glass. Dutch-light greenhouses are ideal for those gardeners whose primary interest is growing tomatoes during the summer, chrysanthemums for late autumn and early winter blooms, and lettuces for early spring. This type of house is used extensively by commerical growers and in this case what is good for them is good also for the amateur gardener – but, of course, on a much smaller scale. The present-day Dutch-light house is much more draught-proof than its predecessors of even a few years ago, the lights fitting closely together to exclude cold winds, and the roofs are constructed in such a way as to prevent rain drip, which as every gardener knows can be as much resented by plants as draughts.

Another advantage of this type of house is its flexibility, for extra lights can be added to the standard unit to make up a house that will exactly suit one's requirements. (Perhaps I should say, too, that a certain amount of flexibility can be built into some span-roof designs, with extensions available for the standard units.)

Dutch-lights are made of softwood or Canadian Red Cedar. I would certainly recommend buying the latter, although they are slightly more expensive, for they last much longer and need very little attention.

The Lean-to Greenhouse. The lean-to type of greenhouse makes use of an existing wall, thus forming one side of the structure and cutting down on the cost of materials. As the wall will usually be a house wall there is likely to be some transfer of heat in winter which is another bonus. In many cases the wall will retain heat much longer than glass and the greenhouse itself will be less exposed to the elements than a free-standing structure.

The lean-to type of greenhouse is ideal for a south-west or south-east facing wall and the wall itself can be used to good advantage for growing a trained peach or nectarine tree or one of the many climbers or flowering shrubs which make such an attractive show when they are trained against a wall.

Like the span-roof greenhouse, the lean-to type can have glass to the ground or have a low wall or boarded base to the height of the staging.

The Three-quarter Span Greenhouse. This type of greenhouse, a mixture of the span-roof and the lean-to designs, is not often seen nowadays although it has many advantages. Greenhouses of this type are built against a wall like the lean-to greenhouse but in this case the house is higher than the wall with a short span between the eaves and the wall which lets in much light. Extra ventilation can be provided by fitting ventilators in this short span to the very considerable advantage of the plants. In some houses, indeed, the entire length of the span may be hinged to provide air as required.

The Circular Greenhouse. A newcomer to the gardening scene is the circular greenhouse. This provides more space for plants in a given overall area than other types of greenhouse. In smaller gardens where space is at a premium, this can be a particularly important factor.

The Sun Lounge or Conservatory. The modern sun lounge (an updated conservatory), preferably with access to the living room, has a value which is becoming more and more appreciated. Many plants which need only frost protection can be grown in such a structure and sun heat will provide acceptable sitting-out conditions on many days in winter, especially if there is a ready transfer of heat from the house through an open door or French window. It is quite usual for the sun lounge to remain unheated except in the coldest weather, when a small heater can be used to keep the temperature above freezing point.

Greenhouse Doors, Hinged or Sliding? Many of the modern greenhouses have sliding doors rather than hinged ones. These can be a considerable convenience if space is at a premium. A minor irritation with sliding doors, however, is that the base runners are liable to have their passage impeded by grit. All doors should be wide enough to allow easy access for a wheelbarrow as there are many occasions when this item of equipment is needed to move such things as compost, plants and flower pots.

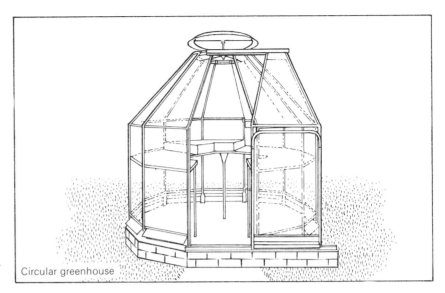

Circular greenhouse

Conservatories

Making a Choice

When choosing a greenhouse much depends on the site selected, the kind of plants one wishes to grow and, of course, the amount of money one is prepared to spend. All modern greenhouses, whether of wood or metal construction, incorporate the minimum amount of either of these materials to allow in the maximum amount of light. With this in mind the strong, lightweight, non-rusting alloys of which most metal houses are nowadays constructed must always win, but wooden houses will always, one assumes, be favoured by many gardeners who find wood a much more sympathetic material both to handle and to look at. The slim glazing bars and large panes of glass in metal houses admit a great deal of light – of special importance in the winter months – and maintenance work is minimal.

On the other hand, greenhouses made of softwood will need painting every other year if decay and general deterioration is to be avoided and they are without question more difficult and costly to maintain. The warmth and moist atmospheric conditions inseparable from the good growing conditions demanded by so many plants has a detrimental effect on unprotected wood. Greenhouses of cedar wood construction need brushing down occasionally with a teak oil or an oil sold specially for this purpose, but they do not need painting. However, their higher price must not be forgotten.

Perhaps it would be helpful if I described briefly my own four greenhouses and what I use them for. My 16 ft. by 8 ft. light alloy greenhouse is divided into two sections, one being kept at a high temperature for the cultivation of those plants needing such conditions during the winter and the other section being reserved for plants needing cooler conditions. In this way heating costs are kept down. This is an arrangement which would suit many amateur gardeners for it greatly widens the range of plants that can be grown, thus creating a greater challenge for the gardener.

My second greenhouse is of cedar wood construction, measures 13 ft. by 8 ft. and is double glazed. This double glazing reduces the cost of heating to less than 50 per cent. of that expended on the metal greenhouse. Because of the high cost of manufacturing these double-glazed greenhouses they are not, unfortunately, on sale any longer but the same effect can be achieved by lining an ordinary greenhouse with thin polythene sheeting available for this purpose. This greenhouse has glass to the ground and one side is used for growing tomatoes during the summer months and chrysanthemums during the winter. Hippeastrums and orchids enjoy the shade under the tomatoes in the summer months, while on the opposite side of the house pelargoniums (geraniums), begonias, fuchsias, impatiens and other flowering plants are grown.

The third greenhouse, measuring 20 ft. by 10 ft., is of the Dutch-light type and represents, I think, the best value for money at the present time. Made of cedar wood and with glass to the ground I have fitted it up with an ash bed on one side for the ring culture of tomatoes and for the accommodation of pot-grown chrysanthemums in the winter months, and on the other side with staging which allows a wide variety of plants to be grown both on and underneath the staging.

The fourth greenhouse, 18 ft. by 8 ft., is of the lean-to kind against a west-facing wall. This is constructed from a mixture of oak and metal and I use it to grow fan-trained peach trees on the wall with a vine growing along the top of the structure. Perpetual-flowering carnations grown in pots on staging facing the peaches provide flowers for cutting throughout the year.

One final piece of advice to all prospective greenhouse owners: do make an effort to visit a centre where greenhouses are displayed before making your final choice. Just walking around a greenhouse and observing its special features can tell you more in a few minutes than many hours of browsing over catalogues. An observant eye will soon spot the strengths and weaknesses of particular models and it will then be possible to relate them to the job you want them to fulfill.

Erecting a greenhouse. **1.** First, the foundations must be constructed with the aid of wooden shuttering and concrete. **2.** Carriage bolts are used to secure the sides and ends of the greenhouse. These can be tapped into position with a hammer. **3.** When the sides and ends have been erected, the roof must be slid into place. Several people may be needed to help with this operation.

Siting and Erecting a Greenhouse

There often seems to be some doubt as to whether a greenhouse should be sited north to south or east to west. In practice I find that this makes little difference. I consider it more important to site the greenhouse so that it fits in with one's other gardening plans: the plants are then positioned in the greenhouse so that their requirements are most nearly matched. Obviously, those plants requiring the maximum amount of sunshine will be placed on the south side, if this can be managed, and those needing less light on the north side. When the sides of the house run east to west then there will be more equable light conditions – but it is really a case of swings and roundabouts.

What is more important is to have the greenhouse near the house or garage so that water and electricity supplies are easily laid on without too much expense, or if the greenhouse is sited elsewhere in the garden, to make sure that both these services are near to hand. Laying electricity cable, in particular, is liable to be expensive for a trained electrician must do this job. If heating is by oil, electricity is needed for the burner and the thermostatic control, and with gas heating, too, the thermostat is run by electricity.

Erecting any structure, let alone a greenhouse with lots of glazing, may not be everybody's idea of fun but as in many other areas nowadays 'do it yourself' is a real money saver. It is possible to get a

4. Each piece of the roof is screwed in securely before the next piece is added

manufacturer to erect a greenhouse for you of any size or pattern desired, but the 'made to order' house is inevitably more expensive than one obtained in standard-sized sections for erecting oneself. Indeed, this is the way most greenhouses are bought nowadays and with the instructions provided by the manufacturer this is nothing like so difficult a task as might be imagined.

The house I am going to use as an example of the processes of erecting consists of the sections of two standard houses bolted together end to end. One is glazed to ground level on one side only and the other, a little shorter, boarded to a height of $2\frac{1}{2}$ ft. all round. The end section is omitted from the longer house, being replaced by the door section of the shorter one. In this way a double greenhouse with a dividing partition is obtained, and one compartment can be kept at a different temperature to the other if so desired.

First, a good foundation is made with concrete prepared with 4 parts all-in ballast to 1 part cement, this being thoroughly mixed dry and then mixed again with water to the consistency of stiff porridge. I do not consider it necessary to cover the whole of the greenhouse floor with concrete. In addition to the base on which the framework of the house will stand, all that is needed is a concrete slab path down the centre of the house with ashes or gravel on either side on which plants can be stood. Gravel or ash under the staging rather than bare soil helps to keep the house clean and in addition to being a good standing place for plants can be used to store such things as dahlia tubers and gladioli corms. Even if the house has a soil bed for growing tomatoes,

Putty is worked down the rebates of the glazing bars before the glass is positioned. Alternatively, glazing tape may be used

Glazing sprigs hold the glass down. These are tapped into position using the edge of an old chisel and a small hammer

lettuces and so on, a solid path which can be washed down is an advantage.

The foundations are shaped by shuttering of 6-in planks spaced 6 in. apart. When the concrete is thoroughly dry, bitumen damp-proof course is rolled out on top of it. One side section and one door section are placed in position and carriage bolts driven through the holes prepared by the makers. For extra stability further bolts are partly sunk in the concrete so that they can project through holes made in the base plates and be secured. In this way the complete structure is bolted down to the foundation.

When the side, end and door sections are in position, the roof sections can be slid into place. These are screwed to the side, end and middle sections.

Glazing can be done with one of the putty-impregnated glazing tapes now available or with plain putty worked evenly down the rebates in the glazing bars. Glazing tape has the merit of being quick and easy but whichever method is used the glass will be firmly secured if the job is done correctly. Glazing sprigs are now driven in to hold the glass down. This is most easily done by holding a piece of flat metal, such as an old chisel, against the sprig and striking the metal with a light hammer. Finally the putty is worked well down into any crevices and the surplus removed. All glazing should be done working backwards from one end of the house to the other, one strip from bottom to ridge being completed at a time.

As I have already remarked, manufacturers provide full instructions on the erection of their greenhouses; these notes merely give an indication of the processes involved.

Greenhouse Equipment

An extremely wide range of equipment is available for greenhouses, some essential and the rest aiming, in one way or another, to make life easier for the gardener. Naturally, we all have our own ideas about what equipment is worth spending money on and what can be done without. My intention now is to briefly outline the most essential and interesting component parts of a greenhouse and related ancillary equipment, defining their role in the scheme of things.

There is certain basic equipment for which every greenhouse gardener will feel a need. For example, staging (even a greenhouse in which the plants are normally grown in beds, can benefit at times from the erection of portable staging), a well-balanced watering-can and, possibly, a water tank, with mains supply. There are few things more irksome than having to carry water from the home to the greenhouse day in day out. A professionally installed supply of electricity is important, too, not only for providing lighting so that work can continue in the greenhouse after dark, particularly on winter evenings, but also to provide power for the many pieces of electrical equipment that are now available for greenhouse use. Ventilators and shading devices are extremely important, but these are described in detail in a chapter of their own on p. 125.

Staging. As I have already said, staging is not always required in the greenhouse, for some crops, such as tomatoes, are best grown on the ground or in rings of prepared soil (for details of ring culture

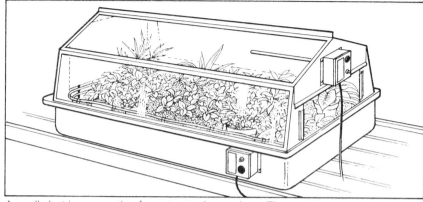

A small electric propagating frame to stand on the greenhouse staging is an invaluable piece of equipment for raising seeds and cuttings. The rod thermostat in this particular model ensures that the correct temperature is maintained

Above: A mist propagator greatly facilitates the rooting of cuttings, and is a boon for the busy gardener. **Below:** Staging can be made of various materials. Here, the top drawings show wooden slats, and the lower one corrugated asbestos covered with gravel. Tiered staging is particularly useful when an attractive display is required in the greenhouse

see p. 108) standing on a bed of ashes or gravel. But staging is convenient for the cultivation of many pot plants and, if it can be screwed or bolted together, it can be removed from the house when necessary.

Staging can be either open, i.e. made of wooden slats, with air spaces between, or closed, i.e. made of asbestos sheeting, concrete or other solid substance usually covered with a layer of gravel or small stone chippings to hold moisture. Open staging causes dry air to circulate around the plants and does not usually provide such a good growing atmosphere for them. For most purposes staging at one height, usually about 2 ft. above ground level, is convenient but in wider greenhouses or where displays of plants are to be arranged, it is sometimes convenient to have tiered staging at several levels.

Insulating Materials. The amount of artificial heat needed to maintain a greenhouse at any desired temperature can be reduced by proper insulation of the side walls and the glass area (with clear

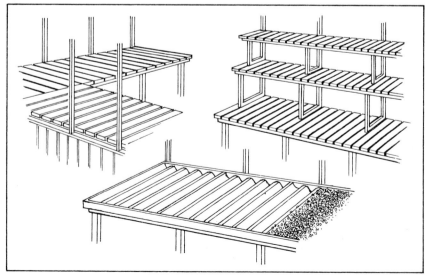

polythene sheeting) and by eliminating all cracks through which cold air may enter or warm air escape. Wooden-sided houses are particularly in need of extra insulation and this may be done with glass wool, asbestos packing or any other heat-insulating material.

Lengths of glass fibre, the kind used by builders for insulation, may be placed against the wood on the inside of the house. They can then be held in place with pieces of asbestos-cement sheet cut to fit. These add further to the insulation and also protect the woodwork from water.

If the greenhouse is lined with clear polythene sheeting during the winter months this gives the effect of double glazing and can reduce the cost of heating the house by almost half. It can be fixed in position very easily with a stapler, placing a piece of strong paper between the stapler and the polythene to avoid tearing. The polythene is stapled or otherwise fixed (drawing pins or tacks can be used) onto the glazing bars, running up and down these rather than across. In this way condensation runs down to the eaves rather than dropping onto the plants. It should not be placed over the ventilators. Naturally, it does reduce the light factor within the house to some extent and this must be balanced against the saving in fuel.

Propagating Frame. A small propagating frame to stand on the greenhouse staging, with soil-warming cables in the sand-covered base and air-warming cables round the sides, is of the greatest value. In such a frame it is possible to maintain a minimum temperature of 16 to 18°C. (60 to 65°F.) for a cost of about 10p. a week. I use such a frame for rooting cuttings such as carnations and chrysanthemums, and even more for seed germination in spring. The great advantage of a propagating frame is that the temperature necessary for plant increase does not have to be maintained in the greenhouse as a whole. Fully automatic models are available with a thermostat giving a wide range of temperature options. It will be readily understood how much more scope such a unit gives the gardener in terms of extended propagating seasons and general interest.

Mist Propagation Unit. A more ambitious aid to propagation is what is known as

A trickle watering system releases water automatically at set intervals from outlet nozzles along its length. The nozzles can supply water directly to the pots, or they can rest on a bed of sand so that the plants receive water by capillary action

a mist propagator, a device which has made it so very much easier to root cuttings of shrubs of many different kinds (some notoriously difficult to root by other means) and other plants. Like so many other ingenious pieces of equipment it is more simple than might be imagined. Basically the unit consists of a device which ensures that the leaves of cuttings are kept permanently moist by subjecting them to a fine mist spray either at set intervals or when moisture evaporation activates a water valve. Further details of this equipment are given on p. 119. Such a unit is normally set up on the greenhouse staging over a bed of sand or other rooting medium. Soil-warming cables are threaded through the bed and can be thermostatically controlled to provide a temperature of about 18 to 21°C. (65 to 70°F.).

Capillary Bench Watering. This method of watering ensures that pot plants get water automatically, when they need it and in quantities appropriate to their needs. The value of this equipment to the busy gardener needs no emphasising. Again, the system of operation is notable for its simplicity.

Water is supplied from a feed tank or large jar (see illustration on p. 125) to a sand tray on which the pot plants are stood. The water is fed by gravity into channels beneath the sand and the height of the water tank is adjusted to ensure that the water level in the sand tray is just below the surface. The water supply comes from a tank connected to the mains supply and controlled by a ball valve, or from a large bottle which must be regularly topped up by hand. The plants in the pots take up water from their compost as they need it, and this in turn is replaced by capillary action between the compost and the wet sand. Plastic pots have a distinctive advantage in this respect over clay ones for their thin bases make it easier for contact between compost and sand, which is essential if capillary action is to take place. Clay pots, however, must have a piece of wick threaded through their base to connect the water supply with the compost. Water is only taken up as it is needed so this is a far more precise method of watering than the traditional way with a watering-can.

Trickle Watering. This system utilises a plastic hose with outlet nozzles at set intervals along the length corresponding to the average distance between quite closely set pots. The hose is connected to a storage tank which fills slowly from the mains and releases its water when full. Plants in pots or beds can thus be given set quantities of water automatically at determined time intervals. It is not such a precise method of watering as the capillary bench, but nevertheless it is useful for the busy gardener. Outlet nozzles which are not needed can be blocked off.

Watering-cans. However much use is made of automatic watering devices, there will always be a place for the watering-can. It is important that it should be well balanced, and the kind with a long spout enabling plants at the back of beds or staging to be reached easily is the best choice for greenhouse use. More and more plastic is taking over from metal in this field, and it will be generally agreed

A soil moisture meter or tensiometer tells at a glance whether plants need watering or not. It is quick and easy to use

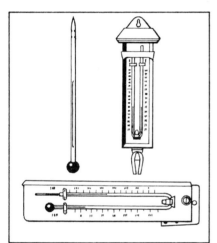

An accurate thermometer is essential for good greenhouse management. A soil thermometer (left) is used when sterilising soil

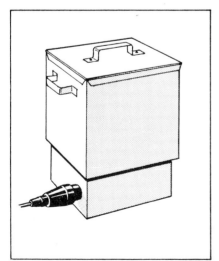

When mixing one's own compost, the loam should always be partially sterilised. An electric steriliser makes this an easy job

that its lightness, durability and, often cheapness give it a distinct advantage.

It is essential to have a fine rose attachment for watering newly potted plants and seedlings and for spraying plants overhead. A coarse rose is also useful for damping down and for other jobs where a heavier spray is required. For watering pot plants I would recommend a can of 1- to 1½-gal. size, but much depends on individual circumstances: how much water do you wish to lift, how far will you have to carry it?

Soil Moisture Meter. A tensiometer or soil moisture meter which indicates whether the soil is dry, moist or wet is a useful item of equipment. When a pointed probe is inserted in the soil a needle gives a reading on a calibrated scale.

Thermometers. Maintaining an equable temperature in the greenhouse is essential if plants are to give of their best. For this reason a thermometer is an essential item of equipment. The most useful kind is that which registers maximum and minimum temperatures by leaving a small needle in position as the mercury retracts. Many thermometers of this type are re-set with a magnet but the more expensive ones have push-button readjustment. A soil thermometer is useful for soil sterilisation, this being calibrated to include the high temperatures involved.

Soil Sterilisers. A small soil steriliser with which to partially sterilise the soil one intends to use for potting and plant propagation, is enormously useful. Several different methods of sterilisation are used but the best and most convenient is steam sterilisation with an electric soil steriliser

Presser

unit. These are compact and reasonably cheap to buy. If you do not wish to go to this expense, though, it is possible to do a good job with an ordinary bucket, standing this in a copper of boiling water. The idea is to raise the temperature of the soil to about 93°C. (200°F.) and keep it at that for about 20 minutes.

Flower Pots. I find it strange to think back to the time when we were told that plants would grow in nothing but porous clay pots. There was the introduction of the glass pot but that did not last long and we went back to clay; but now plastic pots have almost superseded the clay ones. This is not surprising considering the advantages: lightness, durability, ease of storing and cleaning and cheapness compared with their clay counterparts. I do not think that the plants are any the worse for the changeover and the pots are certainly much more pleasant to handle. There is one thing, though, on the debit side; we have to be very much more careful not to overwater. Plants in plastic pots dry out less quickly than those in clay pots, and it is very easy to cause waterlogging.

Watering-cans are available in various shapes and sizes and they are made in plastic or metal. A long spout is particularly important in a greenhouse so that plants at the back of the staging can be reached

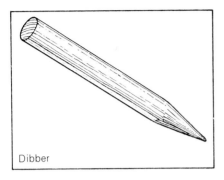

Dibber

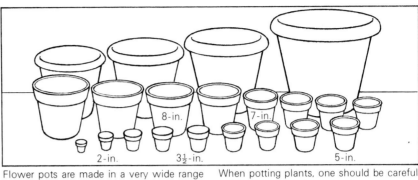

8-in.　7-in.

2-in.　3½-in.　5-in.

Flower pots are made in a very wide range of sizes, but the most frequently used are the 2-in., 3½-in., 5-in., 7-in. and 8-in. sizes.

When potting plants, one should be careful not to choose too large a pot

The accompanying diagram shows the sizes of flower pot available. The most frequently used are the 3½-in., 5-in., 7-in. and 8-in. sizes. The 2-in. size is useful for rooting single cuttings.

Seed Boxes. In seed boxes, too, plastic is rapidly taking over from wood. These have a standard measurement of 14 in. by 8½ in. by 2 in. .

A 'Presser'. This is a wooden block with a short handle which is used for firming and levelling compost before seed sowing. It can be easily made at home.

Sieves. For grading soils to the texture necessary for potting and seed sowing a sieve is essential. For general purposes a ⅜-in. mesh sieve should be used with a finer one for lightly covering seeds with compost after they have been placed in position. This last can easily be made at home from a small wooden box by replacing the bottom of the box with a piece of perforated zinc.

A Measure. There is no need to emphasise the value of a measuring cylinder or jug in the greenhouse. It is needed frequently for measuring liquid feed, insecticides and fungicides.

A Bucket. The uses for this simple piece of equipment need no explanation. In this area, too, plastic now holds top place.

Sprayers. Pest and disease control must always be at the back of one's mind for any infestation or infection in the confines of a greenhouse spreads very rapidly indeed. A small hand sprayer for insecticide and fungicide application is a 'must'. One that can be used for spraying the plants with water during the hot weather is also useful.

Labels. These are available in all shapes and sizes, in plastic, metal and wood. Which one chooses is purely a matter of personal preference.

Tying Materials. There are various

materials that are suitable for tying plants, and one or other should always be close at hand so that plants may be supported as soon as necessary. Raffia has been used for many years and it is reasonably priced. I find that it is easier to handle if it is soaked in water for a few hours before use. When tying small shoots, the raffia can be split and when stronger ties are needed, it can be doubled.

Fillis, a specially prepared soft twine, is available in various plys, and green gardening twine is also suitable. Split rings, the kind used for supporting sweet peas to their canes and small plastic- or paper-covered wires can also be used for greenhouse plants.

A Dibber. This is a small, wooden tool, rather like a thick pencil. It is used to prepare holes for cuttings and seedlings. The end of this tool can be slightly pointed, but if it is too sharp it leaves an air space below the cutting or seedling with, probably, fatal results.

Right: Liquid fertiliser and other chemicals should always be measured accurately. A measuring jug or cylinder provides the most satisfactory method. **Below:** A sprayer is essential if pests and diseases are to be kept at bay. Various designs are made, covering a wide price range

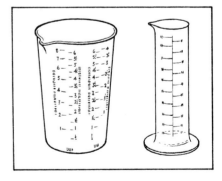

When mixing composts, the loam must first be passed through a ⅜-in. sieve. For seed sowing, a fine-mesh sieve is also useful

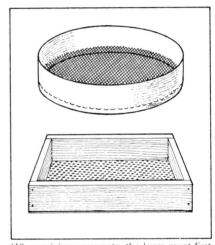

The Unheated Greenhouse

The unheated greenhouse is a valuable asset to any gardener but it is rather limited in its scope. The choice of plants must necessarily be restricted to the more hardy or those which need only slight protection during the winter months.

An unheated greenhouse becomes more useful if it is lined with thin polythene sheeting to serve the same purpose as double glazing. This certainly helps to keep out less severe frosts and maintain a higher temperature, thus making it possible to grow a wider range of plants. It is very important with this type of house to use the ventilators to keep the air circulating freely in winter. Nothing is worse for plants than stagnant air, which, among other things, encourages attacks from botrytis and other fungus diseases. Ventilation must be given throughout the year but obviously with discretion and intelligence in the coldest weather. Watering, too, must be done with especial care in the winter months for plants in unheated houses are barely growing at this time of year whereas their counterparts in heated greenhouses are in more active growth.

One should think of plants grown in an unheated greenhouse as being three weeks to a month later than those in a greenhouse in which a minimum temperature of 4 to 7°C. (40 to 45°F.) is maintained. Such plants will also be roughly as much time ahead of those grown out of doors. Leading on from this, I would add that seed sowing in the unheated greenhouse can be a great success but it is wise to make sowing dates later than those which apply to the heated greenhouse. For example, April and early May

is the best period to sow seeds of half-hardy annuals and these will provide good plants for planting out in late May and early June.

But if there are limitations, the unheated greenhouse can still be great fun. One of the best plants for such a house is, I think, the camellia. Camellias can withstand quite a bit of frost, but with the protection of a greenhouse they will start to flower in late January or February and continue into May and sometimes June. Evergreen azaleas will also flower much earlier than usual in such a structure as will lilac and forsythia. Hydrangeas will over-winter in an unheated greenhouse as long as they are kept on the dry side, to start into growth in the spring and flower in June, July and August.

Hardy annuals like clarkia, cornflower, godetia and mignonette are a good choice for spring flowering. Salpiglossis will also sometimes come through safely in an unheated house and in milder parts of the country so will calceolarias and schizanthuses. Many times, even in greenhouses with some heat, I have seen these last two plants completely frozen after a hard night of frost. They have been sprayed over with cold water while in this condition and have come through unharmed to flower profusely in April, May and into June. The range of plants which can be grown in an unheated greenhouse in summer is almost unlimited – pelargoniums, gloxinias, fuchsias, begonias and so on. They are started off in frost-free conditions in April and May and then transferred to the unheated greenhouse from May onwards when the sun's rays will provide sufficient warmth.

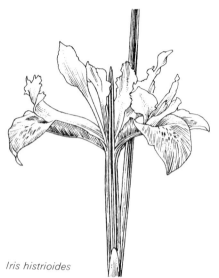

Iris histrioides

A whole range of early-flowering bulbs can be planted in pots and pans to make a splendid display in early spring. For example, the yellow Hoop Petticoat Daffodil, *Narcissus bulbocodium conspicuus*, the lovely cream Angel's Tears, *N. triandrus albus*, the rich yellow *N. cyclamineus*, the yellow and orange *N.* Grand Soleil d'Or and trumpet varieties like the golden King Alfred, as well as hyacinths and dwarf bulbous irises such as the deep purple, golden-blotched *Iris reticulata* and *I. histrioides*, a lovely rich blue marked with white and gold. Lilies like *Lilium speciosum rubrum* and *L. auratum*, the first for late summer and the latter for late summer and early autumn flowering, as well as the more modern varieties and hybrids, bring an exotic flavour to the unheated greenhouse.

Lettuces can be grown in an unheated greenhouse during the winter months if one of the hardy varieties such as Imperial is chosen. Tomatoes can be grown, too, if planting is delayed until late April or May. Tomatoes need a minimum soil temperature of 14°C. (57°F.). Strawberries can be grown in pots and these will be three weeks to a month earlier in fruiting than those out of doors. The Black Hamburgh grape does well in such conditions and if the house is a lean-to, a peach tree is ideal for growing up the wall. It is also exciting to grow apples, pears, plums and cherries in large pots or tubs. The quality of the fruit produced under glass is much superior to that on trees grown out of doors.

Double-flowered camellia

Narcissus Grand Soleil d'Or

The Cool Greenhouse

The cool greenhouse is one which is kept absolutely frost free and in which a minimum temperature of 4°C. (40°F.) is maintained. If the temperature is nearer to 10°C. (50°F.) so much the better for many plants, excluding annuals which much prefer a temperature nearer 4°C. This kind of greenhouse is sheer delight for the adventurous gardener, for compared with the unheated greenhouse the scope is wide indeed. There is no difficulty in having plants in flower during every month of the year. If you wish to make more practical use of such a house it is possible also to grow tomatoes during the summer months and lettuces during the winter.

It is desirable to have a small propagating frame in a cool greenhouse in which a high temperature can be maintained in the spring – say 16 to 18°C. (60 to 65°F.). This is used for germinating seeds of begonias, gloxinias, antirrhinums, lobelias and a host of other plants which are going to be grown on throughout the summer.

I have said that with this kind of greenhouse it is possible to have colour throughout the year, so let us now consider some of the plants which can be grown to provide a succession of colour and interest. If we divide the year into quarters, then in January, February and March we can have *Azalea indica*, cinerarias, *Primula obconica* and the most popular of all flowering bulbs such as daffodils, narcissi, tulips and hyacinths in bloom. The joy these flowers can bring in these bleak, often grey months will be readily appreciated.

In the second quarter, April, May and June, the pleasures are different for plants like the pelargoniums (geraniums) fuchsias, the large-flowered calceolarias and that most lovely of half-hardy annuals, schizanthus, (the Poor Man's Orchid or Butterfly Flower) are coming into flower. Also coming into bloom now are such autumn-sown annuals as clarkias, godetias, stocks and salpiglossis.

In July, August and September even the cool greenhouse can begin to look exotic with begonias, gloxinias and fuchsias continuing to bloom, and achimenes, *Lilium auratum* and *L. speciosum rubrum*, pelargoniums and *Campanula isophylla* all making their contribution.

In the last three months of the year there are chrysanthemums, pre-cooled narcissi, daffodils and hyacinths, abutilons, Zonal pelargoniums, Lorraine begonias, primulas and cinerarias in flower, and *Solanum capsicastrum*, the popular Winter Cherry, will be bearing its orange-red berries.

The perpetual-flowering carnations, or tree carnations as they are sometimes called, are ideal for growing in a greenhouse with a minimum temperature of 7°C. (45°F.) and these will provide a continual display of flowers throughout the year.

The cool greenhouse needs even more ventilation than the unheated greenhouse because of the type of plants grown in it. Most of these need a free circulation of air and can be harmed by too high a temperature. It is, therefore, necessary to use the top and bottom ventilators during the spring, summer and into early autumn, and the top ventilators should also be used throughout the year whenever the weather is what gardeners call 'open', that is to say whenever the air is not cold or damp.

Another point to keep in mind with this kind of greenhouse is that it is inadvisable to sow seed too early. To use tomatoes as an example, I would not recommend sowing seed of this fruit until the middle of March and then only in a warm propagating frame and they should certainly not be planted out in a bed or in pots or boxes until towards the end of April. Tomatoes give a better return if they are planted out later when the days are longer and the sun warmer. Generally speaking, most propagating carried out in a cool greenhouse should be done three weeks to a month later than that in a warm greenhouse.

An important environmental factor in managing a cool greenhouse successfully is that the atmosphere in winter must be kept much drier than that in warmer houses, and the plants must be watered with more care. During winter, watering should be done during the early part of the day rather than in the afternoon or evening. If the atmosphere in this type of greenhouse becomes too moisture laden or stagnant due to faulty ventilation then it is only too easy for botrytis to gain a hold on plants such as pelargoniums and fuchsias and be the cause of many losses.

If these cautionary words are heeded and your cool greenhouse is fully exploited you can be sure that it will give you enjoyment in full measure. If you turn to the Quick Guide to Decorative Plants on pp. 134 to 136 or refer to the notes on individual plants you will see how wide is the scope of the cool-greenhouse gardener.

Primula obconica

Daffodil

Lorraine begonia

The Warm Greenhouse

Having sung the praises of the cool greenhouse, which offers so much for a relatively modest heating cost, let us look now at the warm greenhouse in which a minimum temperature of 10 to 13°C. (50 to 55°F.) is maintained during the winter months. Obviously, such a greenhouse allows one to be even more ambitious and to grow many more plants than would otherwise be possible. A warm greenhouse is appreciated more during the winter and early spring than at any other time of year.

Plants like the winter-flowering begonias, dracaenas, poinsettias and cyclamen can all be grown quite easily in temperatures ranging from 10 to 16°C. (50 to 60°F.). Some ferns are also suitable, for example *Nephrolepis exaltata*, the Ladder Fern. Bulbs, too, like pre-cooled daffodils and narcissi, and specially prepared hyacinths, can be brought into flower much earlier under these conditions.

This interest in terms of plants is very well worth having, and there are other advantages of a warm greenhouse which I shall refer to a little later. But one must be realistic and look at the obverse side of the coin before embarking on this form of greenhouse gardening. For instance, the cost of heating such a structure. If electricity is the source of heat, raising the minimum temperature from 4°C. (40°F.) to 10°C. (50°F.), the difference between the cool and the warm greenhouse, can quite easily double the heating bill. Also, although bedding plants can be raised quite easily in a warm greenhouse they

do need a second, half-way stage before planting out and this makes a garden frame far more necessary than is the case with a cool greenhouse. Bedding plants that have been raised in a cool greenhouse can be stood beside the house in the open to completely harden off before planting out.

On the credit side it is much easier to maintain plants during the winter months in a warm greenhouse without the likelihood of botrytis taking its toll. Also, watering need not be done with the same care in winter time as in houses with less heating or none at all. A warm propagating frame such as I have suggested for the cool and unheated greenhouses is unnecessary in this kind of greenhouse.

Plants grown in a warm greenhouse need more or less the same treatment as those in a cool greenhouse during spring and summer, e.g. free ventilation, shading (particularly where such plants as begonias are grown) and plenty of moisture in the atmosphere.

It is not essential to give melons warm greenhouse conditions but they are easier to grow in this way, provided a warm, humid atmosphere is maintained, and they will mature much earlier. Strawberries in pots can be carrying ripe fruit in late March and early April whereas in a cool greenhouse it would be late April or early May before the first fruits begin to ripen. The same applies to a trained peach or nectarine tree grown on the wall of a lean-to greenhouse.

It is almost impossible to grow codi-

aeums (crotons) of any size or value in a cool greenhouse but these highly decorative foliage plants can be grown most successfully in a warm house. Other plants which can be grown well in the warm greenhouse are allamanda, the greenhouse climber with lovely yellow flowers, streptocarpus, and the trailing columnea which is ideal for a hanging basket. Exotic orchids such as cattleyas and paphiopedilums, can be quite easily grown in a warm greenhouse, provided they are given the correct compost and sufficient moisture during their growing season.

A mist propagation unit is a very useful aid in the warm greenhouse with soil-warming cables maintaining the temperature of the bed beneath the propagator at 18 to 21°C. (65 to 70°F.). This fascinating item of equipment has been with us for a good many years now but not so long that one cannot remember how much more difficult many plants were to increase from cuttings before its introduction.

To sum up then, a warm greenhouse is going to cost you more to run than a cool greenhouse but it will be a considerably easier proposition to provide the right growing conditions for a good many plants. In a very real way, too, it can be looked on as a method of extending one's gardening horizons. It would be quite a good idea to start with a cool greenhouse and move on to the warmer conditions when you feel you are ready to make the change. Again, for a quick check on the plants you can grow in the warm greenhouse turn to pp. 134 to 136.

Codiaeum

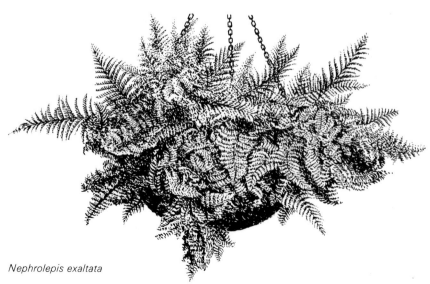

Nephrolepis exaltata

The Sun Lounge and Conservatory

In so far as the plants which are grown in them are the same, the sun lounge and conservatory are virtually synonymous, but of course there are certain differences which make the use of the two terms meaningful. The term sun lounge invariably refers to a light, airy, very glassy structure attached to a modern house whereas the word conservatory is usually applied to the heavier structures (rather more wood or cast iron and rather less glass than in the sun lounge) attached to older houses. Moreover, whereas the sun lounge is very much a room, the old-style conservatory is likely to be very much more a greenhouse-type structure complete with staging and heating pipes. It is another case of changed fashions and different living patterns.

A sun lounge extension to the house can be a great joy. If it is on the south-west or south-east side of the house it becomes a sun trap and a place where all the family can sit and enjoy the sunshine when it is cold and windy out of doors. As my house is on a hill with open country for miles around it is possible that I get more pleasure from such a room than the average house owner, because of the shelter it provides.

But not only is the sun lounge an ideal place for sitting in, it is also ideal as a growing room for many plants, and likewise, of course, the conservatory. We have no heating in our sun lounge except on very frosty nights when we bring in a small electric fan heater. This keeps the temperature just above freezing point and allows us to leave Regal and Zonal pelargoniums, fuchsias and a fruiting lemon there during the winter months. Also there are various ferns and *Begonia rex* which look a little tired in the very cold weather but soon pick up as conditions improve.

The beloperone or Shrimp Plant, the variegated ivies and the tradescantias are other plants which I find useful for this indoor 'garden'. Foliage plants, such as *Grevillea robusta*, are ideal throughout the year. Coleus are splendid summer plants for such conditions, making excellent specimens with brightly coloured foliage because of all the additional light they receive.

Perhaps I should mention here that we have no shading of any kind for our sun lounge. If one chooses one's plants care-

A sun lounge makes a delightful addition to any home, for it extends the house into the garden. On bright days when the temperature outside is not particularly high, it makes the perfect place for sitting and relaxing

fully it is unnecessary and in any case the whole idea is to allow as much sunshine to enter as possible.

In fact, so well do many greenhouse plants grow in modern sun lounges that the tendency is to crowd too much in. This is certainly so in my case. One must always remember that this is a room which should be pleasing to the eye and the plants should be arranged as decorative features. In addition to table level displays, there can be the added attraction of one or more colourful hanging baskets, and

large specimen plants can be stood directly on the floor.

A sun lounge and a cool greenhouse may both be in your possession and in this case it will be possible to have a certain amount of cross movement from one to the other. Plants which need a little more heat than a sun lounge or conservatory normally provides can be brought into top condition in the greenhouse and then moved for short periods to the sun lounge. Such juggling with the available facilities greatly adds to the fun of gardening.

A wooden sun lounge, such as the one illustrated here, would be quite easy for the handyman to erect. The timber can be painted to preserve it, or given a natural finish, whichever blends in most effectively with the surroundings

The Garden Frame

The garden frame is the half-way stage between the greenhouse and garden and, as such, is extremely valuable in many ways. It can also be looked on as a substitute for, as well as an auxiliary of, the greenhouse.

Many plants raised in the greenhouse, but ultimately destined for the open garden must be gradually acclimatised to outdoor conditions. It is here that the garden frame comes into its own. In addition, a garden frame can relieve congestion in the greenhouse and be used as a place for growing plants on before taking them back into the greenhouse.

Frames of many patterns are available and may be made of wood (soft wood or cedar wood), concrete, brick, asbestos or metal sheeting. The traditional frame with a glazed and removable top (known as a 'light') of 6 ft. by 4 ft. dimensions is one of the most favoured, but the best and most convenient, in my opinion, is the kind with lights of standard Dutch light size, where the glass measures 56 in. by 28¾ in. Having one sheet of glass per light rather than numerous panes of glass with glazing bars to hold them in position allows the maximum amount of light to reach the plants – which, after all, is one's real objective, as well as providing controlled atmospheric conditions. Dutch lights are much more convenient to handle than the traditional frame light, which is an important factor to bear in mind when equipment has to be moved frequently. On the other hand it must be said that a broken Dutch light glass is more costly to replace than individual panes of the traditional type.

For the average-sized garden I would recommend a frame with two to four lights, four being the ideal – but, of course, cost must be borne in mind. If the frame is to be used for seeds and cuttings a front wall 12 in. high and a back wall 18 in. high will be sufficient but deeper frames will be needed if pot plants are to be accommodated. It will be understood that deeper frames are much more flexible in their operation than shallow kinds and that with their aid a greenhouse unit can be run with more efficiency.

By the same token, a heated frame offers more scope than an unheated unit, for with soil-warming cables below and air-warming cables around the sides, a

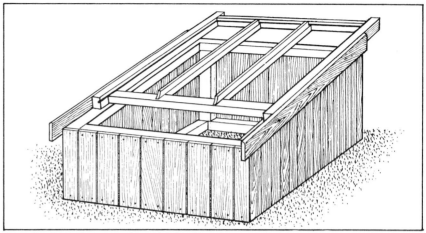

A garden frame is extremely useful for the greenhouse owner, for not only does it serve as a half-way stage between the green-house and the outside garden, but it also provides additional space when the green-house is crowded

frame becomes, in effect, a miniature greenhouse. If a temperature of 13 to 16°C. (55 to 60°F.) can be maintained, seeds of many half-hardy plants can be germinated in early spring or early supplies of such salad crops as lettuces can be produced.

Unheated frames are useful for hardening off greenhouse-raised plants before they are planted out in the garden in spring or early summer. They are useful for raising cuttings in at almost any time of year and for providing slightly tender plants such as penstemons and bedding calceolarias with winter protection. In winter, too, they can be used to house the stools of outdoor chrysanthemums. Seed sowings made in unheated frames can give an advantage of several weeks over outdoor sowings.

An unheated frame is also an excellent place to start off bulbs like hyacinths, tulips, daffodils and crocuses which have been potted up for later forcing in the greenhouse. Lilies and freesias grown in pots can also be started off there.

Cucumbers and melons are popular for frame cultivation and naturally they can be started off much earlier in a heated frame than in an unheated one.

If one wishes to start gladioli into growth early in boxes then the cold frame is the place for these. It is also suitable for raising sweet pea plants in before planting them out in April. Sowings of sweet peas can be made in an unheated frame in October, or in January or February in a frame heated to a temperature of 13 to 16°C. (55 to 60°F.).

These are only some of the uses to which frames can be put. A greenhouse is certainly a less useful item of equipment without them.

Lettuces growing in a Dutch light frame. Other crops which are suitable include melons and cucumbers. The large panes of glass are an important factor in this design, for they allow the maximum amount of light to reach the plants

An A to Z Guide to Greenhouse Plants

Abutilon megapotamicum, with its bell-like flowers on slender stems is an attractive flowering shrub to train against the wall of a lean-to. In a greenhouse the growths may be tied to wires stretched from one end of the house to the other

ABUTILON

A. striatum thompsonii

The abutilons (Indian Mallows) are among the most useful of all plants for the greenhouse and conservatory or sun lounge. These evergreen shrubs have attractive funnel-shaped flowers.

Abutilon megapotamicum with bell-shaped flowers on rather slender stems is the most widely grown species. It is ideal for clothing the wall of a lean-to or for growing on wires, to which the growths can be tied. *A. striatum thompsonii*, with orange-yellow flowers and yellow variegated leaves, and a more recent arrival, the red-flowered Fireball, are also desirable. Fireball will flower through most of the year where a winter temperature of 7 to 10°C. (45 to 50°F.) is maintained. From March to September a temperature of 16 to 18°C. (60 to 65°F.) is suitable. Abutilons do not necessarily need high temperatures and can be grown satisfactorily in a conservatory heated sufficiently to keep out frost.

Propagation. I find it best to raise new plants each year from cuttings, otherwise they become too large for the average-sized house. These are taken in spring, summer or autumn (made from shoots not more than 3 to 4 in. long) and rooted in a close propagating frame in a mixture of peat, soil and sand. Treating the cuttings with hormone rooting powder helps. The young plants are grown on in 3½-in., 5-in. and, finally, 7-in. pots, in John Innes No. 1 Potting Compost.

Species and mixed hybrids can be raised from seed. Make sowings in seed compost in late February, March or April in a warm propagating frame. The resulting plants will flower from June onwards.

ACHIMENES

With flowers in shades of pink, purple, scarlet and white, achimenes is an excellent plant for hanging baskets although it is more often seen as a pot plant. Its common name is Hot Water Plant because it is supposed to benefit from being watered with hot water. In fact, this is not true and watering can be done in the same way as for any other plant.

The Growth Cycle. The small scaly tubers are started into growth in early spring by pressing them into moist peat and sand in pots or boxes which are then provided with a temperature of 13 to 16°C. (55 to 60°F.). New shoots soon develop and the young plants can then be moved to 5- or 6-in. pots, spacing them 2 to 3 in. apart in the compost. John Innes No. 1 Potting Compost is recommended for the purpose.

Hanging Baskets. When making up hanging baskets the small plants can be planted on the top and also pushed gently through the sides of the basket so that eventually the latter will be completely hidden.

Watering and Feeding. Water sparingly at first but as growth develops it should be increased. As the roots begin to fill the pots, feed every 10 days with a soluble fertiliser added to the water supply.

The small, scaly tubers of achimenes are started into growth in the spring by pressing them into a mixture of peat and sand

The brightly coloured flowers ot achimenes are produced in the summer from tubers planted in the spring. These plants are easy to grow, and look particularly effective in a hanging basket

Allamanda cathartica bears its beautiful blooms throughout the summer. The glossy leaves are also a decorative feature

Staking. The stems tend to be straggly, and will need supporting. This can be done with a few twiggy sticks inserted around the edge of the pot.

Shading. Light shade should be given from strong sunshine, and to avoid a dry atmosphere when the weather is hot the floors and staging should be damped down frequently.

Resting. The foliage will show signs of withering in early autumn and at this stage less water should be given until the soil is quite dry. The tubers can remain in the pots and be left in a dry, frost-proof place until repotting time comes round again between February and April and the growth cycle is repeated.

Propagation. These plants can be increased in various ways: by seed sown in March in a temperature of 18 to 21°C. (65 to 70°F.), to provide flowering plants in the second year; by cuttings rooted in spring in a warm propagating frame; and by scales removed from the tubers and raised like seeds.

Varieties. Of the named varieties that are available I prefer Pink Beauty.

ALLAMANDA

A. catbartica

Allamandas are evergreen climbers with trumpet shaped flowers. It must be remembered that they need higher temperatures than many greenhouse plants with a minimum in winter of 13°C. (55°F.). The kinds usually grown are *Allamanda catbartica*, with golden-yellow flowers, and its varieties *hendersonii* with orange-yellow flowers and *grandiflora* with pale yellow flowers. All bloom in the summer from June onwards.

Allamandas can be grown in large pots filled with John Innes No. 3 Potting Compost or be planted in a border. In both cases good drainage is an absolute necessity. Canes pushed in round the side of the pots will give initial support, and they can then be trained on wires up the roof of the house or along the sides. While the plants are in growth they need to be watered freely but at other times only moderate watering is desirable.

Pruning and Propagation. Annual pruning will almost certainly be necessary and it is normal to cut back the sideshoots to within one or two buds of their base in January or February. The tips of these shoots are very useful for propagating purposes, an extra incentive for pruning. They are prepared in the usual way with each shoot bearing two or three buds, and rooted in pots filled with a mixture of moist peat and coarse sand in a propagating frame with a temperature of 18 to 21°C. (65 to 70°F.). When they have formed roots, pot them singly in 3-in. pots and John Innes No. 1 Potting Compost and pot on as necessary until they are in pots of 9- to 10-in. size, or plant out in the greenhouse border.

ANNUALS AS POT PLANTS

Celosia plumosa

There are a number of annuals which make good pot plants for the greenhouse, providing welcome colour from April until July and sometimes August.

Annuals need growing coolly and a temperature near but not below 4°C. (40°F.) suits them well. Too much heat must be avoided or the plants will become drawn and weak. The seed should be sown, with some exceptions, including celosia, exacum and nicotiana, in September and early October. These exceptions, too, have different temperature requirements.

Seed of those annuals included in the main autumn sowing should be sown in boxes of seed compost and germinated either in a cool greenhouse – on a shelf near the glass – or in a cold frame, preferably the latter. Water and ventilate the seedlings with especial care for the greenhouse can soon become cold and clammy at that time of year and damping off may occur.

The seedlings should be pricked out in 3-in. pots as soon as possible using John Innes No. 1 Potting Compost. The pots should be kept on a shelf near the glass during the winter, for good light is essential, and both high and low temperatures must be avoided. Move into 5-in. pots as necessary.

For a spectacular display, three, four or five seedlings can be planted in one large pot but they may become too large for the average greenhouse.

Some annuals are better when stopped, the tips of the shoots being pinched out when they are about 4 or 5 in. high to encourage the plants to develop a bushy habit, but most are best left to grow naturally.

My choice of annuals for pot cultivation is as follows:

Carnations (Annual). Among the annual carnations, strains of *Dianthus caryophyllus,* are the Chabaud Giants, with fringed, double flowers in an attractive range of colours which include shades of red, pink, yellow and white. They are sweetly scented. Pinch out the tips of the shoots when 4 or 5 in. long to encourage the plants to form a bushy habit.

Celosia. The celosias (Cockscombs) are splendid pot plants for greenhouse decoration. *Celosia cristata,* with crests of tightly packed flowers, grows 9 to 12 in. tall and there are dwarf strains like Jewel Box Mixed, only 6 in. tall. *Celosia plumosa* has feathery plumes of flowers which are very decorative. Dwarf Red Plume and Dwarf Golden Plume are only 9 in. tall,

but there are other varieties which reach 18 in. Colours include various shades of red, orange and yellow.

The seed is sown in seed compost in March and germinated in a temperature of 18°C. (65°F.). The resulting seedlings are pricked out into seed boxes of John Innes No. 1 Potting Compost, spaced 2 in. apart, when they are about 1 in. tall and are later moved into 3-in. pots of a similar mixture. A temperature of 16 to 18°C. (60 to 65°F.) is needed at this stage. By June they are ready for moving into the 5-in. pots in which they will flower. Watering must be done with care, particularly when they are young, and they must not be allowed to become dry or over-moist. The foliage should be syringed twice a day and the plants fed once a week with a liquid or soluble fertiliser when the flower buds first appear.

Centaurea cyanus. This plant is the popular Cornflower and there are dwarf strains which make good pot plants. These grow from 1 to 1½ ft. tall and include Polka Dot Mixed with a wide colour range and the blue Dwarf Double Jubilee Gem. Pinch out the tips of the plants when they are 4 to 5 in. long so that they form a bushy habit. Cornflowers like sunshine and dry atmospheric conditions. Grown three or four in an 8-in. pot, they are very effective in bloom.

Clarkia elegans. The double-flowered varieties, 2 to 2½ ft., arising from this species are excellent pot plants. Their colour range embraces purple, mauve, shades of red and pink and white. They are usually very successful when grown three to a 6-in. pot. Pinch out the tips of the shoots when 4- or 5-in. long to encourage the plants to make a bushy habit. Ventilate the greenhouse freely whenever possible.

Dimorphotheca. The South African Star of the Veldt is a delightful annual with daisy-like flowers in orange, apricot, salmon, and yellow and white. The *aurantiaca* hybrids, 12 in. tall, are beautiful and popular; others include the large-flowered Goliath, orange with a green centre, 15 in., and the dwarf Glistening White, 9 in. These also can all be grown three to a 6-in. pot.

Exacum affine. This is an attractive greenhouse plant, up to 12 in. high, which bears fragrant pale 'blue flowers.

Centaurea cyanus

Clarkia elegans

Godetia

It requires warm, moist conditions, with good drainage and shade from hot sun. Although a biennial, seed can be sown in March in seed compost in a temperature of 16 to 18°C. (60 to 65°F.) to provide plants to flower in late summer and autumn. Larger plants can be obtained by sowing in August and overwintering the plants in 3-in. pots. These are then potted on into 5-in. pots the following spring. Such plants need a temperature in winter of 16°C. (60°F.).

Godetia. These are excellent pot plants, providing a display over several months in the early part of the year. They include dwarf varieties and strains of 1 to 1½ ft. in height – especially suitable for pot cultivation – and others growing to 2 to 3 ft. Both double and single varieties are available in colours from mauve and red to pink, salmon, rose and white. The tips of the shoots should be pinched out when 4 or 5 in. long to encourage a bushy habit of growth.

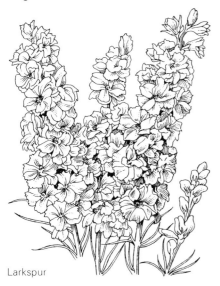

Larkspur

Larkspur. Included amongst the annual delphiniums are varieties of *Delphinium ajacis*, the Rocket Larkspur, 2 to 4 ft., and *D. consolida*, the Branching Larkspur, 3 to 4 ft. The colour range includes blue, lilac, pink and white. The smaller growing *D. chinensis (D. grandiflorum)* includes lovely blue varieties like Blue Butterfly and Blue Mirror. These are strictly speaking perennials, but are treated as annuals.

Mignonette. This plant, botanically *Reseda odorata*, is one of the best fragrant plants for greenhouse cultivation. Seed should be sown in August using John Innes No. 1 Potting Compost in the 6-in. pots in which the plants will flower, the resulting seedlings being thinned to about 1 in. apart as soon as they can be handled. Grow on as detailed for other annuals. Provide very little water in winter but water freely when the plants are coming into bloom. Staking

Reseda odorata

is necessary to keep the growths upright. A spring sowing will provide flowering plants for the cool greenhouse in summer and autumn.

Nicotiana. The nicotianas or Tobacco Plants are attractive, fragrant flowers which make good pot plants. The smaller varieties of *Nicotiana affinis* are especially suitable for this purpose. Colours include red, white and green.

Seed should be sown in February and germinated in seed compost in a temperature of 16°C. (60°F.) and the resulting seedlings potted separately in 3-in. pots of John Innes No. 1 Potting Compost as soon as they can be handled. These are grown on in a temperature of 13°C. (55°F.) and moved to 6-in. pots when their root development makes this necessary.

Salpiglossis. The 2-ft. tall *Salpiglossis sinuata* is a very effective pot plant. It has large, tubular-shaped flowers in many colours, including crimson, scarlet, blue, purple and white with gold markings providing a striking contrast. The plants need staking early as they tend to flop and pinching out the tips is desirable to induce a shorter, more branching habit.

Scabiosa. The Sweet Scabious, *Scabiosa atropurpurea* has double- and single-flowered varieties of many colours from reds and pinks, to purples, blues, lavender and white. The foliage is deeply divided and admirably complements the flowers on their long stems. The double-flowered dwarf strains of about 1½ ft. in height are especially suitable for pot cultivation. If the plants are grown four to a 6-in. pot they will soon make a very bright and attractive display.

Nicotiana affinis

Salpiglossis

ANTHURIUM

A. andreanum

Above: The striking spathes of *Anthurium andreanum*. **Below left:** *Dimorphotheca* Goliath, one of many annuals suitable for the greenhouse. **Below right:** *Exacum affine* is really a biennial but is often treated as an annual

The striking anthuriums have become very popular in recent years, the ladies in particular liking the large white, pink, red or orange spathes for use in flower arrangements. The popular name of Flamingo Flower seems particularly appropriate for these flamboyant plants. However, they are hothouse flowers and young plants need a winter temperature of at least 16°C. (60°F.). Older plants can survive with a few degrees less, but on average 16 to 18°C. (60 to 65°F.) is correct from September to March and 21°C. (70°F.) or more for the rest of the year. They need shade from hot sun.

The species most often grown for their spathes – made more spectacular by the erect or twisted yellow spadices arising from them – are *Anthurium andreanum* with heart-shaped leaves and *A. scherzerianum* with long, narrow leaves. Species grown for their beautifully veined and coloured leaves are *A. crystallinum*, *A. veitchii* and *A. warocqueanum*.

Potting. Anthuriums like a mixture of equal parts fibrous peat and chopped sphagnum moss with a little sand and charcoal added. The crown of the plant should be about 2 in. above the rim of the pot when potting is completed. Annual repotting is essential and this is best done immediately flowering ceases in summer. Those grown purely as foliage plants should be repotted in spring. Water must be given freely from March to November but very carefully during the rest of the year.

Propagation. Increase is by division of the roots, by removing rooted suckers at the time of potting, or by seed. Seed needs a very high temperature to germinate – 21 to 27°C. (70 to 80°F.) – and should be sown in March.

The author tending the plants in his sun lounge. An attractive display can be had throughout the year with a little thought and care

APHELANDRA

A. squarrosa louisiae

Almost everybody must know *Aphelandra squarrosa louisae* as a house plant, but it is in fact much more suitable for the greenhouse than for the home, being sensitive to dry, stuffy air and cold nights. It needs a minimum temperature of 13°C. (55°F.) in winter but in summer it may rise to 24 to 27°C. (75 to 80°F.). The bright yellow bracts of the plant have a splendid foil in its dark green, white-veined leaves.

Cuttings. Plants can be increased readily from cuttings, and young unflowered side-shoots, a few inches long, should be selected. The lower leaves are removed and a clean cut made below a joint at the base. To assist rooting, the lower ends of the cuttings can be dipped first in water and then in a hormone rooting powder and I like to place the cuttings individually in small pots. A suitable rooting medium consists of 1 part loam, 2 parts moist peat and 3 parts coarse sand. The pots may be placed in a propagating frame with a temperature of 18 to 21°C. (65 to 70°F.) or each pot can be enclosed in a polythene bag which is then sealed with a rubber band.

Potting. The rooted cuttings are first moved into 3½-in. pots using John Innes No. 1 Potting Compost and later, when the pots are full of roots, they should be transferred to 5- or 6-in. pots using John Innes No. 2 Potting Compost.

Stopping. The growing tips can be nipped out once or twice to encourage sideshoots and produce plants with a bushy habit.

Watering and Damping Down. During the summer the plants will require plenty of water, and damping down and shading from excessive sun are also important.

Feeding. Once the plants are in their final pots, feeds of a liquid or soluble fertiliser at 10-day intervals will help to keep them growing well. As they come into flower the plants are best kept in cooler conditions.

Pruning. The lower leaves tend to fall as the plants age, particularly if they are kept in a room for too long where the air is hot and dry. In these circumstances it is best to cut back the stems in spring, and, given warmth and moisture, new growths soon develop. These can be used as cuttings if so desired.

ARUM

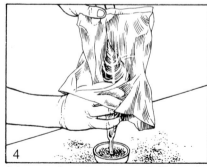

Zantedeschia aethiopica

I have placed this plant under its common name of Arum Lily rather than its botanical name of zantedeschia because it is by the former that it is invariably known to gardeners, and because I believe that more people still refer to it as richardia (its outdated botanical name) than the current zantedeschia. However that may be, there is no doubt that the Arum Lilies (which incidentally are not related to the true lilies) make splendid greenhouse perennials.

The Arum Lily most commonly grown is *Zantedeschia aethiopica*, a handsome plant which is also known as Calla Lily, the Lily of the Nile (although it comes from South Africa!) and Trumpet Lily. There are also several yellow-flowered species including the deep yellow *Z. pentlandii* and the pale yellow *Z. elliottiana*, both of which are more tender than *Z. aethiopica* and so need more protection and slightly higher temperatures.

Taking an aphelandra cutting. **1.** A non-flowering shoot is selected. In this case it is the main stem, which has become rather bare. **2.** After preparation, the base of the cutting is dipped in hormone rooting powder. **3.** The cutting is inserted in a 2-in. pot of sandy compost. **4.** The entire cutting is enclosed in a polythene bag

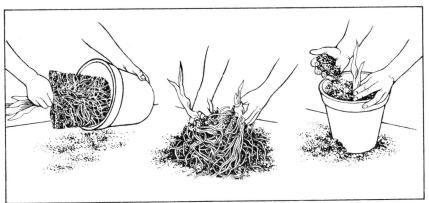

Dividing and repotting an Arum Lily crown. A mature plant is removed from its pot in July or August. The separate shoots are carefully pulled apart, and are then potted up in fresh compost

In June, Arum Lilies are rested for a month or two. The pots are laid on their sides, and water is withheld

The Growth Cycle. *Z. aethiopica* makes a plant 2 to 2½ ft. tall and the pure white spathes on long stems surrounding the true flowers are much in demand at Easter time for flower decorations.

The time to start this plant into growth is in July or August when the old soil should be shaken from the roots. At this stage it can be divided and about three roots or crowns can be accommodated in an 8-in. pot. John Innes No. 2 Potting Compost can be used and it must be worked in well amongst the roots. After a good watering the pots are stood in a sheltered place in the open but they should be taken into a light place in a cool greenhouse before there is any chance of autumn frosts. This is usually by the end of September. Until growth begins, water should be given sparingly. The temperature can be raised gradually to 13 to 16°C. (55 to 60°F.) as the plants develop if early flowers are needed, but they will be quite happy in a temperature of 7 to 10°C. (45 to 50°F.) if flowers are not needed so early.

Feeding. Arum Lilies respond to feeding and once the pots are full of roots regular feeds of a liquid or soluble fertiliser every 7 to 10 days will help to produce good flowers.

Resting. After flowering, watering and feeding must not be neglected but in early June I like to give the plants a rest by laying the pots on their sides in a sheltered spot outside the greenhouse so that the soil is kept dry until repotting is done once again in August, and the cycle is repeated.

Pest Control. Greenfly can spoil the flowers but fumigation with nicotine shreds or BHC smoke pellets will soon deal with them. If reddish globules can be seen on the underside of the foliage the presence of thrips must be suspected. The use of a BHC spray, or malathion as an aerosol, a spray or a dust will be effective as a control.

Division. Propagation is by division of the fleshy roots when repotting.

ASPARAGUS

A. plumosus

Three ornamental species of asparagus are of interest to the greenhouse owner: *Asparagus plumosus*, with fine feathery foliage; *A. asparagoides*, the Smilax, with long green shoots; and *A. sprengeri*, with needle-like, drooping foliage of considerable decorative value. All are splendid foliage plants for the conservatory or greenhouse, and they are easy to grow.

Seed Sowing. New plants can be readily raised from seed sown in the spring, summer or autumn in a propagating frame. A light compost is needed and a minimum temperature of 18°C. (65°F.).

The young seedlings which result are potted singly into 3-in. pots as soon as they are large enough to handle and are later moved on to 5- or 6-in. pots. The John Innes No. 1 Potting Compost is suitable for both stages.

Decorative Uses. *Asparagus sprengeri* is especially well suited for growing in hanging baskets suspended from the roof of the greenhouse but can also be well displayed as a pot-grown specimen. *A. plumosus* and *A. asparagoides* are plants for growing in pots or the greenhouse border. They should be trained to wires which will lead the growths up to the rafters.

Division. Mature plants may be divided by pulling the growths apart in spring and potting each piece separately in a 5-in. pot using John Innes No. 1 Potting Compost.

Cultivation. Frequent spraying with water is necessary in summer and a minimum temperature of 10°C. (50°F.) should be maintained. Potting and planting should be carried out in March.

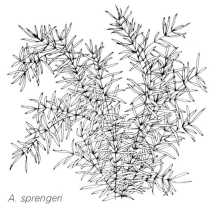

A. sprengeri

AZALEA

The colourful flowers of the Indian azaleas (forced plants of *Azalea indica* which is more correctly named *Rhododendron simsii*) can be seen in most florists' shops in the winter and early spring, and if one has a cool greenhouse, and the plants are given a little attention, they can be kept for many years.

Repotting. After flowering is over the remains of the withered flowers should be removed and the plants repotted, using larger pots if the plants are in 3-, 4- or 5-in. pots, or the same size if in 6- or 7-in. pots. (In this case, some of the old compost should be scraped away.) Rhododendrons and azaleas (the latter are a branch of the large genus *Rhododendron*) will not tolerate lime or chalk in their compost and so a special potting mixture must be used. This can be made by mixing 2 parts of moist peat with 1 part coarse sand. The old drainage crocks must be removed from the base of the plants and fresh compost worked in around the roots, firming it well with the fingers.

Watering. The peaty compost in which the plants are grown must never be allowed to dry out for if this happens it is extremely difficult to get it properly moist again. New growth soon begins after flowering and it is best to keep the plants in a warm part of the greenhouse; sprays of water over the plants will help to encourage good growth. If the tap water is hard, it is wise to use rain water for these plants.

Cultivation. From June to September the plants will benefit from being plunged outside in their pots. It is best to choose a position in partial shade as they do not like strong sunshine.

Above: Azaleas are popular gifts, especially at Christmas. Given the correct treatment, they can give years of pleasure

Below: The large spotted leaves of this *Begonia rex*, with its pink tinges, make it a very handsome foliage plant

As the potting compost contains little plant food it is necessary to feed the plants regularly so that they make good growth and flower well. Numerous liquid or soluble fertilisers are obtainable from garden shops. One can use a dry feed of 2 teaspoonfuls of dried blood to 1 of sulphate of potash for each plant. This can be given once every 14 days in spring and summer.

As the nights become colder in September the plants should be returned to a cool greenhouse. Although high temperatures are not needed, sufficient heat should be turned on to keep the air fairly dry, otherwise the blooms will be spoiled by dampness.

Propagation. The Indian azaleas which are imported to Britain from Continental sources to be forced for Christmas sale, are usually grafted plants. Grafting is a highly skilled job but new plants can be raised from cuttings. It takes longer to produce a sizeable plant by this method but it is a simpler procedure than grafting. Young shoots that have begun to harden at their base are selected and inserted in small pots of moist peat and sand. The pots should be stood in a warm, moist propagating frame until the cuttings have rooted, when they should be potted individually using the special azalea compost.

House Plants. Plants which are taken into the home when in flower are best returned to the greenhouse immediately after flowering has finished as the dry atmosphere causes the leaves to scorch if they are kept there for any length of time.

When azaleas are plunged in the garden, pay particular attention to watering as the roots do not have access to the soil

Above: Tuberous-rooted begonias, with their spectacular flowers make a brilliant display in a heated greenhouse

Below: Winter-flowering begonias are less impressive than the tuberous kinds but even so they are very attractive

BEGONIA

Double begonia

TUBEROUS BEGONIAS

Numerous begonias can be grown in heated greenhouses, but the most popular are the tuberous-rooted kinds with their large double flowers. There are also the tuberous pendulous begonias, seen at their best in hanging baskets.

Tuberous begonias can be grown from dry tubers or seed. Unless one has a heated propagating frame, where a temperature of 18 to 21°C. (65 to 70°F.) can be maintained, though, tubers are the best proposition.

Seed Sowing. Seed sown in January or February will produce flowering plants by mid-summer. The very small seed needs careful sowing in pots or pans filled with seed compost, and should be covered with fine sand rather than compost. After germination, it is best to supply water by holding the pot or pan in a bucket of water until the moisture seeps through to the surface.

Tubers. Dormant tubers started into growth in March will make flowering

plants by late June. These tubers should be pressed hollow side uppermost into moist peat and coarse sand and placed in a warm part of the greenhouse with shade from strong sunshine. Light spraying overhead is appreciated, but overwatering must be avoided, especially in cold weather. When the growths are a few inches high, pot the plants up in 5-in. pots using John Innes No. 2 Potting Compost. Place the tubers half way down the pots, and cover with about ½ in. of compost. Later, when the plants are established they can be topdressed with more compost so that eventually the tubers are about 2 in. below the surface.

Seedlings. When the seeds have germinated, the seedlings must be pricked out into boxes, 1½ in. apart. These are small and difficult to handle and a forked stick is helpful to transfer them to the dibber holes in the box. The tiny plants need a temperature of 18°C. (65°F.) and shade from strong sunshine. When large enough, the seedlings should be moved into 3-in. pots using John Innes No. 1 Potting Compost and be treated in the same way as plants raised from tubers.

The final move for seedling begonias is into 5- or 6-in. pots using John Innes No. 2 Potting Compost. Good drainage is essential.

Staking. As the plants develop, support them with small canes and raffia. Pay particular attention to the flower stems, as the blooms are rather heavy.

Disbudding. The first flowers to appear should be removed so that the plants make good growth before the flowers open. Later on it is wise to do more

Pendulous begonia

disbudding. It will be noticed that the flowers usually appear in threes. In addition to the male double flower there will be two female flowers on either side. These are single and less spectacular and should be pinched out, leaving the double flowers to open to their full size.

Disease Control. Botrytis, the grey mould fungus disease, can be troublesome on begonias. It often makes an appearance in cold, damp weather or in an insufficiently ventilated greenhouse. The fungus may gain entry to the plant through broken leaf stalks. Any withered leaves should be removed with a sharp knife close to the stem, and if the disease appears it pays to dust the infected area immediately with flowers of sulphur.

Watering and Feeding. Begonias need to be watered carefully. Water should be given sparingly after potting and until new roots are made into the fresh compost. Each plant must be treated individually and when the soil in the pot is beginning to dry out the pot should be filled with water to the rim. Water must not be given again until the soil shows signs of dryness once more.

As the plants become established in their final pots, feed with liquid fertiliser at intervals of 7 to 10 days.

Resting. Tuberous begonias must not be dried off too quickly. I like to keep the plants growing for as long as possible into the autumn, but when the foliage shows signs of yellowing, watering can be reduced and the plants laid on their sides under the greenhouse staging. When the

Begonia masoniana

Starting tuberous begonias into growth. The tubers are pressed hollow side uppermost into a mixture of moist peat and sand

stems have withered completely remove the tubers from their pots and shake out the old soil. Then dust with flowers of sulphur and store in boxes of dry peat, sand or old potting soil in a dry, frost-free place until it is time to start them into growth again in the early spring.

REX BEGONIAS

The Rex begonias, which include the striking *Begonia masoniana*, are grown primarily for their handsome leaves as the flowers are not very showy. These begonias have fibrous roots and should not be dried off at any stage. They need a greenhouse with a minimum temperature in winter of 10°C. (50°F.), with shade from strong sunshine in summer. They grow well on the greenhouse floor, just under the staging.

Propagation. These begonias can be propagated from their leaves. The conventional method is to sever the leaf with a piece of stalk attached and then to slit the veins on the underside of the leaf with a sharp knife. It is then laid on the surface of a peat and sand mixture in a pan or shallow box. Small stones placed on the leaf help to keep the cut veins in contact with the rooting medium. Stood in a warm, moist propagating frame with a temperature of 16 to 18°C. (60 to 65°F.), rooting will soon take place where the cuts were made on the veins, and young plants will develop.

Another method is to cut the leaves into small squares and place them on a mixture of moist peat and sand in a shallow box. They are then treated as for whole leaf cuttings. The small plants which result are first moved to 2-in. pots and then to 3½- and 5-in. pots. When the young plants are established in their final pots feeds with a liquid or soluble fertiliser will be helpful.

LORRAINE BEGONIAS

These are the fibrous-rooted, winter-flowering begonias and they are delightful plants. They are more graceful than the tuberous begonias and the stems are more wiry. A minimum temperature of 16°C. (60°F.) is needed to grow them well.

Cuttings. To obtain young basal growths for cuttings the stems of the plants are cut back to within a few inches of their base after flowering. Kept in warm conditions new shoots soon develop and these can be removed in February as cuttings. A suitable rooting mixture consists of 1 part loam, 2 parts moist peat and 3 parts coarse sand, well mixed together.

Each cutting is prepared by trimming the base just below a leaf joint with a sharp knife or razor blade. Several cuttings can be placed round the edge of a 3-in. pot using a dibber. After a good watering the pots should be placed in a propagating frame with a temperature of 18°C. (65°F.).

Potting. The rooted cuttings are first put in 3-in. pots using John Innes No. 1 Potting Compost and firming the soil lightly. With a temperature of 16 to 18°C. (60 to 65°F.) and a moist atmosphere, growth is rapid. Shade must be given from strong sunshine in spring and summer. A further move into the 5-in. pots in which the plants will flower follows when this becomes necessary.

Staking. The fragile stems must be supported by thin canes inserted in the pots. These are held loosely to the canes with fine pieces of raffia. This can be done in such a way that eventually the canes are hidden and the plant is a well-arranged mass of flowers and foliage.

For really large flowers, tuberous begonias should be disbudded. Buds appear in threes, and the two outer ones are removed

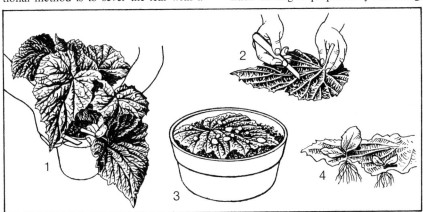

Propagating a Rex begonia. **1** and **2.** A mature leaf is selected and the main veins on the underside are cut. **3** and **4.** Small pebbles keep the cut veins in contact with the rooting medium, and new plantlets soon develop at these points

Supporting the large flowers of a tuberous begonia. The canes and ties should be as unobtrusive as possible

BELOPERONE

B. guttata

Above left: The pink bracts and white flowers of *Beloperone guttata*. **Above right:** *Brunfelsia calycina*, an evergreen shrub for the cool greenhouse. **Below:** *Neoregelia carolinae tricolor*, a brightly coloured member of the Bromeliad family

It is always a pleasure to come across a plant with a particularly appropriate common name. One such is *Beloperone guttata*, the Shrimp Plant. This name refers to the drooping spikes of salmon-red bracts and white flowers which do closely resemble the familiar shrimp.

Beloperone guttata is, of course, a popular house plant as well as a greenhouse subject. It will continue to flower the year through given favourable conditions, and a moderately heated greenhouse, conservatory or sun lounge is a natural choice. The flowers are likely to be borne especially prolifically in summer and autumn. In the home it can be a little tricky in winter if the atmosphere becomes too cold or stuffy, but this is not a role for which we are considering it at the present time.

Cultivation. Established plants should be repotted in spring, using the John Innes No. 1 Potting Compost. They will need quite a lot of water in spring and summer but less during the rest of the year. The best temperature is 16 to 18°C. (60 to 65°F.) but it can fall to 7°C. (45°F.) in winter if necessary.

Cuttings. To increase the Shrimp Plant it is best to cut the established plant back in spring to encourage shoots to form from the base from which cuttings can be made. These can be rooted from April to August in a warm propagating frame. The cuttings will root much more easily if treated with hormone rooting powder before insertion. Rooted cuttings are potted first into 3-in. pots, then into 4½- or 5-in. pots and finally into 6- or 6½-in. pots, using John Innes No. 1 Potting Compost.

BROMELIADS

Billbergia nutans

The Bromeliads – members of the family *Bromeliaceae* – include splendid greenhouse plants of real distinction.

BILLBERGIAS

The bromeliad most commonly and easily grown is *Billbergia nutans*. It is almost hardy but warm, moist conditions are needed if one is to enjoy its drooping flowers of yellow, green, red and blue colouring borne on slender green stems. The distinctive rosette of narrow, toothed leaves, up to 2½ ft. in length, is a permanent decorative feature.

Cultivation. Pot billbergias in early spring using John Innes No. 1 Potting Compost. In spring and summer when growth is active, water freely and keep the cup-like

Cryptanthus fosterianus (top) and *C. tricolor*

centre of the plant, formed by the rosette of leaves, filled with water. This will supply most of the needs of the plant during the winter and the compost need not be watered until almost bone dry. Good drainage is essential.

Offsets. Billbergias are increased by offsets taken in spring or summer and rooted in a sandy, peaty mixture in a propagating frame heated to a temperature of 18 to 24°C. (65 to 75°F.).

A related plant is *Aechmea fasciata* (syn. *Billbergia fasciata*) which bears grey, silver-mottled leaves and rosy-pink bracts in August, provided it is given the warm, moist conditions it likes. Indeed, it should be treated in a similar way to *Billbergia nutans*.

Suckers. Aechmeas are increased by suckers which are produced after flowering. They are rooted in moist, warm conditions, preferably with the temperature at 27°C. (80°F.). A lower temperature can be maintained but rooting will be a much slower process.

CRYPTANTHUSES

Another group of bromeliads well worth considering for the greenhouse is *Cryptanthus*, a genus of dwarf plants which will prosper even in adverse conditions given an orchid-type compost based on peat. To give of their best, though, they need warm, moist conditions. The rosettes of often wavy leaves have a starfish-like appearance and attractive colouring.

Decorative Uses. A popular way to grow these plants is on pieces of bark. Moss is

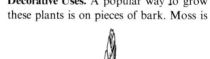

Vriesia splendens

Aechmea fasciata

wrapped around the root ball and the whole plant firmly secured to the bark with wire. The water requirements of the plants are then met by watering the moss as necessary. Also, they can be used for bottle gardens and for decorating the front of the greenhouse staging. The most showy cryptanthus is *C. fosterianus* for it has red and grey variegations. *C. tricolor* is also handsome with cream and green striped leaves and an overall pinkish tinge which is particularly marked in the centre. The flowers of cryptanthuses are of no importance.

Offsets. Cryptanthuses are increased by rooted offsets which are detached in March.

VRIESIAS

Extremely handsome bromeliads are the vriesias, some with spectacular variegations and all forming large rosettes of long, stiff leaves. Spikes of long, narrow flowers are in some cases surrounded by brightly coloured bracts. Perhaps the best for the average greenhouse is *Vriesia splendens* with highly decorative 18-in. long leaves, green on the upper side and with transverse bands of reddish-brown on the under side. Its other attributes are the yellow flowers and red bracts.

Cultivation. For this and other vriesias the temperature in winter must be kept to at least 10°C. (50°F.), and the plants must also be kept drier at this time of year. Full sunshine is much appreciated with frequent overhead spraying and watering in summer. Drainage must be really efficient, and the compost should consist of coarse fibrous peat with some sphagnum moss and charcoal added. Increase is by seed sown in spring or by offsets removed at the same time.

NEOREGELIAS

Neoregelia is a somewhat unusual name many of us have become familiar with since house plants became so popular. (All the bromeliads referred to here, incidentally, are good for growing in the house, at least for reasonably extensive periods of time.) The one usually available is *Neoregelia carolinae tricolor* with cream and green variegated, red-centred leaves arranged in a rosette, at the centre of which are borne the small violet flowers. The cup-like centre of this plant, too, is kept full of water and the cultural conditions needed are as for *Billbergia nutans* except that more water is needed in winter.

ANANAS

Another bromeliad with certain novelty value as well as decorative qualities is the Pineapple, *Ananas comosus*. The widespreading, narrow, grey leaves form a rosette and in some forms have cream, yellow and pink stripes which add to their attractions. As these leaves can be up to 5 ft. long it goes without saying that space is necessary to accommodate this plant. Fruit may be produced if a warm, humid atmosphere is provided but this will certainly not occur under cool house conditions.

Propagation. An interesting exercise is to try to make a new plant from the spiky rosette which forms the top of a bought pineapple. This needs to be cut with a sharp knife and the flesh removed before placing it on a bed of sand in a propagating frame with a temperature of at least 24°C. (75°F.). Increase can also be by suckers, seeds and stem cuttings, again with temperatures not less that 24°C.

Cultivation. Established plants need a winter temperature of 16°C. (60°F.), increasing to 24°C. (75°F.) or more in summer. The atmosphere must be kept moist in spring and summer. A suitable compost consists of 2 parts fibrous loam, 1 part peat and 1 part sand. Good drainage is essential. Water freely in spring and summer when growth is active, but more moderately in winter.

Fruiting Plants. As I have already inferred, fruits are unlikely to appear under typical greenhouse conditions, but if they do, the plants must be kept rather dry while the fruits are ripening.

BROWALLIA

B. speciosa major

This is a popular cool greenhouse plant, although perhaps not quite so popular now as in the time of my youth when it was much grown in the greenhouses or conservatories on large estates. To grow browallias well, all that is needed is a frost-proof greenhouse and cultural attention as detailed below. There are both annual and perennial kinds.

Browallia demissa (syn. *B. elata*) is a half-hardy annual with bright blue or white flowers which it bears from early summer until late autumn. It makes a plant of about 1½ ft. in height and is easily raised from seed sown in early spring. The rather taller *B. speciosa major*, a perennial, bears blue or violet flowers in summer and can also be raised from seed. It is extremely free flowering. Both can be brought into flower in winter by sowing seeds in July.

Seed Sowing. The seed should be sown thinly in boxes filled with seed compost and should be barely covered with fine compost. Germination takes place in a temperature of 16°C. (60°F.).

Seedlings. The seedlings are pricked out into 3-in. pots as soon as they are large enough to handle and moved on into 5-in. pots as they develop further. John Innes No. 1 Potting Compost suits them very well for both these stages. Also, it is possible to grow three plants of *B. demissa* in a 6-in. pot to provide large specimen plants. Place the pots in a light position.

Stopping. Pinch out the tips of the shoots of *B. speciosa major* to ensure that they develop a bushy habit. This should be done when the plants are 3 to 4 in. high and the lateral branches are pinched out also after they have formed four or five leaves.

BRUNFELSIA

B. calycina

The brunfelsia has come to the fore in recent years as a house plant. It is an evergreen flowering shrub which does not last very long in the home, but it is an attractive plant for the conservatory, sun lounge or greenhouse, provided a minimum winter temperature of 7 to 10°C. (45 to 50°F.) can be maintained.

The species usually grown is *Brunfelsia calycina* which bears fragrant lavender-purple flowers intermittently throughout the year, though the main flowering period is in late winter and spring. This native of Brazil will make a specimen up to 2 ft. tall when it is grown in a 5- or 6-in. flower pot.

Cuttings. This plant is propagated by means of cuttings of fairly firm shoots taken in summer and rooted in a mixture of equal parts of peat and sand in a propagating frame with a temperature of 18°C. (65°F.). Cuttings can also be taken and rooted successfully in spring and autumn although I feel that summer is a more suitable time. The cuttings should be 3 to 4 in. long. When rooted they should be potted up singly, first into 3-in. pots and then successively into 4-in. and 5- or 6-in. pots. They need a mixture of lime-free soil, moist peat and coarse sand mixed in the proportion of 1:4:1 if they are to give of their best and should be repotted when the main flowering season is over.

Cultivation. During summer they need warm, humid conditions with ventilation when the temperature rises to 27°C. (80°F.). Weekly feeding with liquid fertiliser is beneficial once the plants have filled their pots with roots.

Pruning. Any pruning necessary to keep the plants shapely should be done before they start to make new growth.

BULBS : SOME POPULAR KINDS

Narcissus
Peeping Tom

I am considering under this heading the more popular kinds of bulbous flowers which are invaluable for providing colour in winter and early spring.

DAFFODILS AND HYACINTHS

Plenty of colour can be created in a cool greenhouse from Christmas until spring with daffodils (narcissi) and hyacinths. Narcissi must be chosen carefully to obtain the earliest flowers, good ones being Paper White and Grand Soleil d'Or. The graceful Roman hyacinths should not be forgotten as they flower earlier than the large-flowered hyacinths.

Treated Bulbs. Pre-cooled bulbs can be obtained which flower earlier than they would normally. Varieties of narcissus for Christmas flowering include Carlton, Cragford and Peeping Tom, the last a lovely *cyclamineus* hybrid. Treated hyacinths can also be obtained.

Potting. Bulbs should be potted in September or October as soon as they can be obtained. If they are being grown in pots use John Innes No. 1 Potting Compost as a growing medium. The bulbs should be placed close together and be so positioned that when potting is completed their tips are just above the surface of the compost. It is not wise to have hyacinths of mixed colours together in the same container as they are likely to come into flower at different times. Bulbs may also be grown in bowls of bulb fibre but it is important to soak the fibre thoroughly with water before it is used. Do not pot too firmly or the roots may push the bulbs out of the compost.

Double-Layer Planting. An interesting way to grow daffodils is in a double layer. For this a bowl 8 or 9 in. deep and with a diameter of 7 or 8 in. is needed. Place a layer of fibre in the bottom, put the bulbs on this and cover with fibre, leaving just their noses showing. Firm the fibre lightly, then place a second layer of bulbs between the noses of the bulbs in the lower layer. More fibre is added and worked around the bulbs. In this way I have obtained up to 45 blooms from one bowl.

Plunging. The pots and bowls must be stood in a cool place for 8 to 10 weeks after potting so that the bulbs can make good root systems. I find it best to stand the pots outside in a sheltered place and, after giving them a thorough watering, cover them with a layer of sand or weathered cinders.

Housing. When the bulbs have made plenty of roots move them into a cold frame to gradually become acclimatised to warmer conditions and allow the shoots to turn green. Then, when the flower buds appear, take the bulbs at intervals into the greenhouse or a warm room. At first a temperature of 7°C. (45°F.) is adequate and the bulbs should only be subjected to higher temperatures gradually. Treated bulbs need slightly different temperatures but instructions are given with bulbs obtained from good bulb merchants.

Watering. Keep the compost uniformly moist and if bulb fibre is used take care it does not dry out. Do not allow water to collect inside the leaves of hyacinths or the buds may rot.

Staking. It is wise to stake the heavy flowers of modern hyacinths, either with hooked pieces of wire or with canes and raffia ties. It is also advisable to support narcissi with raffia looped round their canes to enclose the foliage.

CROCUSES

Large Dutch crocuses make splendid pot plants. Four corms should be potted in October in a 3-in. pot in John Innes No. 1

Hyacinths may be grown in pots, bowls or glass jars. Glass containers are interesting for children, as the roots can be seen

Staking narcissi with canes and raffia. This job should be done well before the plants reach maturity

Plunging newly potted bulbs in a bed of sand. This is important if a good root system is to develop

Planting daffodil bulbs in a double layer. This method gives a really spectacular display of flowers

Potting Compost and covered to a depth of $\frac{1}{2}$ in. Plunge them under ashes out of doors until growth starts and then bring them into the greenhouse. They should not be forced before mid-January, when a temperature of 10°C. (50°F.) is sufficient.

GALANTHUS
Snowdrops (*Galanthus nivalis*) are a source of pleasure when grown in medium-sized pots or pans. Pot the bulbs in September in John Innes No. 1 Potting Compost, setting the bulbs 1 in. below the surface. Start into growth in a cold frame and then bring into the greenhouse.

MUSCARI
Grape Hyacinths are delightful plants. A popular variety is *Muscari* Heavenly Blue. I like to plant about 15 bulbs in a 5-in. pot and John Innes No. 1 Potting Compost is a suitable growing medium. This is done in September or October.

The bulbs should be set about 1 in. below the surface of the compost. Plunge the pots in a cold frame until growth is under way and then bring them into a cool greenhouse.

IRIS
Two dwarf irises are much grown in pots and very attractive they are: the deep purple and gold *Iris reticulata* and the rich blue *I. histrioides* (see p. 20). Several bulbs can be grown in a 3-in. pot and John Innes No. 1 Potting Compost is recommended. The bulbs should be set about 1 in. below the surface of the compost. House in a cold frame until growth starts and then bring into the greenhouse.

Dutch and English irises can be grown in the same way but in 5-in. pots.

SCILLA
The Siberian Squill, *Scilla sibirica*, makes a good greenhouse plant together with

others of the genus. Pot the bulbs, at any time between August and November, in John Innes No. 1 Potting Compost. The bulbs should be set 1 in. deep. Plunge them out of doors until growth starts and then, when a good root system has developed, bring them into the greenhouse.

TULIP
Nearly all varieties of Early Double and Early Single tulips are excellent for a cool greenhouse as well as the Cottage, Parrot, Fringed and Broken tulips and species like *T. kaufmanniana*. They should be potted between September and November in John Innes No. 1 Potting Compost and plunged out of doors until the flower buds appear. They can then be brought into the greenhouse, but the temperature should not rise above 13°C. (55°F.) until the buds are well formed. Tulips can also be grown in bowls, but bulb fibre should be used rather than potting compost.

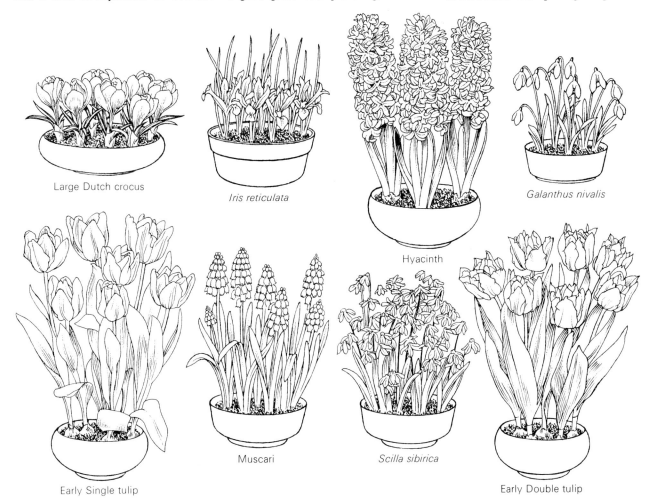

Large Dutch crocus

Iris reticulata

Hyacinth

Galanthus nivalis

Early Single tulip

Muscari

Scilla sibirica

Early Double tulip

CACTI AND SUCCULENTS

Zygocactus truncatus

The cultivation of cacti is a fascinating hobby and most kinds will succeed in a greenhouse with a minimum winter temperature of 7°C. (45°F.). During the spring and summer temperatures can rise to 18 to 21°C. (65 to 70°F.) with sun heat, provided ample ventilation is given. Cacti are sun-lovers and need to be stood in the lightest part of the greenhouse. In summer they can be stood in a sunny cold frame, preferably with the pots sunk in a bed of ashes.

Potting. The time to pot cacti is in the spring just as new growth is beginning. John Innes No. 1 Potting Compost can be used with the addition of two extra parts of coarse sand and two parts crushed brick. Cacti must never be placed in pots which are too big; generally, one size larger than the ones they have been occupying is sufficient.

Handling the plants can be difficult because of the spines and it is wise to make a paper collar which is placed around the plant to serve as a handle. Remove some of the old soil carefully and place the plant in its new pot, firming fresh compost around the roots.

Watering. Growth is made in the spring and summer and during this period plenty of water is needed, but in winter when the plants are resting the soil must be kept dry and watering should only be necessary if the plants begin to shrivel.

Below is a small selection of cacti and succulents:

ZYGOCACTUS

Since the Christmas Cactus, *Zygocactus truncatus*, is such a popular and useful plant, I shall describe its cultivation in some detail.

As its common name implies, flowering usually occurs over the Christmas period, and if not then, certainly very soon afterwards. The colour of the flowers is deep pink and they appear at the end of the leaf-like segments. The habit of growth is pendulous and pieces of zygocactus are often grafted on to another upright cactus, such as pereskia, to make a standard plant.

Cuttings. The usual method of propagation is by cuttings taken in the spring. These should consist of several stem segments and they root readily if inserted in small pots containing a mixture of 1 part loam, 2 parts moist peat and 3 parts coarse sand. Several cuttings can be placed around the edge of a 3-in. pot.

Potting. When rooted, each plant should be potted individually in a 3-in. pot. Use a similar potting compost to the one already mentioned under 'Potting' (left).

Watering. Unlike many other cacti, zygocactus must not be allowed to dry out in the winter, although much less water is needed at that time of year. In the summer the plants in their pots should be plunged in a bed of peat or ashes in a cold frame. This will help to ripen the growths, and will encourage a good crop of flowers. The soil must be kept amply moist and light overhead sprays of water will encourage good growth. Light shade should also be given from strong sunshine.

Feeding. During the summer when the plants are established in their pots feeding can be carried out with a liquid or soluble fertiliser every 10 days.

Housing. In September the plants must be returned to a cool greenhouse. Flowering can be hastened a little by raising the temperature provided the air is kept fairly moist with light sprays of water.

LOBIVIA

The lobivias are attractive small cacti which flower while still young. One I have a regard for is *Lobivia famatimensis*, a yellow-flowered species which has numerous varieties with flowers of other colours, including red, pink and white. This cactus likes a sunny position.

EUPHORBIA

Euphorbia is a huge family including plants of many different kinds but the one I would mention now is *Euphorbia splendens*, the Crown of Thorns, a species which bears scarlet bracts and sharp thorns. This will make a succulent, shrubby plant up to 3 ft. tall. It likes a sunny position.

LITHOPS

The lithops are the Living Stone or Pebble Plants, all natives of South-west Africa and intriguing in their mimicry of stones or pebbles as the common names suggest. *Lithops olivacea*, with yellow flowers, is a species often grown. Drainage must be specially good for these plants. They need a fair amount of water between May and November but no water at all from then until April.

CEPHALOCEREUS

Some of the columnar 'woolly' cacti are of especial interest, like the striking *Cephalocereus senilis* or Old Man Cactus,

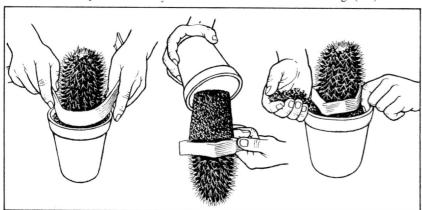

Repotting a cactus can be quite a hazardous job because of the sharp spines. A strong paper collar wrapped round the base of the plant makes handling much easier and potting can then be carried out in the normal way

Conophytum nobile

Lithops olivacea

Lobivia famatimensis

Euphorbia splendens

Sedum bellum

Cephalocereus senilis

which comes from Mexico. The long white hairs give it a distinctive appearance. This plant needs full sun and very careful, restrained watering. Extra lime added to the compost is beneficial.

CONOPHYTUM
The conophytum are related to the lithops and, like them, come from South-west Africa. These need plenty of sunshine and good drainage, a fair amount of water during August and September when they are growing and very little from then until July. Species grown include *Conophytum bilobum* and *C. nobile*.

SEDUM
A sedum with attractive glaucous foliage and white flowers which is worth adding to a collection is *Sedum bellum*. A sunny position is needed.

ECHEVERIA
The easily cultivated, winter-flowering *Echeveria retusa* illustrated on p. 51 is excellent for a cool greenhouse, mature plants being grown in 5- or 6-in. pots in John Innes No. 2 Potting Compost. The stems should be neatly staked as they develop to support the clusters of coral-red flowers.

KALANCHOE
The species grown in greenhouse and home is *Kalanchoe blossfeldiana* in one or other of its various forms. These attractive succulent plants have glossy, fleshy leaves and red, pink or yellow flowers. They make rounded domes some 9 in. tall. A variegated type is illustrated on p. 51.

APOROCACTUS
Another cactus with an appropriate common name is *Aporocactus flagelliformis*, the Rat's Tail Cactus. It has long, trailing, ribbed stems, covered in small spines, and bears pink or red flowers freely.

Propagating a zygocactus by stem cuttings. **1.** Suitable pieces consisting of several segments are selected from the parent plant. They can be easily snapped off with the fingers. **2.** The cuttings are then inserted round the edge of a 3-in. pot, with the aid of a dibber. **3.** When rooting has taken place, the plants can be potted up individually

CALCEOLARIA

The bright and gay colours of the greenhouse calceolarias with their curious, pouched flowers always attract attention in the spring. Plants can be raised easily from seed sown from May to July, the earliest sowings providing plants for flowering in April, May and early June of the following year.

Seed Sowing. The seed should be sown on the surface of sifted seed compost, and because the seed is so fine, no covering of compost is required. The pots should be covered with a sheet of glass and stood in a cold frame until germination takes place, usually within ten days. The resulting seedlings should then be pricked out into boxes and, before they become too large, be moved again into 3-in. pots of John Innes No. 1 Potting Compost. In October another move into 5-in. pots can be given, using a similar compost.

Cultivation. During the winter the plants are happy in a minimum temperature of 7°C. (45°F.) – they do not like high temperatures – but the air must be kept

As the flower buds appear on calceolarias, weekly feeding is beneficial. A liquid or soluble feed is the most convenient

fairly dry by careful ventilation. Water should be given sparingly at all times, and during winter it must be kept off the leaves and crowns of the plants as much as possible, or damping off may occur.

I like to give the plants another move to 6-in. pots in February to obtain really good specimen plants. This is well worth doing if there is sufficient space available in the greenhouse. Plants measuring 2 ft. or more across can thus be obtained.

Feeding. When I am aiming to grow very large specimens, I water the plants once with ½ oz. of nitrate of soda dissolved in a gallon of water just when they are beginning to show their flower buds. From then onwards feeding the plants once a week with a liquid or soluble fertiliser until they begin to flower will benefit them considerably.

Pest Control. Greenfly are often a nuisance on calceolarias and as soon as the first signs of this pest are seen fumigate with nicotine shreds or BHC smoke pellets. Alternatively, use a systemic insecticide as a control.

CAMELLIA

C. japonica

The evergreen camellias are fine flowering shrubs for a greenhouse from which frost can be excluded. The kinds most commonly grown are varieties of *C. japonica*, their flowers ranging in colour from shades of red to pink and white.

Propagation. One way of increasing camellias is by removing leaves from the shoots in March, each with a bud and portion of stem attached. The cuttings are inserted around the edge of 3-in. pots filled with a mixture of 2 parts coarse sand and 1 part moist peat. After a good watering, place the pots in a warm, moist propagating frame. As the roots form, new growth will develop and the young

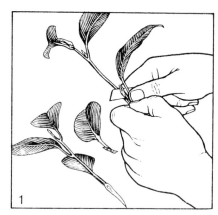

Taking leaf bud cuttings of camellias. **1.** Using a sharp knife a small portion of stem bearing a bud and a leaf is removed from a mature shoot. **2.** The cuttings are inserted in the normal way round the edge of a pot. **3.** After a while, rooting will occur, and the bud in the axil of the leaf will start to develop into a new shoot. **4.** Potting up into separate 3-in. pots can then take place using a compost prepared from lime-free loam

plants should be potted individually in 3-in. pots. Compost consisting of 2 parts peat, 1 part lime-free loam and 1 part coarse sand is ideal. Young plants will be happy in a cold frame with shade from strong sun in summer.

Cuttings can also be taken in late July but these are made from shoots produced in the current season that have begun to harden at their base. They should be treated in a similar manner to the other cuttings.

Both types of camellia cutting will root much more easily under a mist propagator. Raised in this way they can be taken in late summer or autumn and rooted before winter.

Repotting. When the plants begin to fill their small pots with roots, move them into 5- or 6-in. pots using the peaty compost referred to earlier. Finally, the plants can be grown in 8- or 9-in. pots or tubs.

Established plants should only be re-potted when this is really necessary – in early spring before new growth begins. Some of the old soil should be removed and fresh compost worked in among the roots, using a rammer to firm it. Good drainage is essential.

Summer Treatment. If possible, stand the plants out of doors in summer in a partially shaded place and never let the roots dry out, otherwise the flower buds may drop later. Feeding with a liquid or soluble fertiliser each week will help to keep the plants growing steadily in summer, and in hot weather overhead spraying with water will keep them in good condition.

Housing. In early autumn return the plants to a fully ventilated, unheated greenhouse. A little heat can be provided in cold weather but not too much must be given. Avoid damp, stuffy conditions at all times and keep the ventilators open whenever the weather is favourable.

CAMPANULA

C. isophylla

The most popular campanula or Bell Flower is the trailing *Campanula isophylla* with blue star-shaped flowers, and its white variety *alba*. This perennial is a splendid plant for hanging baskets. The other campanula grown under glass is *C. pyramidalis*, the Chimney Bell Flower, which makes a plant sometimes as much as 4 ft. tall and is often too large for the amateur's greenhouse. This biennial also has blue flowers and a white variety.

Propagation. *Campanula isophylla* can be raised from cuttings taken at any time between March and September, the best cuttings being made from the young shoots growing from the base of the plant. These can be rooted in a propagating frame in a mixture of equal parts loam, peat and sand or in a soilless seed compost. The temperature required is between 10 and 16°C. (50 to 60°F.). It can also be

raised from seed sown in an unheated frame in March or by careful division and repotting of the old plants, also in March. The plants should be grown on in John Innes No. 1 Potting Compost.

Seed of *C. pyramidalis* is sown in a cool greenhouse or frame in March or April in seed compost. A temperature of 16°C. (60°F.) is needed. The resulting seedlings should be pricked off singly as soon as they can be safely handled into 3-in. pots using John Innes No. 1 Potting Compost. From now onwards they need cool conditions and should be hardened off in a cold frame. The pots can be stood out of doors in summer and overwintered in a cold frame. The plants will finally need pots of 6- to 10-in. size. They come into flower in July and should continue to bloom for many weeks.

Decorative Uses. As previously mentioned, *C. isophylla* is an ideal plant for a hanging basket. I value it, too, for trailing along the side of the staging – a picture in summer when the blue or white flowers are borne particularly freely. It will also flower in winter if given a reasonable temperature. I never grow *C. isophylla* in pots of more than 5-in. size; in fact, I prefer half-pots or seed pans as receptacles for they are less noticeable when placed along the edge of the staging.

C. pyramidalis is useful for placing at the back of a display of flowers, or as a 'dot' plant to give variation in height amongst shorter plants.

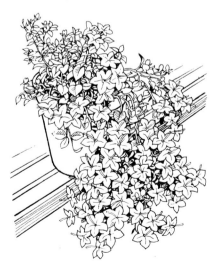

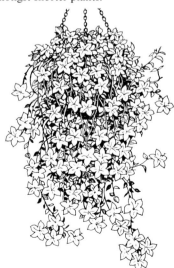

Two ways of using the attractive *Campanula isophylla* in the greenhouse. On the left of the illustration it hangs gracefully over the edge of the staging, and on the right it trails from a hanging basket

CARNATION

There is a widely held view that perpetual-flowering carnations should be grown in a greenhouse on their own, or at least have one part of the house reserved for them. I used to think the same myself but I have proved to my own satisfaction that they will grow perfectly well in association with pelargoniums, cinerarias and all the general run of cool greenhouse plants provided they are given plenty of light, space and ventilation. Some gardeners also hold the view that carnations do not grow well in plastic pots. My experience is just the opposite for my plants in these containers have always done exceptionally well.

The joy of perpetual-flowering carnations is that there are always a few flowers on the plants whatever the time of year, with the main flowering period coming in

Stopping a carnation plant. **1.** When the young plants have about eight pairs of leaves they must be stopped. **2.** This is done by carefully pinching out the growing tip with the finger and thumb. **3.** As a result, sideshoots are encouraged to grow from the buds in the leaf axils, and a bushy plant is produced

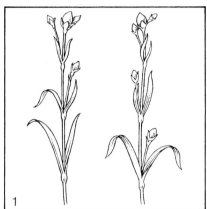

Disbudding carnations. In order to produce large, good quality blooms, disbudding is essential. **1.** Shoots before disbudding.

winter. In my opinion a dozen plants is sufficient to provide a few flowers for cutting and arranging whenever they are required.

Perpetual-flowering carnations do not need a high temperature and a winter temperature of 7°C. (45°F.) is adequate. Ventilation must be provided whenever the weather allows, to prevent the atmosphere becoming damp and stuffy, conditions which these plants are not able to tolerate.

Starting a Collection. Those wishing to start a collection can buy young rooted cuttings in spring ready for potting into 3-in. pots. Many varieties are offered by specialist carnation growers and, as with so many other special-interest plants, making a choice is a question of personal preference.

Potting. John Innes No. 1 Potting Compost is a suitable growing medium for the rooted cuttings and when they have filled their pots with roots they should be moved into 5-in. pots and, subsequently, into

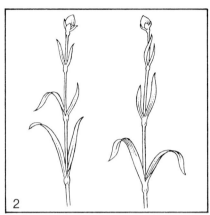

2. Shoots after disbudding, with only the terminal bud remaining

8-in. pots. Take care not to pot the plants too deeply.

The plants can, of course, be grown in beds instead of pots but this is a less flexible method of cultivation, especially as pot-grown plants can be housed in a deep frame during the summer allowing the space they normally occupy in the house to be used for other purposes. The plants can be put in the frame at the beginning of July and returned to the greenhouse at the end of September. Plants grown in beds should be planted out from the 3-in. pots when they have developed a good root system.

Stopping. The plants should be stopped when they have made about eight pairs of leaves, the young growing tip being taken out to induce sideshoots to develop and so create the desired bushy habit. This task is best carried out early in the morning when the stems are full of moisture and are therefore brittle.

The sideshoots are also stopped, their tips being pinched out when they have

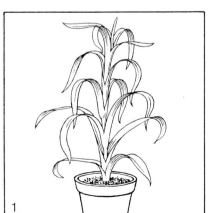

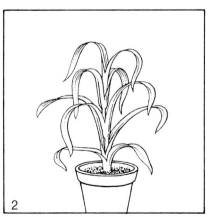

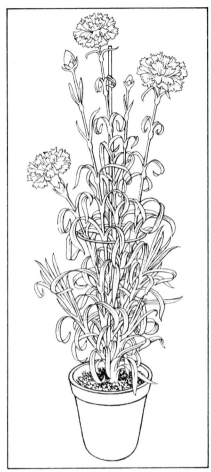

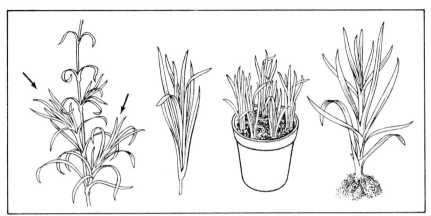

Propagating carnations by cuttings. Short, non-flowering sideshoots, as indicated by the arrows, provide suitable material. The cuttings should be trimmed cleanly at the base below a leaf joint, and rooting is best in pure sand

A well-grown carnation which has been staked with the aid of a bamboo cane and a specially designed split ring

made about four pairs of leaves. Disbudding is necessary if large blooms of good quality are to be obtained. As the terminal buds begin to develop so the side buds which form round them should be pinched out.

Watering. Perpetual-flowering carnations need watering freely in summer but more moderately in winter when their moisture needs must be fully met but the soil must not be allowed to become wet. Syringing over the plants with water on fine days when the greenhouse atmosphere is buoyant (airy) is very beneficial in discouraging red spider attack.

Staking. The plants grow several feet tall and the growths must be supported. I consider the best way to do this is with bamboo canes, 4 to 5 ft. tall, and the specially designed split rings which are used in conjunction with them. These are much easier to use than raffia or twine and

save much time and effort. Also, just as important, it makes it much easier to cut the blooms. When cutting blooms sever these within 9 or 10 in. of the pot for this encourages young shoots to form low down on the plant and keeps its habit bushy and sturdy.

Shading and Feeding. The plants should be provided with shade during hot, sunny parts of the day in summer. Feeding should begin as soon as the plants have filled their final pots with roots using a liquid or soluble fertiliser with a fairly high potash content.

Propagation. It will usually be found that plants need replacing every second or third year. Cuttings can be rooted between November and March, these being made from short non-flowering side growths. Those taken from mid-way up the flowering stems are the most satisfactory. They should be 3 to 4 in. long and a clean cut should be made immediately below a leaf joint.

The cuttings will root best in pure sand in a propagating frame heated to 16°C. (60°F.). With sand as the rooting medium, though, the rooted cuttings must be moved on into pots as quickly as possible. Use small pots for this purpose filled with John Innes No. 1 Potting Compost. From now onwards they are treated like mature plants and are repotted into larger pots as their present ones become full of roots.

Carnations can also be raised from seed but the plants so obtained will be of variable quality and some will not be worth keeping. On the other hand it is possible to obtain very attractive forms in this way. Flower colour, habit and

robustness will all vary. Seed should be sown in spring in boxes filled with seed compost. A temperature of 16°C. (60°F.) is required for germination. The resulting seedlings are then grown on in the same way as plants raised from cuttings.

Pest and Disease Control. The most important pest of these plants is possibly greenfly which causes distortion of the leaves and young shoots. This pest can be brought under control by fumigating with BHC or spraying with malathion. Another damaging pest is, of course, red spider mite which delights in dry atmospheric conditions. As already noted, syringing the plants with water on fine days in summer is a great help in combating this pest. Fumigation with azobenzene will kill red spider mites when an attack is seen to be in progress. Mottling of the foliage is a symptom and it will be possible to see these very small mites with a magnifying glass.

Also liable to attack perpetual-flowering carnations are thrips which, like red spider mites, thrive in a hot, dry atmosphere. The foliage of attacked plants is mottled with silver and the flowers are streaked and mis-shapen. When the pest's presence is noted, fumigate or spray with malathion or BHC.

One of the worst diseases is rust, a fungus which causes raised brown spots to form on the leaves. This is combated by spraying with thiram or lime-sulphur.

Pale stripes and sunken spots of a greyish colour on the leaves indicate virus attack for which there is no cure and the plants should be burned immediately an attack is noticed.

Above left: The Rat's Tail Cactus is an appropriate common name for *Aporocactus flagelliformis* which bears its flowers freely on long, spiny stems. **Above right:** *Camellia japonica* will flower out of doors but often the blooms are damaged by the weather. Given the protection of a cool greenhouse, they are able to develop to perfection

CHLOROPHYTUM

C. comosum variegatum

The Spider Plant, *Chlorophytum comosum variegatum*, is another of those excellent, easily grown plants which has a dual role as a cool greenhouse and a room plant. Its common name comes from the rosettes which develop on the ends of the flowering stems. It is grown mainly for its attractive green-and-cream striped foliage as the white, starry flowers, borne on long, arching stems, are insignificant. They are soon followed, however, by rosettes of leaves which add to the decorative value of the plant. It is this attractive waterfall effect which endears the chlorophytum to so many gardeners.

This is, indeed, a most tolerant plant which will thrive in sun or light shade and quite a wide range of temperatures. It does, however, need plenty of water and a rich compost is appreciated.

Propagation. As the plants age and decline in vigour the rosettes of leaves can be detached. These are, in fact, small plants and root initials are usually present. If they are placed in small pots of good soil new

Increasing a chlorophytum. **1.** Small plants are produced on the end of long arching stems. If these are detached from the parent they can be grown on as separate plants. **2.** The plantlets should be potted up individually. **3.** A good root system will soon develop, and the plants can then be moved to larger pots

Above left: The distinctive pouched flowers of greenhouse calceolarias have a curious appeal. **Above right:** A succulent which has become increasingly popular over the last few years is kalanchoe. This one has attractive variegated leaves

Below: *Echeveria retusa*, an easy succulent for a cool greenhouse. The small flowers appear in winter

roots will soon develop. Eventually they can be moved on to 5- or 6-in. pots.

Indoors, it may be more convenient to place the rosettes in the top of a jar of water into which new roots soon develop.

Another way to increase this plant is by simple division in spring. Chlorophytums have a tuberous root system and the tubers, with shoots attached, can be separated and potted individually.

Feeding and Repotting. These plants soon use up all the goodness in the soil and to keep them growing steadily when they are established in their final pots, it pays to feed regularly with a liquid or soluble fertiliser. The best time for repotting is in spring and this should be done when inspection shows that the plants have filled their pots with roots.

Decorative Uses. With its rather distinctive appearance, *C. comosum variegatum* gives opportunities for attractive display. A position should be found for it which will show off the elegant trailing growths to full advantage, such as the edge of the staging, or a hanging basket.

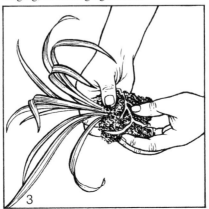

CHRYSANTHEMUM

Incurved chrysanthemum

Reflexed chrysanthemum

Anemone-centred chrysanthemum

Few plants provide so much colour in the greenhouse in autumn as late-flowering chrysanthemums. High temperatures are not required but some form of heat is necessary to overcome cold, damp conditions which can spoil the blooms. The plants can be grown in pots throughout their life or be planted outside for the summer, in which case they are lifted carefully in the early autumn and re-planted in the greenhouse border. I prefer the former method.

Varieties. A bewildering number of varieties come into flower from October until the end of the year and new ones are constantly appearing. They are classified according to flower formation and time of flowering. The incurved types have almost globular blooms with tightly packed petals while the reflexed varieties have outward pointing petals. Some reflexed types have reflexing outer petals and incurving inner petals. There are

Chrysanthemums should be staked after their final potting. Note how the canes slope outwards to allow room for development

also single, pompon and anemone-centred types.

Heat Treatment. Part of the reason why new varieties are constantly being produced is that stock gradually loses vigour. Virus diseases, for which there is no cure, can cause this weakening. However, heat-treated plants are obtainable from specialist nurserymen and these will overcome the virus problem.

Stools. After flowering, the stems of the best plants of each variety should be cut

Pompon chrysanthemum

back and, after some of the old soil has been shaken off, the stools packed close together in boxes of potting compost. Kept in a light place in a cool greenhouse new shoots soon develop around the base of the old stems. Cuttings can be made from these in January and February.

Cuttings. Use only sturdy, short-jointed shoots, about 3 in. long. The lower leaves are removed and each cutting trimmed below a joint at the base with a sharp knife. Rooting powder is helpful.

A suitable compost consists of 1 part loam, 2 parts moist peat and 3 parts coarse sand. Insert the cuttings round the

edge of 3-in. pots filled with this mixture and place them in a propagating frame, or put them directly into a bed of sandy soil in a propagating frame. Water them thoroughly and label all batches of cuttings with their variety. They will root in a temperature of 7°C. (45°F.). Shade with newspaper if there are bright spells of sunshine, and wipe the condensation from the glass of the frame each day. Little water will be needed, but the compost must not be allowed to dry out.

Single chrysanthemum

The First Potting. Use 3-in. pots and John Innes No. 1 Potting Compost for the first potting. Afterwards, give the plants a good watering and stand them on the staging, well spaced out and in full light. Encourage sturdy growth by maintaining a temperature of 7°C. (45°F.) and opening the roof ventilators each day unless there is severe weather or fog.

In March the plants may be moved to a cold frame, provided protective material, such as sacking or straw, is available to cover the frame on cold nights – if the frame is heated so much the better. Water carefully. After potting little water

Boxing chrysanthemum stools. New shoots will develop around the base of the old stems, and these can be used for cuttings

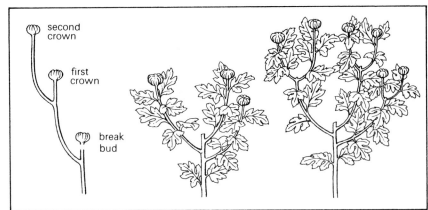

Stopping chrysanthemums to encourage the production of flower buds. First crown buds, as in the centre picture, appear after the removal of the break bud. Second crown buds, as on the right, are the result of removing the first crown buds

will be needed until new roots develop. When cold, keep the soil on the dry side.

Stopping. The term stopping means removing the tip of the shoot to induce sideshoots to form. It is not always necessary as some varieties 'break' or produce side stems naturally. These will produce flower buds at their tips in due course called first crown buds. Some varieties, mainly late-flowering ones, are given a second stopping to induce more side growths to develop. The buds which form on these are called second crown buds.

One cannot generalise about stopping; each variety must be treated individually. Most chrysanthemum specialists give stopping dates in their catalogues which can be followed or varied slightly.

The Second Potting. When the young plants begin to fill the 3-in. pots with roots, pot on into 5- or 6-in. pots using John Innes No. 2 Potting Compost. Give

the plants a good soaking first so that they can be knocked out of the pots easily. Firm the new compost well around the root ball and leave about 1 in. of space between the compost and the rim of the pot for watering. Label the pots with the varietal names immediately, then return the plants to the frame and give little water for the first few days after the initial watering. As the plants become re-established, open the frames fully by day to encourage sturdy growth.

The Final Potting. This is usually carried out in early June, as the roots begin to fill the 6-in. pots. Water the plants well a little while before repotting. Use 8-in. pots and John Innes No. 3 Potting Compost which must be made firm with a rammer. Leave space for later topdressing with fresh compost. Remember to transfer the labels.

Staking. It is convenient to stake the plants at this stage. I place three stout

bamboo canes in each pot, looping raffia around them to keep the plants secure. Make further ties as the plants grow.

Standing Out. The plants are stood outside in rows for the summer on an ash base or on pieces of slate to prevent worms getting into the pots. To secure the plants, stretch wires between strong posts at a height of about 4 ft. and secure the canes in the pots to them.

Watering and Feeding. Inspect the plants at least once a day in summer; two or three waterings may be needed each day in very hot weather. As the plants fill their pots with roots, topdress with fresh potting compost and feed with dry or liquid fertiliser to keep them growing steadily. Feed only when the compost is moist to avoid scorching the roots. Water dry fertiliser in well.

Pest and Disease Control. Regular spraying with a suitable insecticide or fungicide will prevent most troubles. Capsid bugs,

Preparing chrysanthemum cuttings. The base of the cutting should be trimmed with a sharp penknife or razor blade

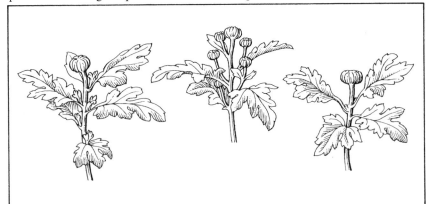

Sideshooting and disbudding are both important tasks for the chrysanthemum grower if large blooms are required. Side-shoots (left) and buds (centre) should be removed as soon as they are large enough to handle, except with spray varieties

leaf miners and aphids are common pests – all can be checked with BHC. Mildew, causing a white powdery deposit on the leaves, can be controlled with thiram applied as a spray, or dinocap as a smoke under glass. Another suitable fungicide is sulphur, applied as a dust.

Side-shooting and Disbudding. The young growths forming in the joints of the leaves on the flower stems must be removed as they appear except for varieties grown as sprays. Do this with the fingers or a sharp knife. Also disbud to leave one bud on each stem, pinching out the surplus ones while they are quite small.

Housing. The plants must be taken into the greenhouse in the latter part of September, first removing all dead or shrivelled leaves and spraying with a combined insecticide and fungicide. Allow them plenty of space and keep the ventilators fully open whenever the weather permits. A little heat at night in the autumn will keep the air circulating.

CINERARIA

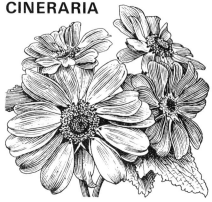

Any gardener who can maintain a temperature in his greenhouse in winter of at least 7°C. (45°F.) can grow cinerarias. Their brightly coloured daisy flowers provide a wonderful splash of colour in late winter and early spring. In small greenhouses it is probably best to grow the Multiflora Nana strains, which grow about 15 in. tall. My favourites are the large-flowered Grandiflora hybrids which have great appeal and grow about 2 ft. tall. Even taller are the Stellata cinerarias which have a branching habit and bear masses of small flowers.

Seed Sowing. Seed can be sown in April, May and June to provide a succession of blooms. Plants from an April sowing should flower in December or January.

Above: Goya, an early-flowering chrysanthemum belonging to the reflexed decorative group

Below: Charm chrysanthemums make bushy, spreading plants. Unlike other types, they need little support

Seed compost should be used, and for the later sowings the seed pans or pots can be stood in a cold frame and covered with glass or paper. This should be removed as soon as the seedlings appear, and when the seedlings are large enough to handle they must be pricked out into boxes of John Innes No. 1 Potting Compost. The young plants should be kept in a light place but be given shade from strong sunshine.

Potting. Before the seedlings become overcrowded in the boxes, move them individually to 3½-in. pots using John Innes No. 1 Potting Compost. Water the boxes thoroughly before disturbing the plants and, provided the potting compost is moist, give no more water for a few days after potting. The final potting is into 5- or 6-in. pots of John Innes No. 2 Potting Compost. The soil level in the pot must be about 1 in. below the rim to allow for watering. Potting should be done as soon as the roots begin to fill the small pots. At all stages, adequate drainage must be given as cinerarias will not tolerate waterlogged soil. In the case of clay pots this can be provided by crocks, and with plastic pots extra sand can be added to the compost.

Summer Treatment. Cinerarias do not like high temperatures and for the summer they are best kept in a cold frame, preferably standing on or plunged in a bed of ashes to prevent rapid drying out. The plants must be given shade from the sun otherwise they will soon wilt, and watering must be attended to carefully. Greenfly and leaf miner can be a nuisance and at the first signs of these pests, spray with a suitable insecticide.

Stopping. The tops of some of the plants can be pinched out – when they are in their final pots – if it is desired to delay flowering and so provide a longer display of flowers.

Feeding. Feed with a liquid or soluble fertiliser throughout late summer and autumn until the flowers appear. Then in late September take the plants into the greenhouse allowing them plenty of space. Ventilate freely in suitable weather and water very carefully when temperatures are low.

Although cinerarias are perennials, they are best treated as annuals, raising new plants from seed each year.

Above: One of the many varieties of perpetual-flowering carnation. These plants like cool, light, spacious conditions

Below: Cinerarias add colour to the cool greenhouse in late winter and spring. Careful watering is essential

CITRUS

Orange

Citrus fruits include the lemon, orange, tangerine and grapefruit. Generally, it takes eight to ten years for such plants to produce fruits if they are grown from pips. Increase by budding or grafting on to seedling stock or by cuttings are quicker methods of securing fruiting specimens, and are essential for specific varieties. Budding is done in early spring, grafting in late summer.

I grew some lemons from cuttings which are now in 9-in. pots and produce 30 to 40 fine large fruits each year. (One is shown in the picture of my sun lounge on p. 31.)

Cultivation. As a growing medium for the lemons I use John Innes No. 3 Potting Compost to which a little more peat has been added for citrus fruits seem to appreciate a slightly acid soil. They also need a moist atmosphere and free ventilation in the growing season.

They do not need high temperatures during winter and will come to no harm if the temperature falls to 4°C. (40°F.). Their greatest enemy is brown scale which I control with white oil emulsion or a weak solution of malathion.

In time the trees can become far too large for the sun lounge or conservatory. This can be countered by not allowing the trees more root area than that provided by a 9-in. pot. If this is done, then the plants should be removed from their

pots each year so that some of the old soil can be teased out from among the roots and new soil added when they are returned to the pots.

Propagation. The easiest way to increase citrus plants is by seed, but as already mentioned it will take several years for fruits to appear. Germinate the pips in seed compost in a propagating frame with a temperature of 13°C. (55°F.). Pot up the seedlings singly using 3-in. pots and John Innes No. 1 Potting Compost.

Cuttings can be taken from April to September and rooted in a propagating frame at a temperature of 18°C. (65°F.).

CLIVIA

C. miniata

The clivia or Kaffir Lily is a tender evergreen with attractive lily-like flowers of yellow, red or orange colouring. The flowers are borne between March and June, depending on the temperature which is provided; the higher the temperature the earlier the flowers appear. Most of those grown are forms of *Clivia miniata*, or, less commonly, *C. nobilis*.

Cultivation. The fleshy roots should be potted in February into 5- to 10-in. pots (depending on the size of the roots), using John Innes No. 1 Potting Compost. Place the pots in a sunny position and provide a temperature of around 13°C. (55°F.). From the time growth commences until September water the plants freely and feed with liquid or soluble fertiliser at regular intervals. Such feeding

– and topdressing in spring – is particularly important as this is a plant which should not be repotted too often. It likes to be pot-bound and dividing and repotting most certainly hinders flowering. Shade should be provided against strong sunshine to prevent scorching, and the handsome leaves need occasional sponging over to keep them glossy.

The plants can be stood in a sunny frame or outside under a south- or west-facing wall or fence from June to September, provided watering and feeding is not neglected.

From September to spring watering must be done with especial care – only enough being given to avoid drying out – and the temperature must be kept at or above 7°C. (45°F.).

Propagation. The usual method of increase is by division of the crowns in February at the time of repotting, but plants can also be raised from seed sown at a temperature of 21°C. (70°F.). In the latter case, though, it will be three or four years before the plants which result bear their first flowers.

CODIAEUM

A plant which is grown for its colourful foliage is the codiaeum, or croton. It is by the latter, outdated, name that it is still, perhaps, best known. The colouring of the foliage varies with the variety and there are also variations in leaf shape – some are long and strap-like while others are more rounded.

Cultivation. To grow codiaeums successfully a minimum winter temperature of 13°C. (55°F.) is needed. In summer, temperatures can rise to 24°C. (75°F.), provided a humid atmosphere is main-

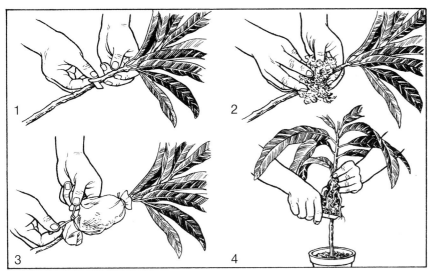

Air layering a codiaeum. **1.** A short upward cut is made in the stem. **2** and **3.** After dusting with rooting powder, damp moss is wrapped around the cut and the moss is enclosed in polythene. **4.** When roots appear, the new plant is severed from the parent

tained. The colour of the leaves is more intense in good light but it is wise to provide some shade against strong sunshine.

Air Layering. As codiaeums age they tend to lose their lower leaves and the best way of obtaining young plants with foliage down to soil level is to air layer an older plant. This is done by making a cut, about 1 in. long, part way through a stem to form a tongue. The cut surfaces are dusted with hormone rooting powder and then surrounded with damp moss. This is enclosed with a piece of polythene and tied above and below with raffia or twine. The polythene prevents moisture evaporating from the moss. When roots are seen twining amongst the moss the new plant can be severed from the parent just below the new root system.

Potting. The roots at this stage are rather brittle and they must be handled carefully. Put the new plant in a 3-in. pot of John Innes No. 1 Potting Compost without removing the moss and keep it in a warm part of the greenhouse until more roots have developed. Later, move to a 5- or 6-in. pot filled with John Innes No. 2 Potting Compost.

Feeding. Codiaeums soon fill their final pots with roots and to keep them growing well they should be fed each week with a soluble or liquid fertiliser.

Cuttings. Instead of air layering plants, cuttings can be made from the ends of young shoots. Do not remove too many of the lower leaves otherwise the new plant will have a bare stem. Cuttings root without difficulty in pots of sandy soil in a propagating frame with a temperature of 18 to 21°C. (65 to 70°F.).

Pest Control. A careful watch should be kept on the plants for signs of such pests as mealy bugs and red spider mites. The latter increase rapidly in the hot conditions which codiaeums enjoy. Regular sponging of the foliage with a white oil emulsion insecticide will help to keep the plants clear of these pests and it will also enhance the appearance of the foliage.

COLEUS

The handsome leaves of *Coleus blumei* are available in a variety of colours, including many shades of red, purple and green. The plants are grown for their beautiful leaves, and the flowers, which are not very decorative, are pinched out whenever they appear. If the flowers are left on the plants, the leaves lose much of their colour.

To grow coleus well a minimum temperature in winter of 10°C. (50°F.) is needed. At lower temperatures, or if plants receive a check in growth, they are likely to drop their leaves, but given a warm greenhouse, coleus are not difficult plants to grow.

Propagation. It used to be the case that coleus raised from seed were of poor colour. This is no longer so and raising plants in this way, rather than from cuttings, saves the bother of over-wintering old plants.

Seed Sowing. Seed should be sown in February or March in a seed compost and germinated in a propagating frame with a temperature of 16 to 18°C. (60 to 65°F.). The resulting seedlings should be potted singly in 3-in. pots of John Innes No. 1 Potting Compost as soon as they can be handled. When they have become well rooted in these pots they can be potted on into 5-in. pots using a similar compost.

Cuttings. Particularly attractive plants should be propagated by vegetative means, i.e. by cuttings, as this is the only way in which they will come true to colour and form. The cuttings are made from young sideshoots taken from mature plants in spring or summer, inserted singly in small pots filled with sandy compost and placed in a propagating frame with a temperature of at least 16°C. (60°F.). Young plants have the most colourful foliage and it is wise to take cuttings several times in the summer so that there are always new plants available as the older ones are discarded.

Potting. Rooted cuttings are put first into 3-in. pots filled with John Innes No. 1 Potting Compost and are later moved into 5- or 6-in. pots.

Cultivation. Give the plants plenty of light to encourage good colour, and when temperatures are high, a humid atmosphere should be maintained by damping down the floors and stagings in the greenhouse. This will help to prevent the plants from flagging.

Stopping. The tops of the shoots should be nipped out at intervals to induce a bushy habit.

Streptocarpus, gloxinias and coleus form
the centre of attraction in this greenhouse
scene. Other plants include ivies, fuchsias
and *Begonia rex*, with *Hoya carnosa*
trained along the roof

Above: *Clivia nobilis*, with its large clusters of flowers and strap-like leaves. **Below left:** A fine display of codiaeums, with the striped leaves of an aphelandra in the foreground. **Below right:** The widely varied leaf colourings of coleus

COLUMNEA

C. gloriosa

The columneas are plants of a trailing nature which are ideal for growing in hanging baskets or in 5- or 6-in. pots which are then suspended by wire from the greenhouse roof. Of the species available, the best known and most attractive is the red-and-yellow flowered *Columnea gloriosa*. These tubular flowers are borne in profusion on the growths during winter, a cheery sight which is especially welcome at that time of year.

Cultivation. When making up a basket of these plants, line the wire frame with moss and then add a compost mixture. This should be reasonably rich, and the John Innes No. 2 Potting Compost would be a suitable choice. The young plants should be positioned fairly close together around the rim of the basket.

Columneas need a minimum winter temperature of 13°C. (55°F.), but in summer it may rise to 24°C. (75°F.), provided the atmosphere is kept moist and there is shade from strong sunshine.

The plants need plentiful supplies of water in summer but more moderate amounts must be given during the rest of the year, especially winter. Just give them enough at that time to keep the compost from becoming dry.

Propagation. This is quite an easy plant to increase from cuttings. These should be made from half-ripened wood in spring, the shoots being cut into pieces 2 to 3 in. long and rooted in sand and peat in a warm propagating frame. When the cuttings have rooted they should be moved into 3½-in. pots.

CUCUMBER

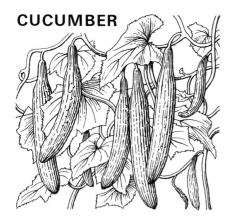

Most of us appreciate the value of cucumbers for use in salads and sandwiches, and they are a crop well worth growing if a minimum temperature of 16°C. (60°F.) can be maintained. The best and biggest crops are obtained from greenhouse-grown cucumbers but they can also be grown in frames if so desired. Whichever method is chosen, the plants need close attention to detail if they are to flourish.

Seed Sowing. The seeds can be sown singly in 3-in. pots of seed compost at intervals between January and the end of April and germinated in a temperature of 18 to 21°C. (65 to 70°F.). The seedlings will appear within three or four days given warm, moist conditions. They should be watered freely.

Planting. Before the plants fill their pots with roots they should be planted out in a bed on the greenhouse staging or in large pots filled with good soil such as the John Innes No. 3 Potting Compost. If planting out has to be delayed it is wise to move the plants from their 3-in. pots into 5-in. pots to prevent them becoming starved and setting back their growth.

To prepare the bed, make a ridge of rich compost about 15 in. wide and 7 in. deep in the centre for the young plants and plant these 3 to 5 ft. apart. A suitable mixture would be the John Innes No. 3 Potting Compost.

Topdressing and Feeding. When the white roots of the plants break through the surface, topdress by adding a thin layer of similar compost. Feeds of a suitable fertiliser will maintain good growth.

Training. The main stem of each cucumber should be tied to a vertical wire or bamboo cane and allowed to grow until it reaches the top of the roof before the tip is removed. Side stems or laterals will form and the tips of these should be removed at one leaf beyond the first fruit. The shoots should be tied carefully to horizontal wires and sub-laterals must all be kept stopped at one leaf beyond the first fruit. All male flowers must also be removed to prevent fertilisation of the female flowers as this would make the fruits bitter.

If the plants are grown well, fruit can be cut within 12 to 14 weeks of sowing the seed.

Watering. Shade is needed from strong sunshine and copious supplies of water are needed as the plants develop. Syringe the plants daily with tepid water.

Frame Cultivation. If the plants are to be grown in frames, sow the seed in March as already described. The young plants can be planted in a similar compost to that used in the greenhouse. In heated frames they should be planted in April and in unheated frames at the end of May or in early June. Soon after planting the plants are stopped by pinching out the growing point. Four lateral growths are then allowed to develop and these are trained to the four corners of the frame and stopped at the fourth leaf. Shade the glass to prevent the sun scorching the plants. Cut the cucumbers regularly when they reach a suitable size. Again, the plants will need a lot of water and weekly feeding with a compound fertiliser when they are established will pay. Topdress the beds as already described for greenhouse cultivation.

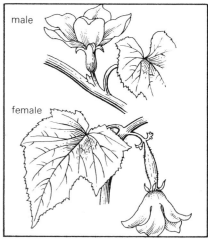

Male and female cucumber flowers are easily distinguishable for the female has an embryo fruit directly behind the petals

Varieties. Butcher's Disease-resisting is a splendid old variety which is much favoured and Simex is a recently introduced, non-bitter, all female F$_1$ hybrid. Improved Telegraph is especially suitable for frame cultivation

Cucumbers can be grown in a greenhouse border, in beds on the staging or in large pots. A good rich compost is needed for these plants, such as the John Innes No. 3 Potting Compost

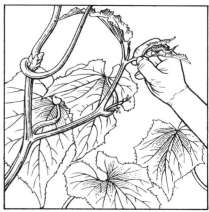

Stopping a cucumber lateral at one leaf beyond the first fruit. Sometimes a cucumber fruit will develop at this point too

CYCLAMEN

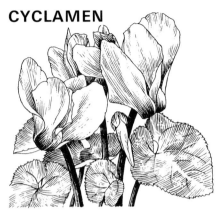

Cyclamen give a wonderful display of colour from autumn until spring, and they are one of my favourite pot plants. To grow well, the plants need a minimum temperature in winter of 10°C. (50°F.). Plants are raised from seed and there are strains available with pink, red, white, violet and crimson flowers. There are also types that have frilled edges to their petals and these make charming companions for the usual kinds.

Seed Sowing. I sow cyclamen seed in June but sowing can also be done in August to provide plants for flowering at the end of the following year. Some gardeners also sow in January but at that time of year it is often difficult to provide sufficiently high temperatures to germinate the seed.

The seed should be spaced out evenly on the surface of a pan of seed compost, and covered lightly with sifted compost which is then firmed. The pan should be covered with a pane of glass and a sheet of newspaper to prevent rapid drying out of the compost. Wipe the condensation from the glass daily and remove the coverings as soon as the seed germinates. The pan is then stood in a warm, shaded part of the greenhouse.

Pricking Out. When the seedlings are large enough to handle, lift them carefully with a dibber and prick them out into boxes of John Innes No. 1 Potting Compost. This must be done before the seedlings have too many roots. Some seeds take several weeks longer than others to germinate so the seed pan should not be discarded until the required number of seedlings has appeared. Hold the seedlings by their seed leaves to avoid bruising the delicate stems. Space the seedlings about 1½ in. apart.

The First Potting. New growth is soon made in warm, moist conditions with shade from the sun. Before the seedlings become overcrowded pot them singly in 3-in. pots, using John Innes No. 2 Potting Compost to which extra coarse sand has been added to give the plants really good drainage. Firm the soil around the roots with the fingers and be careful not to set the plants too deeply. Leave a space between compost and pot rim for watering. A winter temperature of 10 to 13°C. (50 to 55°F.) is adequate and the pots can be stood on a greenhouse shelf so that they get the maximum amount of light available.

The Final Potting. As the plants fill their pots with roots they should be transferred to their flowering pots, the strongest going into 6-in. pots and the weaker ones into 5-in. Use John Innes No. 2 Potting Compost, making it moderately firm, and keep the top of the corm just above soil level to prevent it from rotting off.

Summer Treatment. Cyclamen like cool conditions in summer and the best place for them is a cold frame with shade being provided from the sun. Sinking the pots in a bed of ashes reduces the frequency of watering. Overhead sprays of water are beneficial and the frame lights can be removed entirely at night. Allow plenty of space between the plants, and as the roots fill the pots, feed the plants each week with a suitable fertiliser.

Housing. Towards the end of September and before hard frosts arrive the plants must be returned to a frost-free greenhouse. At this time remove any dead leaves and green slime from the pots. Free ventilation is needed, and on warm days damp the floor and staging with water to maintain a humid atmosphere.

Pest Control. If aphids are seen spray the plants thoroughly with a suitable insecticide. Small cream-coloured grubs are often found feeding on the roots of cyclamen. These are the grubs of the vine weevil (which also attack begonias). The use of BHC insecticide will destroy them and where this pest is troublesome, dust the potting compost with BHC.

Ventilation. As the weather becomes cooler and there is less heat from the sun pay particular attention to ventilation to avoid conditions becoming damp and stuffy. Sufficient heat should be provided to keep a steady temperature of at least 10°C. (50°F.) at night. Should signs of the grey mould fungus (botrytis) appear, which is common when conditions are too damp, a fungicidal dust can be

Cyclamen must be watered carefully, particularly when applying liquid fertiliser, as the leaves are easily scorched

When potting cyclamen, care must be taken not to cover the corm with compost, otherwise it will tend to rot off

In order to build up strong plants, the first flower buds of cyclamen are removed. This is done by giving them a sharp pull

The delightful blue, star-like flowers of
Campanula isophylla, and its variety *alba*.
The trailing habit of these plants makes them
ideal for growing at the edge of the staging

Above: Cyclamen, one of the most popular of all greenhouse plants. They need careful attention to detail

Below: Spring is an attractive time in the greenhouse. This fine display includes cyclamen, cinerarias, primulas and narcissi

applied with a small puffer. Any leaves that shrivel must be removed as botrytis often starts to develop on a damaged leaf.

Removing Flowers. The first flowers appear in early autumn but I remove these until the main 'flush' of flowers develop. The way to remove a flower is to hold the stem between the thumb and first finger and give a sharp tug. The stem should then come away cleanly without leaving a piece at the base which could rot and cause trouble later on.

Watering and Feeding. This must be done very carefully in winter. The compost must not be kept too wet otherwise the flower and leaf stalks will rot. When applying liquid fertilisers take care to see that none of the liquid touches the leaves or scorching will occur.

Faded Flowers. As the flowers fade they should be removed – by giving the stems a sharp tug – so that the plant does not waste energy on producing seed.

Keeping Corms. The best plants can be kept for another year and once flowering has finished they should be put to one side in the greenhouse where they can continue to grow for a while.

Resting. During the summer the corms should be allowed to rest by withholding water, although I do not think it is wise to dry them off completely as it is very often difficult to start dry corms into growth again.

Watering. In July watering can begin again and if plants are sprayed overhead with water it will help to encourage new growth.

Repotting. As young leaves appear the plants should be repotted. All the old leaves should be cleared away and the plants tapped out of their pots. Some of the old soil can be scraped away so that the plant can be put in a clean pot of the same size: 5- or 6-in. Fresh John Innes No. 2 Potting Compost should be used. Keep the corm slightly above the level of the compost.

The plants soon make progress if stood in a shaded cold frame and given similar treatment to younger plants. Water sparingly after repotting but give more water once roots have formed. The plants should flower at about the same time as those raised from seed. Plants more than two years old lose vigour and are not worth keeping, in my opinion.

DIEFFENBACHIA

D. amoena

This attractive foliage plant has the common name of Dumb Cane. It is a warm greenhouse plant, needing a temperature of 16 to 21°C. (60 to 70°F.) from April to September and 13 to 16°C. (55 to 60°F.) from October to March. It makes a splendid house plant where the required temperature can be maintained.

Dieffenbachias eventually grow several feet tall and have stems of substantial thickness. The leaves are large and, in the varieties usually grown, spotted to a greater or lesser degree in white.

A moist atmosphere is appreciated and a warm, even temperature essential. Fluc-tuations in temperature soon have their effect on the foliage.

The kinds usually grown are forms of *Dieffenbachia picta.* Another handsome species is *D. amoena* with large, shapely, heavily marked leaves.

The common name I mentioned earlier has a story attached to it which is worth telling. The plant contains an acrid sap which is poisonous and must on no account be brought near the mouth or eyes. If it does contact the mouth, it may cause choking and an inability to speak – hence the name Dumb Cane. However, since dieffenbachias smell so unpleasant when they are cut, it is very unlikely that this would happen.

Propagation. Dieffenbachias can be increased quite readily by rooting pieces of stem 2 to 3 in. long containing at least one bud. These should be dried off for a couple of days after cutting and then be placed in sand which is kept warm and moist. Watch for signs of sprouting and pot singly when sufficient roots have been formed.

Propagating a dieffenbachia by stem cuttings. **1** and **2.** The old bare stem is cut up into pieces about 2 or 3 in. long, each bearing a dormant bud. **3.** The cut ends should be allowed to dry off for a day or two before rooting the stems in warm, moist sand. **4.** Eventually, small shoots will grow from the previously dormant buds and the young plants can then be potted up

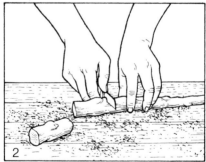

DIZYGOTHECA

D. elegantissima

Like the dieffenbachias described earlier, the dizygothecas – formerly called aralias – need warm greenhouse treatment, or, if grown in the home, warm, equable, non-stuffy conditions. Perhaps it should be pointed out, too, that this is a shrub (or dwarf tree if you like) which cannot be kept in good condition for more than a few years. Adult forms are unknown of two much-grown species: *Dizygotheca elegantissima* with green and white leaf stalks, and *D. kerchoveana* with wavy-edged leaflets. Another species grown is *D. veitchii* which has glossy leaflets with red undersides. All come from islands in the South Pacific.

These foliage plants have a very attractive appearance. Their leaves, which radiate from a central stem, consist of narrow leaflets with toothed edges. They are excellent for combining with flowering plants in a composite display, but draughts will cause the leaves to drop.

Cultivation. All dizygothecas like rich, acid soil with plenty of peat or leaf-mould added. Potting is best carried out in March using pots which are just large enough to accommodate the roots comfortably. Good drainage is essential.

The plants should be watered freely in summer, sparingly at other times. A temperature of 18°C. (65°F.) or more is needed from April to September and one of 13 to 16°C. (55 to 60°F.) from October to March.

Propagation. Increase is by cuttings rooted in sand in a propagating frame at a temperature of 18°C. (65°F.).

DRACAENA

D. terminalis

Grown for their handsome, colourful foliage, dracaenas need a temperature of 16°C. (60°F.) or more from April to September, and 13 to 16°C. (55 to 60°F.) from October to March. They thrive in a hot, humid atmosphere. *Dracaena terminalis* is more correctly called *Cordyline terminalis* – the two families are rather confused – and it has numerous varieties with foliage variously tinged rose, green and white. *D. fragrans victoriae* is even more showy with handsome green and cream striped leaves. *D. godseffiana* Florida Beauty is a trailing variety with green leaves speckled with white. As dracaenas age they tend to lose their lower leaves and if young plants are propagated each year these can take their place.

Propagation. There are several ways of increasing dracaenas. Some kinds can be raised from seed but special forms or varieties must be propagated from cuttings. Pieces of stem can be cut into 1-in. lengths and if these are placed in a warm, moist propagating frame in sandy, peaty soil dormant buds will soon develop to form new plants. Another method is to take root cuttings or 'toes' from the plants.

D. fragrans victoriae

These are cut off with a sharp knife and placed in small pots containing sandy potting soil. The best time for taking these cuttings is in spring and summer, and in a warm propagating frame new growth soon forms.

Potting. The young plants are moved first to 3-in. pots filled with John Innes No. 1

Preparing root cuttings of dracaena. **1.** Sturdy pieces of root, about an inch in length are cut with a sharp knife. **2** and **3.** These are placed in pots of sandy compost and covered with a similar mixture. **4.** In a warm propagating frame, new roots will soon form, and eventually a small shoot will be produced

D. godseffiana Florida Beauty

Potting Compost and they should be kept in the warmest part of the greenhouse until they are growing away well. Later, they can be potted on into 5- or 6-in. pots. After taking root cuttings, the old plants must be repotted. Use the same sized pots and John Innes No. 2 Potting Compost which should be well firmed round the roots.

Syringing and Shading. During hot weather the plants benefit if they are syringed overhead. Rain water is best for this purpose as hard tap water will mark the foliage. The leaves are particularly susceptible to damage in the winter and they should not be sprayed overhead at that time. Sponging of the leaves is necessary to keep them healthy and to bring out their full beauty. The variegated kinds need good light but shade should be given from strong sunshine.

Watering and Feeding. Once the plants have filled their pots with roots, water should be given liberally and regular feeds of liquid fertiliser supplied.

House Plants. The dracaenas are nowadays used as house plants but, as already pointed out, they have rather exacting temperature and atmospheric requirements and it is as well to remember this when considering them for house display.

FERNS

Asplenium bulbiferum

There are several ferns which are invaluable for their decorative effect. These include *Asplenium bulbiferum* and *A. nidus*, adiantum (Maidenhair Fern), platycerium (The Stag's Horn Fern), pteris, nephrolepis and woodwardia.

ASPLENIUM

Asplenium bulbiferum is the well-known Spleenwort. This needs a temperature in winter of 7 to 10°C. (45 to 50°F.). Potting should be carried out in March and John Innes No. 1 Potting Compost would be a suitable growing medium. Water must be supplied freely in summer.

This fern produces small plants or bulbils on the veins of the fronds. These can be removed and laid on the surface of a mixture of 2 parts moist peat and 1 part coarse sand in a seed box. The bulbils can be held close to the compost in the box with bent pieces of wire. If they are kept moist and in a temperature of 16°C. (60°F.), roots will soon develop. The small ferns can be potted into 2-in. pots of John Innes No. 1 Potting Compost.

Asplenium nidus, the distinctive Bird's Nest Fern with undivided fronds up to 4 ft. long and 8 in. wide, is a plant which needs more heat – not less than 16°C. (60°F.) in autumn and winter, rising with sun heat during the rest of the year. Shade from strong sun must be provided. A suitable compost consists of equal parts coarse peat and sphagnum moss.

This species is increased by means of spores which can be germinated on fine peat and brick dust and kept shaded under a glass covering. The compost should be sterilised at least 12 hours before sowing by scalding it with boiling water.

ADIANTUM

There are various adiantums or Maidenhair Ferns which can be grown in shady positions in heated and unheated greenhouses. For the former, heated to 16 to 18°C. (60 to 65°F.), *Adiantum cuneatum*, *A. decorum* and *A. williamsii* are suitable, for the latter *A. capillus-veneris*, *A. pedatum* and *A. venustum*.

Adiantum cuneatum and *A. decorum* can be moved to rooms in the home for limited periods provided they are placed in cool, well-lit positions but without direct sunshine falling on them. To maintain good health the atmosphere must be kept moist, which is possible in the greenhouse but more difficult indoors.

The three species I have named as suitable for an unheated house must also be given humid atmospheric conditions. They are not difficult to grow well and can be progressively potted on to make large specimens. Potting should be done in early spring using John Innes No. 1 Potting

Compost. Water should be supplied freely from April to August and moderately for the rest of the year when growth is less active.

Adiantums can be increased by dividing the crowns of the plants between March and April. This must be done carefully to avoid damaging the fronds and roots, preferably with two hand forks placed back to back and then prised apart, as one would divide herbaceous plants with garden forks. Spores can also be germin-

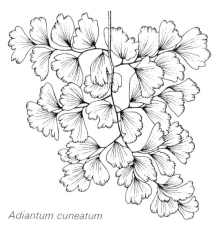

Adiantum cuneatum

ated as recommended for *Asplenium nidus* but this is a much slower process.

PLATYCERIUM

The platycerium or Stag's Horn Fern (the common name is really appropriate) is an imposing plant for the greenhouse whether grown in pots or, even better, on a piece of bark or wood. All the platyceriums except one, *Platycerium bifurcatum* (syn. *P. alcicorne*) need really warm greenhouse conditions but this fine species is prefectly happy in a cool greenhouse.

The most satisfactory form of display, as I have indicated, is to suspend the plants on bark or wood from the roof or sides of the greenhouse. The roots should be covered with a layer of sphagnum moss and fibrous peat, these being retained in position with pieces of copper wire. Topdressing with the same materials should be done in February or March.

Water should be given freely from April to September and moderately for the rest of the year. Shade must be given from direct sun but this plant needs good light.

Platycerium bifurcatum is increased by division in spring as with adiantum.

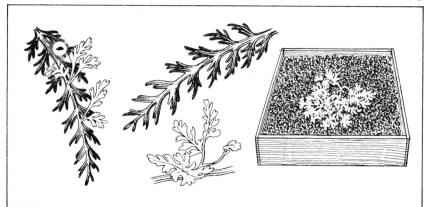

Asplenium bulbiferum is an interesting fern, for it produces small plants on the veins of mature fronds. If these are detached and pegged down in a sandy compost, roots will soon develop and the young plants can be potted up individually

Above left: *Asplenium nidus*, the Bird's Nest Fern. The beautiful, undivided fronds can reach as much as 4 ft. in length if the plants are given the conditions they like.

Above right: *Woodwardia radicans*, an ideal fern for a cool greenhouse or conservatory. Cool conditions are essential to avoid damage from thrips and scale insects

PTERIS

The pteris are popular ferns for the cool greenhouse, especially *Pteris cretica* which has pretty fronds up to a foot in length, and the handsome *P. ensiformis victoriae* with variegated foliage. This last needs shade from strong light to get the best effect from the variegation and *P. cretica* needs shade in summer.

Pteris should be potted in March using John Innes No. 1 Potting Compost. In spring and summer they need plenty of water but less during the other seasons. A winter temperature of 7°C. (45°F.) is desirable.

Pteris are increased by division in spring, carried out with care to avoid damaging the roots and fronds.

NEPHROLEPIS

The nephrolepis (see p. 22) are ferns noted for their beauty and desirability as hanging basket plants. One, *Nephrolepis exaltata*, the Ladder Fern, has especial appeal with its arching fronds over 2 ft. long. This fern needs a winter temperature of 13 to 16°C. (55 to 60°F.).

Potting should be carried out in February or March using John Innes No. 1 Potting Compost. Water should be given freely from April to September and moderately during the rest of the year.

Increase is by division of the crowns between February and April.

WOODWARDIA

Woodwardia radicans is a delightful fern to grow in a cool or unheated greenhouse, and may even be grown out of doors in sheltered gardens if covered with bracken fronds or similar protective material during winter. It is best of all planted out in a greenhouse border, when the fronds reach 5 or more feet in length but it can be grown in pots or hanging baskets, in which case the fronds are much shorter.

Increase is by bulbils, as described for *Asplenium bulbiferum*, or by division of the crowns.

Platycerium bifurcatum

Pteris cretica

FICUS

F. elastica

F. benjamina

Numerous species and varieties of ficus are grown nowadays as greenhouse and room plants. By far the best known and most widely grown is the stylish Rubber Plant, *Ficus elastica*, and especially its variety *decora*. This last has dark red undersides to the young leaves and a pink sheath to the terminal bud. The bold, ovate leaves are of a dark green colour, glowing and handsome when the plant is in good condition. A comparative newcomer but not so easy to grow as well as *F. e. decora* is the variegated variety *tricolor* which has leaves marked with cream, pink and green, a pleasing com-

bination of colours. This must be given a lighter position than the ordinary green-leaved kinds. It is also a much slower growing variety, as is common with variegated plants.

A ficus of great charm is *F. benjamina*, with spreading, arched branches from which hang pointed, glossy green leaves to give the impression of a miniature weeping tree, hence its common name of Weeping Fig. Another choice ficus, but one which is harder to please than the Rubber Plant, is *F. lyrata*, the aptly named Fiddle-leaved Fig with large leaves of distinctive shape and a slightly paler green than the Rubber Plant. Two trailing kinds are the small-leaved, almost hardy *F. pumila* (syn. *F. repens*) and the larger-leaved *F. radicans*, which also has a silver-variegated form, *F. r. variegata*.

Cultivation. These plants should be potted or planted in February, March or April using John Innes No. 2 Potting Compost. Water should be given in only moderate quantities from October to March but freely at other times. In hot weather all ficuses will benefit if the paths and staging of the greenhouse are damped down to provide a more humid atmosphere. Creeping species like *pumila* and *radicans* are best planted in beds where the shoots can cling to walls or to mossed supports which can be kept damp. These ficuses need rather lower temperatures and a moister atmosphere than the others if they are to flourish.

For the rest, a temperature of 10 to 16°C. (50 to 60°F.) is suitable from October to April and 16 to 21°C. (60 to 70°F.) for the remainder of the year.

Disorders. As I have said, all these ficuses are grown nowadays as house plants, in the case of *F. elastica decora* very widely indeed, but it should be remembered that low or fluctuating temperatures and hot, stuffy conditions are likely to cause brown or yellow marks to appear on the foliage – and the same unwelcome result is likely to follow overwatering in winter. Another possible cause of trouble is overpotting which leads to stagnant root conditions and consequently leaf fall.

Air Layering. As the Rubber Plant ages it tends to lose its lower leaves and become rather leggy. A new plant can be made from the old plant by air layering. This is best done in the spring and summer when the weather is warm, for the plant is growing actively and rooting will therefore be quicker.

A diagonal cut, about $1\frac{1}{2}$ in. long, should be made in the stem about 9 to 12 in. from the tip. If necessary, one or two leaves

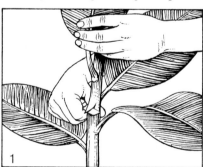

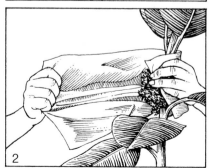

Air layering a rubber plant. **1.** A diagonal cut is made halfway through the stem. **2.** Hormone rooting powder is dusted around the cut, which is then enclosed in damp moss and polythene. **3.** After a few weeks, roots will be seen in the moss. **4.** The polythene is removed, and after severing from the parent, the new plant is potted up

should be removed so that this is possible. To keep the cut open a match stick can be inserted between the two surfaces. To assist good roots to develop at the cut surfaces the wound can be treated with a hormone rooting powder. The area is then surrounded with thoroughly moistened moss into which roots will develop. To keep the moss in a moist condition for some time it is necessary to enclose it in a piece of polythene film which is sealed at the top and bottom with string or raffia. The plant should be kept in a warm part of the greenhouse where the atmosphere is moist and watering should be carried out normally.

Inspect the layer occasionally for signs of root development, and when a good root system can be seen through the polythene the plant can be severed below the new roots. As the polythene covering is removed a mass of white roots will be seen twining among the moss. Care must be taken not to damage the young roots, which will be quite brittle.

Potting. Before the plant is potted the old piece of stem immediately below the roots should be cut off cleanly with a sharp knife. Potting may then be done without removing the moss and, depending on the size of the plant, a 5- or 6-in. pot can be used. John Innes No. 1 Potting Compost is suitable to use at this stage and it should be worked around the roots of the plant as it is held in position. The compost must be made firm around the roots without being rammed hard. Afterwards, a good watering may be given, and to help the plant

F. lyrata

F. elastica tricolor

establish itself quickly it should be stood in a warm, shaded part of the greenhouse. By air layering a plant in this way, a sizeable and attractive specimen is obtained in a very short period of time, which should be potted on as necessary.

When the top of the old plant has been removed the dormant buds in the leaf axils will begin to develop and form sideshoots. When these have produced several leaves they, in turn, can be air layered. They will give rise to slightly smaller plants than an air layering from the main stem.

Leaf Bud Cuttings. Although air layering provides a few good plants fairly quickly more plants are obtained if leaf bud cuttings are taken in spring or summer. These consist of small pieces of stem each

containing a bud and a leaf. They are placed singly in 2-in. pots containing a mixture of moist peat and coarse sand in equal parts. A propagating frame with a temperature of at least 21°C. (70°F.) is needed and the pots can be plunged in a bed of moist peat inside the frame. To prevent damage to the leaves from drips of condensation it is most important to wipe the glass covering of the frame each day. When the cuttings have rooted and the buds begin to develop they can be moved to 5-in. pots and be grown in a temperature of 16 to 18°C. (60 to 65°F.). John Innes No. 1 Potting Compost should be used for this potting, and the atmosphere around the new plants should be kept moist until they have become well established.

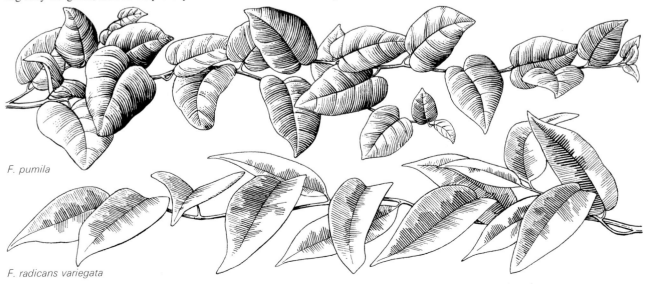

F. pumila

F. radicans variegata

The author removing the faded flowers
from a group of pelargoniums.
By doing this, the colourful display
will be considerably prolonged

FREESIA

During the summer seedling freesias can be housed in a cold frame or stood in a sheltered part of the garden

Freesias growing in 6-in. pots on the greenhouse staging. An alternative to pots is to use 6-in.-deep wooden boxes

Freesias are colourful, scented flowers on thin, wiry stems and are among the most beautiful of winter-flowering plants for the cool greenhouse. Anyone who has a greenhouse which can be heated enough to exclude frost and to maintain a temperature of 4 to 7°C. (40 to 45°F.) can grow these lovely flowers. Freesias have been developed considerably in recent years and strains can now be obtained in numerous shades, including yellow, white, orange, crimson and lavender.

Cultivation. There are two methods of

The pendant flowers of the easily grown fuchsia are always popular. This particular variety is called Mission Bells

growing freesias – from seed and from corms, but named varieties must be grown from corms.

Corms. Seven or eight corms can be placed in a 6-in. pot of John Innes No. 1 Potting Compost in August and covered with about 1 in. of compost. The pots are then placed in a cold frame under a thick covering of moist peat. This is to keep the corms cool and ensure that they will form a good root system. After a period of about six weeks the layer of peat can be removed and the pots taken from the frame and placed in a greenhouse which must be kept well ventilated.

Seed. Good strains of freesia seed are available in a mixture of lovely colours. Seedlings take about nine months to flower and if seed is sown in heat in February or March, flowers can be expected in time for Christmas. They need a temperature of 18°C. (65°F.) in which to germinate. Freesias are often sown and grown on to maturity in the same container. Boxes with a depth of 6 in. should be used for this purpose or about six seeds may be sown in a 6-in. pot. As germination is often erratic, some gardeners 'chit' the seed before sowing by mixing it with moist peat in a jar. Kept in a warm place there should soon be signs of germination and within a few days the seedlings can be spaced out in pots or boxes of John Innes No. 1 Potting Compost, taking care not to damage the young shoots or roots. During the summer the seedlings are best housed in a well-ventilated cold frame or they can be stood outside in a warm, sheltered place.

The compost in the boxes must never be allowed to dry out and ample water must be given in hot weather in the summer. In late summer feed once a week with a liquid or soluble fertiliser.

Housing. The seedling freesias must be taken into the greenhouse in September and their treatment then follows the same pattern as those started from corms. A temperature of 7°C. (45°F.) is adequate but a damp atmosphere must be avoided by careful ventilation. Less water is needed in the autumn and winter but when the soil begins to become dry, watering must be carried out.

Staking. Some support is needed to keep the foliage upright, and thin, twiggy sticks can be used for this purpose, placing them around the edge of the pot. Alternatively, insert three canes around the edge and loop raffia between them. Most of us would probably agree that the first-mentioned method is the least obtrusive, for the leaves and flower stems will soon hide the twigs.

Resting. When the flowers fade, continue to water the plants until the foliage shows signs of yellowing. Water supplies can then be reduced and the pots laid on their sides under the greenhouse staging. The corms must be kept dry in the summer while they are at rest but in August they can be removed from the pots and started into growth once more in fresh potting compost. Only the largest corms are likely to flower but the smaller ones can be grown separately to produce larger corms and these will eventually flower in a year or two.

FUCHSIA

F. Mrs Rundle

Few other plants give such a long display of colour in the cool greenhouse as the easily grown fuchsias. Many lovely varieties are available, including numerous kinds with a pendulous habit which are excellent for growing in hanging baskets. Some vigorous, upright varieties, such as Rose of Castille and Duchess of Albany, can be treated as permanent greenhouse climbers if planted in a border. There are also some interesting species, such as *Fuchsia corymbiflora* with clusters of deep red flowers and *F. fulgens* with slender reddish flowers.

Cuttings. Cuttings taken in July to September will provide plants for flowering the following summer. A temperature of 16 to 18°C. (60 to 65°F.) is needed to root the cuttings. Young sideshoots, a few inches long, are removed and trimmed below a joint with a sharp knife. Any flowers or buds are removed, also some of the lower leaves. Dipping the cuttings in hormone rooting powder aids rooting.

A suitable compost consists of equal parts of moist granulated peat and coarse sand or, alternatively, 1 part medium loam, 2 parts moist peat and 3 parts coarse sand. Insert the cuttings round the edge of a 3-in pot with the aid of a dibber. Label immediately and give the cuttings a good watering before putting the pots in a propagating frame in a warm, shaded part of the greenhouse. Wipe condensation from the underside of the glass covering each day to prevent drips spoiling the foliage.

Potting. The rooted cuttings are first put in 3-in. pots of John Innes No. 1 Potting Compost and grown in a warm, light part of the greenhouse. The young plants must be kept growing slowly through the winter and not be given a partial rest like mature

Training a young standard fuchsia. **1** and **2**. The plant is moved into progressively larger pots until a 6-in. size is used. **3**. Staking is important at all times. A larger cane should be provided as necessary, and the main stem must be tied in with raffia or garden twine at regular intervals. **4**. When the desired height is reached, the growing tip is pinched out to produce a bushy head

plants. When they have filled their pots with roots, pot on into 5- or 6-in. pots of John Innes No. 2 Potting Compost.

Stopping. To obtain plants with the desired bushy habit, take out the tips of the main stems when they are about 6 in. tall. Sideshoots will form which are themselves pinched back when 6 in. long to build up a good plant. Remove any early flower buds which form, so that the plants make plenty of growth before the main flowering period.

Feeding. When the plants are in their final pots, feed weekly with liquid or soluble fertiliser. This keeps the plants flowering well into autumn.

Watering. Water freely in summer when the soil dries out, and provide shade from strong sunshine. Damp down the floor and staging regularly to create the desired humid conditions.

Resting. Mature fuchsias are given a partial rest in winter. Very little water should be given but the soil must not be allowed to dry out completely. A dry shed or garage makes a good storage place with straw or bracken protecting the stem from possible frost damage.

Pruning. In early spring side branches made in the previous year are cut back to within two or three joints of their base, otherwise there will be a tangled mass of growth and poor quality flowers.

Repotting. After pruning, some of the old soil is teased out from among the roots and the plants are repotted in the same size pots, firming the new compost with a rammer. In a warm greenhouse and with light overhead sprays, new shoots soon develop. Afterwards they are treated exactly as for young plants, new growth being stopped to encourage a bushy habit, and feeding being carried out regularly each week.

Standards. To train standards it is best to start with young plants. These are not stopped until they reach the desired height. The main stem is tied to a thin cane

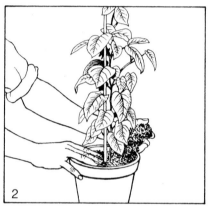

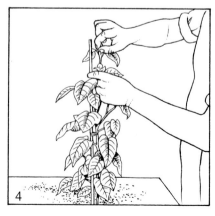

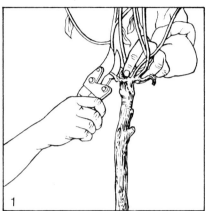

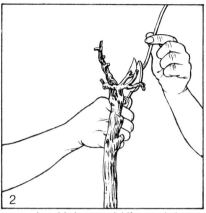

1

2

Pruning a standard fuchsia. **1.** In the spring all sideshoots are cut back to within two or three joints. **2.** The result may look rather severe, but this is essential if a tangled mass of growth is to be avoided

and the plant moved first to a 5-in. and then a 6-in. pot, using John Innes No. 2 Potting Compost for the final potting. Longer canes will be needed as the stems lengthen.

If a main stem of 3 ft. is required, let it grow to 3½ ft. before taking out the tip. This induces strong sideshoots to form at the top of the plant and these in turn are stopped to produce a good 'head'. Sideshoots on the main stem are left until the head has developed as these will help the growth of the plant but they should be stopped at the first pair of leaves. When the head has formed, they can be removed or left, whichever is preferred.

After resting, standards are treated

exactly as bush plants. Any unwanted shoots on the main stem should be rubbed out and the stakes should be checked and replaced where necessary.

Pest Control. Pests can do a lot of damage. Greenfly congregate on the underside of the leaves and can be controlled with a BHC or malathion spray. Red spider mites cause mottling of the foliage which, in bad cases, will wither and drop. This pest increases rapidly in hot dry conditions and damping down and syringing is the antidote, especially in hot weather. Spray with malathion or fumigate with azobenzene. Capsid bugs, which puncture and distort the leaves, can be controlled with BHC in spray or smoke form.

Repotting a mature standard fuchsia. **1.** A pointed stick is used to tease out some of the old soil from amongst the roots, taking care not to damage them. **2.** The plant is then returned to a clean pot of the same size. **3.** Fresh compost is trickled in around the sides of the pot, and is firmed with the aid of a rammer

GARDENIA

G. jasminoides

There is no mistaking the greenhouse in which a flowering gardenia is growing; as soon as the door is opened the scent is almost overpowering. This evergreen shrub bears its white flowers in spring, summer and autumn, and it is the double-flowered forms of *Gardenia jasminoides* which are usually grown. The best flowers are borne on one- to two-year-old specimens but older plants flower very freely. This is a lime-hating plant and if one is making up one's own John Innes compost the ground limestone or chalk must be omitted. If the compost is bought, half as much peat should be added, measured by bulk.

Cultivation. The plants should be potted or planted in February or March and be pruned for shapeliness during the same two months. The temperature from September to March should be between 13 and 18°C. (55 and 65°F.), and from March to September 21 to 24°C. (70 to 75°F.). Water moderately in winter but more freely at other times with daily syringing except in winter or when the plants are in flower.

Once the plants are established in their final pots (of 5- or 6-in. size), feed once a week with liquid or soluble fertiliser in spring, summer and autumn and once a fortnight during the winter months. If a minimum temperature of 13°C. (55°F.) is maintained the plants will flower in winter as well.

Cuttings. Heel cuttings can be rooted in February in a propagating frame with a temperature of 21°C. (70°F.). When rooted, these are potted into 3-in. pots and then into 5- or 6-in. pots. Pinching out the growths once will make the plants bushy, and flowering is likely to occur later in the same year.

1

2

3

The rich velvety texture of gloxinia
flowers, and their spectacular colouring
make them extremely rewarding to grow.
Plants may be raised from seed or tubers

GLORIOSA

G. rothschildiana

The Glory Lily, as this plant is called, is a tender, bulbous-rooted climber for the warm greenhouse which much appeals to me for it has unusual and attractive flowers. These have spotted, narrow, wavy and recurved petals. Two species are usually grown: *Gloriosa rothschildiana* with crimson flowers, and *G. superba* with blossoms of orange and red. *G. superba* needs rather less heat than the other. They climb by means of tendrils on the ends of the leaves and reach a height of about 6 ft. It is usual to train the growths to the roof or to trellis work.

A temperature of 13°C. (55°F.) is needed from September to January rising to 21°C. (70°F.) from February to August.
Cultivation. The bulbs are potted in February or March, three or four bulbs to an 8- or 9-in. pot or one to a 6-in. pot. They are planted 2 in. deep in John Innes No. 2 Potting Compost. Water should be given in moderate quantities until growth is well advanced and then more freely. During the summer, too, the plants need feeding regularly with liquid or soluble fertiliser.

When the leaves go yellow in the autumn, water should be gradually withheld and the soil left completely dry in the winter months. The pots can be stood under the greenhouse staging to keep them out of the way.
Propagation. Increase is by seeds sown singly in 2½-in. pots of seed compost in January. Germinate them in a propagating frame with a temperature of 21°C. (70°F.). The young plants should be moved without disturbing the roots into 7-in. pots. Alternatively, offsets can be removed from the parent bulbs at potting time, this being done with great care as the bulbs are very brittle.

GLOXINIA

These are popular summer-flowering plants which also have handsome foliage. The velvet-like blooms are available in shades of red, purple, rose and white.
Seed Sowing. Gloxinias are best raised from seed and if this is sown in a temperature of 16 to 18°C. (60 to 65°F.) in January or February, flowering plants will be available by mid-summer. The seed is fine and must be sown thinly in pots of seed compost. It is not necessary to cover it. Stand the seed pots in a propagating frame and the seedlings should appear in 14 to 21 days. Prick these out into boxes of John Innes No. 1 Potting Compost and place in a warm atmosphere with shade from the sun. Growth is rapid.

Tubers. When high temperatures cannot be maintained in the early part of the year, plants can be raised from tubers in March and April. These are pressed into boxes of sand and peat, hollow side uppermost, and kept in a warm, shaded part of the greenhouse. A moist atmosphere should be maintained by spraying overhead with water. Before the plants grow

Raising gloxinias from seed. **1.** The seed should be scattered as thinly as possible over the surface of the compost. Since it is very fine, no covering is necessary. **2.** As soon as the seedlings are large enough to handle, they should be pricked out

The showy flowers of the gloriosa. Despite their exotic appearance, they are not difficult to grow

too large move them into 5-in. pots of John Innes No. 2 Potting Compost, covering the tubers with ½ to 1 in. of compost.
Seedlings. Plants raised from seed and pricked out in boxes are first put in 3½-in. pots of John Innes No. 1 Potting Compost and moved subsequently to 5- or 6-in. final pots. Keep the developing tubers at or slightly below soil level and do not make the compost too firm.

Shading and Ventilating. A summer temperature of 16°C. (60°F.) is ideal for plants raised from seed or tubers. Shade from sunshine, and maintain a moist atmosphere by damping down, but keep mois-

Raising gloxinias from tubers. **1.** The tubers are started into growth in boxes of sand and peat. **2.** Before they become too large the plants should be lifted from the box and potted up in 5-in. pots

ture off the leaves. As the plants come into flower lower the temperature by increasing the ventilation whenever possible.

Watering and Feeding. Little water will be needed for a few days after potting but then it must be given as the soil dries out. Feed with liquid or soluble fertiliser at 7- to 10-day intervals.

Resting. After flowering gradually give less water and ripen the tubers by standing the plants in a cold frame. Then, in autumn, return them to the greenhouse to dry off completely. Store tubers during the winter in a warm, dry place.

Leaf Cuttings. This method of propagation is not often adopted but it is the best way to increase a particularly good plant. Remove a mature leaf with the leaf stalk, preferably in early summer, and insert it in a bed of peat and sand in a warm propagating frame. Small tubers soon form and can be potted individually.

Alternatively, treat the leaves in the same way as those of *Begonia rex*. Cut the main veins on the underside of the leaves at intervals and place on a mixture of moist peat and sand in a warm propagating frame. Young plants will appear where the cuts were made.

GRAPES

Many gardeners have the idea that high temperatures are needed to grow grape vines. This is not altogether true as by choosing varieties carefully it is perfectly feasible to grow a vine in a cold greenhouse (there are, in fact, several varieties that can be grown successfully in the open). The vines themselves are perfectly hardy but some need a longer season than others to ripen their fruit.

Varieties. One of the best grapes for a cold greenhouse is Black Hamburgh, and Buckland Sweetwater, a white grape, is another. One of the finest dessert grapes is Muscat of Alexandria, but it is not so easy to grow and must have heat to ripen the fruit.

Vines can be grown in a border but where space is limited a large pot or tub can be used if only a few bunches of grapes are needed each year.

The Vine Border. To grow a vine successfully the soil must be prepared carefully. The border can be inside or outside the greenhouse. In an outside border the main stem of the vine is passed through a hole

in the side of the greenhouse. Good drainage is important and if there is any doubt about this it pays to excavate the soil and lay rubble at the base of the border with tile drains to take surface water away to a lower level. In heavy, sticky soils it is also wise to have an enclosed border with brick or concrete sides so that the roots of the vine cannot penetrate into unsuitable soils. In poorly drained soils vine roots cannot function properly and troubles such as shanking will develop. Unless the existing soil is good and well drained the border is best filled with a prepared mixture composed of 8 parts decayed turves to 1 part grit or coarse sand. Add a 5-in. pot of coarse bonemeal to each barrow load of the mixture.

Planting. Dormant vines grown in pots can be planted just before new root growth starts in late winter. The roots should be disentangled so that they can be spread out when planting and covered with about 2 in. of soil. Vines must never be planted with their roots in a tight ball. Plants raised from 'eyes' in February in a warm greenhouse can be planted direct in borders inside the greenhouse in the summer, but as the roots are active at this time of year they need not be disentangled.

Pruning. Vines flower and fruit on the new growths made each year and the usual method of pruning in winter is called spur pruning. All the sideshoots made in the previous season are cut back in November or December to within one or two buds of their base. Afterwards, it is wise to remove all the loose bark on the main stems of the vine because this forms

Stopping is essential to keep a vine under control. Shoots should be pinched back at two leaves beyond the flower

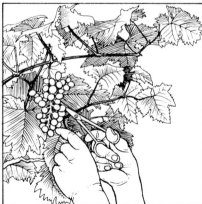

The developing grapes must be thinned to allow room for them to expand. Long, pointed scissors are used for this operation

an ideal hiding place for pests such as mealy bugs or the overwintering eggs of aphids and red spider mites. It can be done by scraping carefully with a knife or by twisting with the hands. Care must be taken not to expose the green rind beneath the bark.

Propagation. The growths removed when pruning can be used to produce young vines. The best and sturdiest shoots can be bundled together and put outside, partly burying them in the soil. In February the shoots are cut up into 'eyes'. These consist of pieces of stem each containing a single bud or 'eye'. Trim the cut surfaces with a sharp knife and place the eyes horizontally in sandy soil in 3-in. pots. Add a little soil to keep them in position but do not cover completely, and place in a propagating frame with a temperature of 18°C. (65°F.).

New growth soon develops from each bud and good roots appear in about six weeks. The young plants can be moved to a border in the summer or to 5- or 6-in. pots. In the following winter they are repotted in 10-in. pots if they are to be grown permanently in pots and not in a border.

Repotting. Pot-grown vines should be repotted after pruning. Scrape away some of the old soil, and return the plant to a clean pot of the same size. John Innes No. 3 Potting Compost can be used or the mixture recommended for vine borders. Firm the new compost with a rammer.

Supporting. After potting, make a framework with stout stakes or bamboo canes on which the new growths which appear in the spring can be supported. One arrangement is to have a stout central stake with a circular wooden hoop fixed at the top with cross pieces. The new growths are trained and tied to the hoop.

Stopping. The new growths made in the spring must be curbed if they are not to become a tangled mass. They should have their tips pinched out two leaves beyond the flower or embryo bunch of fruit. Secondary growths will develop and these should have their tips taken out at one leaf. Tendrils must also be pinched out.

Watering and Feeding. Vines in pots soon dry out in summer and watering must be attended to carefully. A vine border dries out less rapidly but also needs examining regularly. When the border is watered,

Preparing vine eyes. Strong sideshoots are cut up into small pieces, each bearing a single bud or 'eye'. The cut edges should be trimmed with a sharp knife and then the pieces are placed in pots of sandy compost to root

sufficient must be given to penetrate deeply to all the roots. A mulch of decayed manure over the border greatly conserves soil moisture. A topdressing can be given to vines in pots using fresh potting soil and to make space for it a zinc collar can be placed round the rim of the pot. Feeds of a well balanced fertiliser must also be given to keep the plants growing well.

Pest and Disease Control. Pests which attack vines include aphids, mealy bugs, red spider mites and scale insects. These can be controlled by spraying each year with malathion when the new shoots first appear. Mildew may affect the fruits and can be controlled with a dinocap spray when the flowers have set.

Thinning. Developing grapes must be thinned so that each berry has space to enlarge. Surplus berries are removed with a pair of long, pointed scissors. Start at the bottom of each bunch and work upwards, removing the smaller seedless ones first. To avoid touching the berries, and thereby spoiling their bloom, a small forked stick is useful.

Autumn Treatment. After the fruit has been picked, vines in pots can be stood outside to ripen the wood. Watering must continue until the leaves fall and in December they should be brought into the greenhouse for pruning and repotting.

Winter Treatment. When the vines are dormant it is a good idea to untie the main stems (rods) and let them hang down on long strings. This will prevent the sap rising too quickly in spring and will encourage buds at the base of the rods to develop. When the new shoots are 2 to 3 in. long, the rods should be tied back in position.

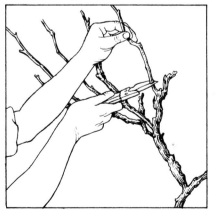

When pruning vines, all sideshoots made in the previous season should be cut back to within one or two buds of their base

All the loose bark on a vine should be rubbed away after pruning to prevent insect pests hiding under it during the winter

Above: A grape vine is an interesting plant for a greenhouse border. If space is limited, it can be grown in a large pot

Below: The huge flowers of the hippeastrum, borne on a stiff, upright stem. Colours include red, orange, pink and white

GREVILLEA

G. robusta

Some plants are grown purely for their foliage, and *Grevillea robusta*, the Silk Oak or Silk Bark Oak, is one of them. The finely cut, fern-like leaves of this Australian plant, silvery-bronze in colour, make it attractive for greenhouse decoration. When stood between begonias, gloxinias, primulas and similar plants they set the flowers off admirably.

In addition to its usefulness as a greenhouse plant, *G. robusta* is used for summer bedding and window-box decoration.

Cultivation. Cool, airy conditions suit this plant best; indeed the leaves tend to drop if the air is hot and stuffy. It is quite happy with a temperature of 4°C. (40°F.) during the winter months. Rapid growth is made in summer and water is needed in some quantity.

Seed Sowing. This plant is increased by sowing seed in a propagating frame between April and September. A temperature of 16°C. (60°F.) is needed for successful germination. It should be noted that the seed can sometimes take many months to germinate.

Potting. When the seedlings have developed their second pair of leaves, they should be potted separately in 3½-in. pots using John Innes No. 1 or 2 Potting Compost. When the root system has permeated the compost, pot on into 5-in. and subsequently into 7-in. pots. When these have been outgrown the plants are too large for the greenhouse and should be discarded. I sow seed each spring to maintain a regular supply of young plants for growing on.

Above left: *Hoya bella*, with its delicate clusters of pendant flowers, is particularly suitable for a hanging basket. **Below:** Ipomoea or Morning Glory is an attractive addition to any cool greenhouse with its continual succession of trumpet flowers throughout the summer. **Above right:** A variegated variety of the ever popular Busy Lizzie or impatiens

HEDERA

H. Glacier

There are numerous ivies with ornamental leaves that make excellent pot plants for the greenhouse or the home. A great many of the kinds that are available are varieties of *Hedera helix*, the hardy common ivy. *H. h. cristata* is an interesting example with crimped edges to the green leaves. One of my favourites is Glacier which has silvery-green leaves with white margins. *H. h. sagittaefolia* is attractive; its small green leaves have pointed lobes. *H. canariensis*, the Canary Island Ivy, is more tender than the others

H. canariensis variegata

but it is a delightful plant with large, bright green leaves. It is usually offered in one of its variegated forms, like *H. c. variegata* which has handsome dark green leaves shading into silver and edged with white.

If carefully trained these plants can be use effectively to provide a pleasing foil for more spectacular plants.

The varieties of *H. helix* like cool, partially shaded conditions but abhor draughts. Similarly, they will react adversely to hot over-dry atmospheric conditions which cause the leaves to wither and drop. They are happiest when the greenhouse temperature in winter is kept just below 10°C. (50°F.). Watering must always be done carefully, but especially so in winter. *H. canariensis* needs rather warmer conditions. All appreciate fairly frequent overhead sprayings with clear water.

Propagation. Ivies are very easy plants to increase. Two methods are adopted – tip cuttings and leaf bud cuttings. The former are made from the tips of the stems. The lower leaves are removed and each cutting is trimmed below a leaf joint to make a

H. h. sagittaefolia

cutting a few inches long. Several of these cuttings can be placed round the edge of a 3-in. pot filled with a mixture of equal parts of sand and peat, or seed sowing compost.

A leaf bud cutting consists of a leaf with a small piece of stem attached. This is cut just above and just below the bud in the joint of the leaf and the cuttings are rooted in a similar mixture to that recommended above.

Cuttings are best taken in the spring and summer and rooting soon occurs if they are placed in a propagating frame with a temperature of 16°C. (60°F.).

Potting. Once rooted, the young plants can be put in 2-in pots of John Innes No. 1 Potting Compost and later repotted into 3½-in. pots. Ivies can be grown for some time in small pots if they are well watered and fed. Only when they are really pot bound need they be moved into 5-in. pots.

HIPPEASTRUM

One of my favourite bulbs for the greenhouse is the hippeastrum, incorrectly but frequently called amaryllis. The huge trumpet-shaped flowers in colours which include scarlet, crimson, pink and white, on stiff, sturdy stems, 2 ft. in length, appear in late winter and spring depending on the temperature they are given.

Potting. A single bulb can be grown in a 5- or 6-in. pot and good drainage is essential. John Innes No. 2 Potting Compost is a suitable growing mixture and the top part of the bulb should be left exposed above the level of the compost. Complete repotting is necessary only every three or four years as the bulbs resent root disturbance and will flower better when pot bound, but each year before starting the

Before starting hippeastrums into growth the surface soil should be scraped away and replaced with fresh compost

bulbs into growth the surface soil should be scraped away so that a topdressing can be given with fresh potting compost. This is normally done in February but if early flowers are needed and a temperature of 16°C. (60°F.) can be maintained the bulbs can be started into growth in December or January.

Watering. Water should be given sparingly until growth is active although the soil must not be allowed to dry out once growth has started.

Prepared Bulbs. Hippeastrum bulbs can now be obtained that have been specially treated so that they flower early, the blooms appearing in time for Christmas. They are available for planting in early November. The bulbs are placed in pots in the normal manner and for Christmas flowering they must be placed in a constant temperature of 21°C. (70°F.). At lower temperatures the flowers will not start to show until mid- or late-January. In subsequent years these bulbs will flower at the normal time.

Staking. To prevent the flower stems being damaged by accident it is a good idea to support them with thin canes and raffia ties.

Feeding. After flowering, when the foliage has developed fully, the plants must be looked after well to build up the bulbs for the following year. They should be placed in a warm part of the greenhouse and given feeds each week with a liquid or soluble fertiliser.

Resting. Towards the end of the summer, when the foliage begins to turn yellow, watering should gradually be reduced and when the soil is dry the pots can be laid

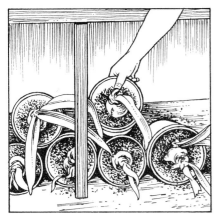

Resting hippeastrums under the greenhouse staging. Water is withheld until early in spring when growth is started again

on their sides under the staging. To ripen the bulbs thoroughly the pots can be stood on the staging in full sunlight for a few days before laying them on their sides.

I nave practised this method of cultivation successfully for many years but some gardeners feel that the bulbs should not be given a complete rest. The plants are kept cool but are not allowed to dry out entirely, enough water being given to keep the compost just moist. In this way the plants get a partial rest.

Pests. Mealy bugs with their white, woolly covering can be troublesome and are usually found in the brown outer covering of the bulb. When dormant, inspect the bulbs carefully by removing the brown skin. Painting with a brush dipped in malathion or white oil emulsion will destroy the insects.

Staking is important with hippeastrums because of the large blooms which tend to be rather top heavy

HOYA

H. bella

Two hoyas of quite different habit are *Hoya carnosa* and *H. bella*. The climbing *H. carnosa* has glossy green leaves and waxy pink and white flowers and *H. bella* is a much smaller, pendulous plant with white, crimson- or violet-centred flowers. It is excellent for hanging baskets and for growing as a pot plant.

Cultivation. *H. carnosa* grows well when planted in the greenhouse border, but where space is limited it can be grown in large pots of John Innes No. 2 Potting Compost. A temperature of 18 to 24°C. (65 to 75°F.) is needed from March to October, and 7 to 13°C. (45 to 55°F.) in winter. Water freely from March to September, but only moderately during the rest of the year. Feed regularly with liquid or soluble fertiliser during summer and autumn, and in spring, pot-grown specimens can be topdressed with fresh compost. The vigorous branches will need some support, and it looks particularly attractive if trained to horizontal wires

H. carnosa

so that the clusters of flowers can hang downwards. Any pruning that is necessary to keep the plants in shape should be done in February.

Hoya bella is a more tender plant than *H. carnosa*, requiring slightly higher temperatures throughout the year. It is also much less vigorous, and care should be taken not to overwater it.

Propagation. Increase is by cuttings of the previous year's growth, taken in spring. Insert in sandy compost in a propagating frame with a temperature of 24°C. (75°F.). Strong shoots of *H. carnosa* can also be layered by removing a few leaves and pegging the stem down into a pot of John Innes No. 1 Potting Compost.

HYDRANGEA

H. macrophylla

The many garden varieties of *Hydrangea macrophylla* make excellent pot plants which flower in spring. Plants are best raised annually from cuttings between March and May.

Cuttings. These are prepared from strong non-flowering shoots. Each should be 4 to 5 in. long and be cut cleanly just below a joint. The bottom pair of leaves should be removed and the base of the cutting dipped in hormone rooting powder. Insert them in equal parts of peat and sand and root them round the edge of a 3½-in. pot. Place them in a propagating frame with a temperature of 16°C. (60°F.), or they can be enclosed in a polythene bag, sealed with a rubber band. In this case, if the cuttings are well watered beforehand they will probably need no further attention until they have rooted in two to three weeks time.

The First Potting. The rooted cuttings should be potted individually in 3-in. pots of John Innes No. 1 Potting Compost. If blue rather than pink or red flowers are desired chalk or limestone should be omitted from the compost and a proprietary blueing compound used instead. Note, however, that white varieties cannot be made either blue or red.

The Second Potting. When the plants have filled their pots with roots move them into 5-in. pots using John Innes No. 2 Potting Compost, but again minus chalk or limestone for blue flowers.

Stopping. When well established in 5-in. pots each plant should have its growing tip removed to make it branch. This should not be done after mid-July. Cuttings rooted later than mid-May should not be stopped as side growths would be made too late to flower well the next spring. Instead, let them grow on a single stem and produce one good-sized flower truss per plant.

Summer Treatment. After stopping, move the plants to a cold frame, keeping them well watered. Watch for greenfly, and if they appear spray with derris. Remove any leaves which turn yellow or show signs of decay.

From late September keep the lights on the frames at night and a month later return the plants to the greenhouse.

The Final Potting. Well-grown plants will require a further move in October into 7-in. pots using John Innes No. 2 Potting Compost with the variation already referred to.

Flowering. By November the terminal buds, from which next spring's flowering shoots will be produced, should be well developed. It is vital that these should not be lost by cold or decay during the winter. Little water is needed now and just enough heat to maintain a temperature of 7°C. (45°F.). In January, if desired, growth can be speeded up by raising the temperature a little. A few weeks later clusters of flower buds will be seen and feeding should start with liquid or soluble fertiliser. Good plants should produce four to eight heads each.

Staking. It will be necessary to support the stems, and the stakes, which should come just below the flowers, should slope outwards to open up the plants.

Aftercare. When the flowers fade cut them off together with a little stem to keep the plants compact and encourage further branching. Carry out repotting now, using the same size or slightly larger pots, and a similar compost to the one used for the final potting. Place the plants out of doors for the summer in a sheltered position, or in a cold frame, plunging the pots in sand or peat.

IMPATIENS

I. sultanii

The Busy Lizzies, *Impatiens holstii* and *I. sultanii* and their offspring, with gay flowers and glossy looking stems are popular plants for the greenhouse as well as for the home. The flowers appear throughout the summer, and into autumn and winter when conditions are to their liking. Good choices include the varieties Scarlet Baby and Orange Baby, and splendid F_1 hybrids with large flowers are available, like the 9-in. tall red-and-white striped General Guisan. A less usual plant is *I. petersiana*, which has scarlet flowers and dark red stems and leaves.

Cultivation. Impatiens can be grown quite successfully in soilless compost but I prefer to use John Innes No. 1 or No. 2 Potting Compost which I find gives harder plants which flower more freely. I prefer not to use pots larger than 5 in. in diameter. If the plants become pot bound they will flower better than ever, but it will be necessary in such circumstances to feed once a week in spring, summer and autumn with a liquid or soluble fertiliser. They should be placed in a sunny position. Repotting should be done in the spring.

I. petersiana

Preparing hydrangea cuttings. **1.** Strong non-flowering shoots make suitable cuttings. **2** and **3**. After dipping in rooting powder they are inserted in a mixture of sand and peat. **4.** Enclosing the cuttings in a polythene bag makes rooting easier

Copious supplies of water are needed from March to September but winter watering must be done with considerable care or rotting may result. Keep the temperature at 7 to 13°C. (45 to 55°F.) from October to February and 13 to 18°C. (55 to 65°F.) from March to September.

Propagation. Seed is by far the best means of increase. Sowings can be made from late February to May for summer flowering, or in June and July for autumn and winter flowers. The seed should be sown in seed compost and germinated in a temperature of 16°C. (60°F.).

Cuttings of young sideshoots from the base of the plant inserted in sandy compost in a temperature of 18°C. (65°F.) between March and September are another method of increase.

IPOMOEA

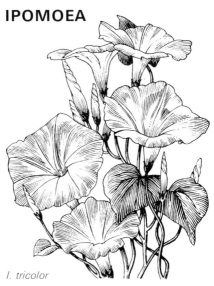

I. tricolor

The climbing Morning Glory, as *Ipomoea tricolor* (syn. *I. rubro-caerulea*) is called, is a splendid pot plant for the cool greenhouse with its beautiful blue trumpet-shaped flowers. Botanically it is now called *Pharbitis tricolor* but it is still listed by seedsmen under its former name. Heavenly Blue, a bright azure blue, is the most popular of its varieties; Flying Saucers has large blue and white striped flowers; Pearly Gates is pure white; and Scarlet O'Hara dark red. The flowers themselves last only one day but there are always buds opening to provide a continuity of colour over quite a long period.

Cultivation. Ipomoeas are raised from seed sown in late March or early April. Place them separately in 3-in. pots of seed

compost and germinate at a temperature of 16°C. (60°F.). The seed coat is rather hard, and seed germinates best if it is chipped or soaked in water for 24 hours before sowing.

The resulting seedlings should be accustomed to full light as soon as possible and should subsequently be potted on into 4-in. and 6-in. pots when they are ready for these moves, using the John Innes No. 1 Potting Compost. The growths must be given the support of canes or wires to which the stems can cling and twist themselves around, for well-grown plants can reach a height of 8 to 10 ft.

Sometimes three plants are grown in an 8-in. pot with twigs, light trellis or wire for support. These plants should have John Innes No. 2 Potting Compost.

Plants raised in the greenhouse can also be planted in a sunny position in the garden in June. Again, they must be given support, and trellis on a sunny wall would be ideal.

JASMINUM

J. primulinum

The most popular jasmine for growing in a cool house or conservatory is the delightful *Jasminum polyanthum*, a species which bears clusters of white flowers from late November or early December to March. These blooms are very fragrant, and are pink in the bud stage which heightens their attractions. It can be grown in pots or in the border.

Another species for greenhouse cultivation is the spring-flowering, *J. primulinum*. This has bright yellow flowers and makes a useful pot plant, although it is better when planted out in the border. It needs much the same conditions as *J. polyanthum*.

Cultivation. Pot the plants in February or March in John Innes No. 2 Potting

J. polyanthum

Compost, or plant out in a greenhouse border containing a similar compost. Water should be given freely from March to October but moderately for the rest of the year. The foliage should be syringed over daily in spring and summer.

When plants are being grown in 5- or 6-in. pots they need the support of three 3- to 4-ft. canes, these being pushed in around the side of the pot and the long, slender growths tied around and around the canes to form a pillar. When the plants are covered in flowers this can be a delightful spectacle. Plants grown in the border will require the support of trellis or wire.

Pot-grown specimens can be stood outside the greenhouse in a sunny position from June to September. I find that plants respond well to this treatment, as the wood ripens better than it would in the greenhouse, and flowering is more prolific the next season.

Cuttings. Jasmines are generally propagated by cuttings taken in the summer. Firm shoots should be selected, about 4 in. in length, and inserted in a sandy compost in a propagating frame with a temperature of 18 to 21°C. (65 to 70°F.).

LACHENALIA

L. bulbifera

The beautiful Cape Cowslips – South African in origin as the name implies – are splendid plants for the cool greenhouse, flowering normally from February until May. Many species and hybrids are grown in a good range of colours. Two popular kinds are *Lachenalia aloides nelsonii*, with spikes of golden-yellow flowers, and *L. bulbifera* (or *L. pendula* as it is often listed in catalogues) which includes coral-red, yellow, purple and green in its floral colours. These and many other lachenalias have spotted leaves as an added attraction.

The Growth Cycle. The bulbs should be potted in August or September and I find it best to plant five to seven in a 5-in. pot. Use John Innes No. 1 Potting Compost and cover the bulbs to a depth of 1 in. They must be kept cool in the early stages and the best place of all for them is a shaded cold frame. Water must be given very sparingly until the leaves start to develop. When the leaves begin to appear the pots should be brought at once into a cool greenhouse with the temperature being best at around 7 to 10°C. (45 to 50°F.). High temperatures in particular are resented by lachenalias. The amount of water supplied must now be stepped up with still more being provided as the plants come into flower. With flowering completed, progressively reduce the water supply and allow the plants to die down and then spend the summer ripening off in a sunny position. Repeat the growth cycle in August by repotting in fresh compost.

Propagation. Increase can be by offsets removed from the parent bulbs when repotting or by seed sown in the normal way in a temperature of 16 to 18°C. (60 to 65°F.).

LAPAGERIA

L. rosea

In some favoured parts of the country the evergreen Chilean climbing shrub, *Lapageria rosea* – the only species of this genus – is grown out of doors in sheltered, sunny positions but for most of us it must be considered as a plant for the cool greenhouse. The pink, bell-shaped flowers, which are borne in the summer and autumn, are especially lovely. There is also a white variety. Ideally this is a plant for a greenhouse border with trellis or wires for it to climb up, but it can be grown in a large pot or tub and trained around canes.

Cultivation. Planting or potting should be carried out in March using a loamy, lime-free compost to which peat has been added. The drainage must be first-class and water should be provided freely in spring and summer with daily syringing of the foliage. Maintain a temperature of 7 to 10°C. (45 to 50°F.) in winter, 13 to 16°C. (55 to 60°F.) in summer and ventilate freely in summer whenever conditions allow. Shade from strong sunshine should be provided. In winter reduce the water supply considerably. Little pruning is necessary, but remove overcrowded or weak growths in March.

Greenfly can be troublesome and appropriate spraying or fumigating measures should be taken. Also, slug damage should be watched for with young plants.

Layering. This shrub is quite easily increased in spring or early summer by layering young shoots. These are pegged down in John Innes No. 1 Potting Compost and roots will form at the leaf joints. The shoots can be cleanly cut away from the parent plant when well rooted and the new plants potted individually.

LETTUCE

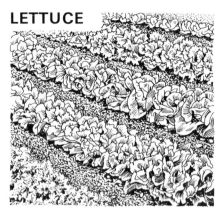

Lettuces are often grown during winter and early spring to complete the chrysanthemum-tomato cycle, and they are a useful crop when a temperature of 10 to 16°C. (50 to 60°F.) can be maintained. One of the best varieties is Kordaat; another is May Queen and a third, the longer-established Cheshunt Early Giant.

Cultivation. Sow the seed in late autumn or early winter in boxes or pots in a temperature of 13°C. (55°F.) and when the seedlings have formed their second pair of leaves pot them up separately into 2-in. peat pots. When the roots show through the sides of the pots they can be planted out in the greenhouse border. A rich, well-drained soil is best, for this is a crop which must grow and mature quickly. Space the plants 9 in. apart each way, and place them so that the top of the soil ball or the pot is slightly above the level of the surrounding soil. This helps to keep the leaves off the soil and the plants are less likely to be affected by

Winter lettuces are useful in a greenhouse when a minimum temperature of 10 to 16°C. (50 to 60°F.) can be maintained

botrytis. Water the plants in carefully to settle the soil around the roots, and afterwards at weekly intervals except when the weather is very dull or damp. Avoid wetting the leaves as this can lead to infection.

Lettuces can be started in the greenhouse and then planted out in a heated frame, successional sowings making it possible to harvest from December right through to when the earliest plants are ready in the garden. In a greenhouse when a border is maintained for tomatoes, lettuce can normally be grown in this area until late March or early April.

In a greenhouse without a border, lettuces can be grown in pots – one to a 5-in. pot – but this is not a way in which many gardeners choose to use valuable space on the staging.

LILIUM

L. auratum

Lilies are exciting plants to grow in the greenhouse. At one time the most popular type was *Lilium longiflorum*, the white-flowered Easter Lily, but nowadays there are many others which are also grown as pot plants. Those I like to grow for early flowering include *Lilium regale*, the popular Regal Lily; followed by Golden Clarion, Enchantment and *L. tigrinum*, with *L. speciosum rubrum* for late summer and *L. auratum* which flowers in late summer and early autumn. All are excellent for the cool or unheated greenhouse.

The bulbs should be potted between September and the beginning of December, the earlier the better. I prefer to use 8-in. pots, putting three bulbs in each. The drainage must be extremely good

for lilies will not tolerate stagnant compost. John Innes No. 3 Potting Compost, to which a little extra peat has been added is an ideal growing medium. In the case of stem-rooting lilies I also add a little well-decayed manure to the mixture. With these lilies only half fill the pots with compost and leave the tops of the bulbs showing above the mixture. They will later be topdressed to bring up the compost level. Pots containing non-stem-rooting lilies are filled with compost to within about $\frac{1}{2}$ in. of the rim at the time of potting, the bulbs being covered to a depth of 2 in.

The pots can now be put in a cold frame or be stood outside and covered with straw, leaves or even polythene sheeting. Alternatively, they can be placed under the staging of an unheated greenhouse. No heat should be given during the winter months. As the shoots of stem-rooting lilies develop and reach a height of about 9 in., the plants can be topdressed with similar compost to bring the level to within 1 in. of the rim. Staking will be necessary as more growth is made.

The plants, when well advanced, can be brought into the greenhouse in batches, depending on their time of flowering but none, with the exception of the Easter-flowering *L. longiflorum*, should be brought into a heated greenhouse before March or April. If the plants are allowed to develop naturally they will be stronger with longer-lasting flowers.

The greenhouse should be ventilated freely and overwatering must be avoided.

L. speciosum rubrum

L. Enchantment

Keep the temperature below 10°C. (50°F.) if possible. The plants will benefit from feeding with liquid fertiliser when the shoots are 12 to 15 in. high.

In the autumn when the leaves and stems begin to yellow, the plants can be moved to a cold frame. They can be cut down to soil level and the amount of water gradually reduced. They must not, however, be allowed to become completely dry for the bulbs are never really dormant.

Lilium speciosum rubrum can be used for pot cultivation a second time, also *L. longiflorum*, although it loses some vigour after the first year, but the rest I plant out in the garden. Brief descriptions of the lilies referred to are as follows:

L. longiflorum. White trumpet flowers, 3 ft. Stem rooting.

L. regale. The Regal Lily. Trumpet flowers suffused maroon and pinkish-purple on outside, white within and flushed yellow in throat. 3 to 6 ft. Stem rooting.

L. Golden Clarion Strain. Trumpet flowers in shades of yellow, gold and orange, $3\frac{1}{2}$ to 4 ft.

L. Enchantment. A splendid nasturtium-red Mid-Century Hybrid, $2\frac{1}{2}$ to 3 ft.

L. tigrinum splendens. The Tiger Lily. Rich salmon-orange flowers, 4 to 5 ft. Stem rooting.

L. speciosum rubrum. Rose and carmine, purple-spotted flowers. 4 ft. Stem rooting.

L. auratum. The Golden-rayed Lily of Japan, huge flowers 9 to 12 in. across, gold on a white ground and heavily spotted crimson. 6 ft. Stem rooting.

MARANTA

M. leuconeura kerchoveana

The marantas are popular plants nowadays both as greenhouse and room plants, and they are as good for one purpose as the other. I find that they grow best, like *Begonia rex*, if they are stood on the floor of the greenhouse, where they get partial shade and take up moisture from the soil or ashes on which they are standing. They need a minimum winter temperature of 13 to 16°C. (55 to 60°F.) rising to 24°C. (75°F.) from spring to autumn.

The most widely grown variety is *Maranta leuconeura kerchoveana*, the Prayer Plant, which has pale green leaves with oblong purple markings changing to brown as the leaves age. The leaves fold inwards at night as though in prayer – hence its common name. Another variety with beautifully marked leaves is *M.l. erythrophylla*. This newcomer has fresh green foliage boldly marked with red and brown stripes and blobs.

Cultivation. I find that marantas grow well in the John Innes No. 1 Potting Compost or in a soilless type. Potting should be done in February or March and

M. leuconeura erythrophylla

drainage must be good. The largest pots the plants will need is the 5-in. size. Watering must be heavy from spring to autumn but much lighter in winter, indeed they should be kept almost dry from December to February. In the summer, feed with a liquid or soluble fertiliser which can be given once a week with benefit. These plants need careful attention, especially in winter. If they die down at that time do not discard the plants for new growth often develops later.

Division. Increase is by division in February or March. Loose soil is shaken from the roots and separate shoots with roots attached can be potted in 3-in. pots and potted on as necessary.

MELON

I am always surprised that more gardeners do not grow melons in their greenhouses or garden frames. It is an exciting crop to grow and it is impossible to buy a melon with a flavour approaching that of home-grown fruits.

Greenhouse Cultivation. Melon seeds are sown singly in 3-in. pots at any time from January to the end of May, but I would recommend the average greenhouse owner to wait until April before making a sowing. Alternatively, sow two seeds in each pot and remove the weakest seedling of each pair when these emerge. Before the plants become pot bound they must be planted out.

Planting. Make a ridge of soil – more than one if necessary – on the greenhouse bench, first placing polythene sheeting (or old polythene fertiliser sacks) on the bench to stop the soil coming in contact with the shingle base. The bed should be 2½ to 3 ft. wide and have a 6 in. depth of soil spread over it with a narrow ridge of

soil a further 6 in. deep towards the back on which the plants will be set 2 ft. apart. John Innes No. 3 Potting Compost is a suitable growing medium and the plants must not be planted too deeply. The cotyledons or seed leaves must be well clear of the soil or foot rot may be experienced.

Training. The plants are trained as single stems to wires strained from one end of the house to the other, 6 in. away from the roof glass. When the plants have reached a height of about 30 in. the tops are pinched out. The laterals which develop are reduced to between four and six and are pinched out beyond the second leaf.

Pollinating. The female flowers which form – they can be recognised by the small embryo fruit just behind the flower – must be fertilised with pollen from the male flowers. All the female flowers on one plant should be fertilised at the same time. Four fruits per plant should be considered a good crop to carry, and any extra fruits which form should be removed. The fertilising should be done at midday when the pollen is dry, removing the petals of the male flower and running the stamens inside the female flower.

Feeding. Regular feeding with liquid or soluble fertiliser is necessary from the time when the fruits begin to swell, and I topdress the bed with well-decayed manure at this time.

Supporting. As the fruits develop and become heavy they must be supported, either with melon nets or raffia bags which can be obtained for this purpose.

Spraying. It should be remembered that

Young melon plants growing on the greenhouse staging. The stems are supported with the aid of bamboo canes and strained wires

The laterals of melon plants should be stopped after the second leaf. This is done by pinching out the growing tip

the melon, like the cucumber, is a tropical plant which likes warmth and moisture. The plants will grow better if they are sprayed over in the morning and afternoon on fine days, with the ventilators closed to raise the temperature.

Ripening. When the fruits are nearly ripe they give off a characteristic aroma and at this stage watering – formerly given freely – must be reduced, indeed almost stopped, or the fruits will split.

Frame Cultivation. Seed sowing for frame cultivation should be done in April or May and the plants set out early in June. Two plants can be housed in a 6-ft. by 4-ft. frame and they should be planted in John Innes No. 3 Potting Compost. Stop the plants at the fourth rough leaf and retain four side growths for flowering and fruiting. In other respects cultivation is the same as in greenhouses. Growing the plants over soil-warming cables or in a raised bed made by mounding up the compost is an advantage.

Varieties. There are numerous varieties to choose from and everybody will have their personal choices. The white-fleshed Hero of Lockinge is a variety well suited for greenhouse or frame cultivation, and the Cantaloupe variety Dutch Net – an early, large-fruited kind with orange-pink flesh – is especially well suited for frame cultivation as well, together with others of this type. Other varieties for greenhouse cultivation include the green-fleshed Emerald Gem, with an especially fine flavour, and the scarlet-fleshed Superlative.

NERINE

Nerines are splendid bulbous plants for the cool greenhouse giving a colourful display from August into the autumn. The umbels of distinctive flowers, up to a dozen in each cluster, now include pink, salmon, orange and white as well as red.

The Growth Cycle. Nerines flower best when the bulbs are pot bound. Potting up should be done in July and August when the bulbs are dormant, four to five being planted in a 6-in. pot. John Innes No. 3 Potting Compost can be used and the bulbs should be positioned to leave them half-exposed.

Place the newly potted bulbs in a sunny, unheated greenhouse and water sparingly at first, increasing the amount as growth appears. The showy flowers will appear in a month or two, before the leaves have developed, and will continue into October and sometimes November. As the flowers fade the leaves will increase in size and as soon as the plants have filled their pots with roots, they should be fed once a week. Keep the plants growing steadily in a minimum temperature of 4°C. (40°F.), giving plenty of ventilation and full sunshine. It is during this period that the plants are building up a supply of food for flowering the following autumn. In May the leaves will begin to die down. Watering should stop, and the pots should be stood on a shelf near the glass so that the bulbs can ripen in the sun. No more water should be given until growth starts again in August, when the pots should be thoroughly soaked, and the growth cycle repeated. Repotting should be done every three to four years when the bulbs become overcrowded.

Offsets. Propagation is by offsets removed from the plants when repotting.

NERIUM

N. oleander

The neriums are evergreen shrubs for the cool greenhouse which grow up to 10 ft. in height and bear terminal clusters of attractive flowers. The foliage is narrow and leathery and reminiscent of willow. The best known species is *Nerium oleander*, the Oleander or Rose Bay, and another is *N. odorum*, both being available in double- and single-flowered forms in colours from white to deep pink. They flower from June to October.

Cultivation. The plants should be potted in tubs or large pots in February or March using John Innes No. 3 Potting Compost or be planted in well-drained beds of loamy soil in a light sunny greenhouse. The temperature from September to March should be between 7 and 13°C. (45 to 55°F.) with normal cool house temperatures for the rest of the year. The plants do not require shading.

Watering and Feeding. The plants need large quantities of water between March and September but only moderate quantities from then until November and hardly any between November and March. Feeding with liquid fertiliser is advisable once or twice weekly between May and September, and syringe twice daily from March to June. Young shoots which emerge from the base of the flower trusses should be removed as these will rob the flowers of their food and they will wither.

Propagation. Cuttings can be rooted in spring or summer in a propagating frame with a temperature of around 16°C. (60°F.). Firm young shoots, 3 to 6 in. long, should be chosen for this purpose, these being trimmed and inserted in 2-in. pots filled with a sandy compost. Another method is to root cuttings of mature wood in water during the summer.

ORCHIDS

Odontoglossum crispum

Orchids are, all too often, looked on as specialised plants which need a greenhouse to themselves. This is not the case. Certain orchids can be grown in the average-sized amateur's greenhouse together with other plants. Cymbidiums are possibly the easiest of all, with paphiopedilums the next easiest. Others which can be grown are *Coelogyne cristata*, dendrobiums, cattleyas and odontoglossums.

Ordinary compost is not suitable for orchids and the special requirements of each genus is detailed in the notes which follow. Osmunda fibre is expensive for it is imported from Japan, but bracken fibre has been used successfully on many occasions as a substitute. Other ingredients of orchid composts are turf fibre from which the loose soil has been shaken away, flaky decayed oak or beech leaves, farmyard manure at least 12 months old and broken up into pieces the size of walnuts, peat fibre and sphagnum moss.

All orchids must have good drainage with broken crocks in the base of the pots supplementing the free-draining compost mixture.

CYMBIDIUMS

The many cymbidium hybrids available have an enormous colour range. They flower from January to May or June, depending on the temperature and conditions under which the plants are grown. A minimum temperature of 10°C. (50°F.) is desirable but it can go down to 7°C. (45°F.) if necessary.

Cymbidiums are best grown in light, fibrous loam with a little sphagnum moss and peat fibre added. When potting, allow the thick fleshy roots plenty of room and make sure that the drainage is good. Repotting is necessary every second year and is done when flowering has finished. While they are in active growth from May to August or early September, cymbidiums need plenty of water and a feed with liquid or soluble fertiliser about once a fortnight (it must be given at much lower strength than for other plants – about 50 per cent.). Shade from strong sunshine is needed in summer. Water supplies should be reduced in winter without allowing the plants to dry out.

Cymbidiums are increased by division or by repotting the pseudo-bulbs in March. Plants should, however, be left undisturbed for as long as possible as they take a long time to develop flowering stems.

PAPHIOPEDILUMS

The Lady's Slipper Orchids are still familiar to many people by their old name, cypripedium. They are extremely handsome plants with beautiful flowers – excellent for cutting – and, usually, large, leathery, mottled leaves. The two most frequently grown are *Paphiopedilum insigne*, with purple-spotted greenish-yellow flowers, and its yellow and white variety *sanderae*. They flower in winter and spring.

These plants should be grown in a mixture of equal parts peat and fibrous loam with sphagnum moss and broken brick added. Drainage must be excellent. Potting is done in spring, after flowering.

Paphiopedilum insigne

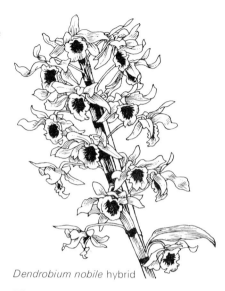

Dendrobium nobile hybrid

They need plentiful supplies of water at all times but rather less in winter than during the rest of the year. Shade is needed from strong sunshine in summer, and a temperature of 13 to 18°C. (55 to 65°F.) in winter. Increase is by division of the plants in spring.

COELOGYNE

Another interesting orchid is *Coelogyne cristata* with white blooms attractively marked with yellow in the centre. It flowers in the spring, and sometimes into early summer and is a good plant for a hanging basket in a greenhouse, sun lounge or conservatory. It needs very similar treatment to cymbidiums. Increase is by division.

DENDROBIUMS

This is a huge genus which includes some-

Coelogyne cristata

Cattleya hybrid

thing like a thousand species, both evergreen and deciduous, and countless hybrids needing varying cultural conditions. A popular range for the amateur gardener are the hybrids of *Dendrobium nobile* in colours which range from purple and pink to yellow and white. These need a minimum temperature of 10°C. (50°F.) in winter when they are resting, rising to 16 to 29°C. (60 to 85°F.) in summer. The flowers are borne during late winter and early spring.

Pot in spring in a mixture of 3 parts osmunda fibre and 1 part sphagnum moss. The plants must be watered freely in summer, given light shade against strong sunshine, and kept in a moist atmosphere. The water supply must be much reduced in winter, at the same time not allowing the pseudo-bulbs and leaves to shrivel. Increase is by division.

CATTLEYAS

The very handsome, epiphytic, large-flowered cattleyas are plants for the warm greenhouse needing a minimum temperature of 13°C. (55°F.) in winter, then increasing to 18 to 21°C. (65 to 70°F.) in summer. Mauve, purple, white and yellow are colours found in cattleyas, and flowers appear in summer and autumn.

Potting is done in spring or early summer using a mixture of 3 parts chopped sphagnum moss and 2 parts osmunda fibre, with a sprinkling of broken charcoal added. Shade is needed against strong sunshine in summer and a moist atmosphere must be maintained. Water freely in summer, but much less so for a month or two after flowering and in the spring. Increase is by division of the pseudo-bulbs when repotting.

ODONTOGLOSSUMS

These are orchids for the moderately heated greenhouse needing a temperature of 16°C. (60°F.) in summer and winter. There are many lovely hybrids of *Odontoglossum crispum* with long, arching sprays of flat flowers produced most of the year. The white petals are marked with such colours as yellow, pink and purple.

Pot odontoglossums in March in a mixture of equal parts chopped sphagnum moss and osmunda fibre. Water should be given sparingly at first but in greater quantities later as growth develops. Fairly heavy shade is needed from May to September and keep the atmosphere moist at this time by syringing. While the plants are resting in winter they should be kept only just moist. Increase is by division.

Orchids are often grown in specially designed wooden-slatted baskets, known as rafts. These can be hung from the greenhouse roof and are particularly suitable for trailing types

PEACH

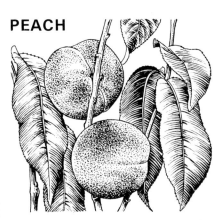

Peaches and nectarines are ideal for growing in a lean-to greenhouse where they can be trained on the back wall, the growths being tied in to horizontal wires set 9 to 12 in. apart. Both these fruits are suitable for growing in unheated and cool greenhouses (heated to a temperature of 10°C. [50°F.]) but there are certain disadvantages in growing them in a house shared with other plants which need more than modest amounts of heat in winter for the heat can excite the trees into premature growth and cause bud dropping. In an unheated house they rest during the winter and only start into growth when the weather improves in early spring.

Varieties. I consider one of the best peaches for the greenhouse is the self-fertile Peregrine which starts ripening from early August onwards in an unheated house and a little earlier in a heated one. Hale's Early is another good variety but it needs another variety near it for pollination purposes. My choice of nectarines is the yellow-fleshed Pine Apple and Humboldt. These ripen late in the season, in late August, September and early October. A mature fan-trained tree will virtually fill the wall of an 18 ft. lean-to greenhouse.

Planting. Peaches and nectarines need a reasonably rich deep soil and it is advisable to dig out the existing soil in the border to a depth of 2 to 2½ ft. and spread a 4- to 6-in. layer of broken bricks, broken flower pots or weathered ashes over the bottom of the border to secure good drainage. Then add a layer of upturned turves, a layer of well-decayed manure and finally rich loamy soil to which the coarsest grade of bonemeal has been added at the rate of 1 lb. to each barrow-load of soil. This mixture should be made

Jasminum primulinum, a superb climbing shrub for the cool greenhouse or conservatory. It flowers in the spring

The spectacular flowers and heady scent of lilies make them very popular plants with many people. This pure white species is

Lilium longiflorum, the Easter Lily, which bears its flowers on 3-ft. stems

firm and the trees planted so that they are at the same depth as they were in the nursery. The soil mark on the stem will indicate the correct depth for planting.

Training. The trees are grown as fans and a young tree when purchased will normally have six or eight branches trained in the shape of a fan. These are tied in to bamboo canes to give even coverage of the wall.

Note that peaches and nectarines bear fruit on the previous year's wood, and that there are two kinds of buds – round

fruit buds and pointed growth buds. The former cannot produce shoots.

In the spring, as the young shoots begin to develop, disbudding is important if the tree is to keep its shape. All badly placed shoots must be rubbed out; these include those growing towards the wall, those growing out from the front of the branches, and those growing on the back of the branches. The remaining shoots should be thinned so that they are spaced 12 to 15 in. apart, and these will be sufficient to form a well-shaped tree with

plenty of fruiting branches the following year.

All shoots should be tied in to the training wires as they develop, so that the fan shape of the tree is maintained.

Winter pruning consists only of cutting out old or diseased branches where necessary.

Watering and Feeding. As the roots of a peach or nectarine grown in a greenhouse border are closely confined, watering is necessary at frequent intervals during spring, summer and autumn. I allow a

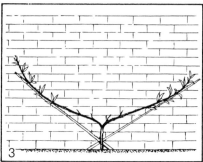

Fan-training a peach tree. **1.** When a young tree is planted the side branches should be supported with bamboo canes, which are, in

turn, attached to the wall. **2.** The central stem should be removed when the side branches are about 1½ ft. long. **3.** In

February, these branches are cut back to an upward-growing bud 1 to 1½ ft. from the main stem. **4.** About four buds are selected

Originating from South Africa, the Cape Cowslip or lachenalia is a fine bulbous plant for the cool greenhouse. The bulbs are potted in August, and flowers appear in the spring

The beautiful flowers of nerine are borne in the autumn, making them excellent plants to continue the year-round display

free-flowing hose-pipe to run on to the bed for anything up to two hours, moving it along at intervals.

Feeding is essential once the tree is established. It is not wise to feed in the early stages as the tree would become too vigorous but once it has begun fruiting feeding should be carried out in the spring, top-dressing the bed first in late winter with John Innes No. 3 Potting Compost. I use a general purpose fertiliser applied at the rate of 4 to 6 oz. per tree and water this in well.

Pollination. Peaches and nectarines grown under glass must be assisted with their pollination. This is best done with a rabbit's tail attached to a bamboo cane, a piece of soft cotton wool on a cane or a small camel hair brush. Pollinate the flowers about midday when the pollen is dry, just touching the flowers to transfer the pollen from stamens to stigma. This should be done every day while the trees are in flower as the pollen does not all ripen at the same time.

After pollination, the humidity of the

greenhouse should be raised by damping down the floor and lightly spraying the trees. Close the ventilators for an hour or so after this.

Fruit Thinning. Often more fruits are set than the tree can carry without reducing its vigour and the size of the following year's crop. These should be thinned, but not until stoning is completed. When the fruits are about the size of walnuts and have been stationary for about three weeks, this stage can be assumed to have been reached. Where two or more fruits are clustered together reduce these to one, and when the final thinning is done leave only one fruit to every 9 to 12 in. of branch. Watering and feeding should be increased at this stage.

Pest and Disease Control. The main pests are aphids, red spider and scale. Aphids can be controlled by spraying or fumigating with BHC, red spider with sprays of clear water or white oil emulsion, and scale by spraying with a winter wash of DNOC. The main disease is peach leaf curl. Remove the infected leaves and twigs and spray with Bordeaux mixture at bud burst.

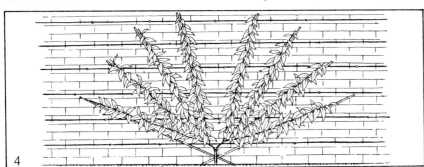

on each branch to train into the fan shape and the unwanted buds are rubbed away. All the branches should be carefully tied in to the training wires to give them full support

PELARGONIUM

Zonal pelargonium

Four distinct types of pelargonium (or geranium to give this plant its popular name) are grown: the Regal, Zonal and Ivy-leaved types, and the fragrant-leaved kinds. All are good greenhouse plants and all need plenty of room and light. In addition to being grown as pot plants the Regal, Zonal and Ivy-leaved kinds can be planted in beds and trained up the wall. They will then produce a mass of flowers throughout the summer.

REGAL PELARGONIUMS

These splendid plants have large flowers, often in two colours. They make showy pot plants, flowering from spring until July or August, and are particularly easy to grow. They must have full sun.

Cuttings. The Regal pelargoniums are grown from cuttings of firm young growth. These can be rooted in summer or early autumn, but for convenience are usually

After flowering, Regal pelargoniums should be pruned quite severely to prevent them from becoming weak and straggly

taken in July after flowering. Non-flowering shoots of 3 to 5 in. in length are required, each being cut cleanly at the base immediately below a leaf. The lower leaves are removed and the base of the cuttings dipped in hormone rooting powder. The cuttings are rooted in $3\frac{1}{2}$-in. pots in a mixture of 1 part medium loam, 2 parts peat and 3 parts coarse sand, with a little extra sand spread over the top of the compost. As each cutting is dibbled in around the side of the pot, a little of the sand falls into the hole and lies at the base of the cutting, so providing improved drainage and aeration and assisting rooting. Label the pots immediately, and water the cuttings in well. If shaded from direct sunshine, well watered, and syringed once or twice daily, the cuttings will root on an open greenhouse bench. Alternatively, they may be placed in a propagating frame with a temperature of 10 to 13°C. (50 to 55°F.).

Potting. When well rooted the cuttings should be potted individually in 3- or $3\frac{1}{2}$-in. pots of John Innes No. 1 Potting Compost, but for later pottings it would be better to use the stronger No. 2 mixture.

Grow on the young plants in a light, airy greenhouse in a temperature of around 10 to 13°C. (50 to 55°F.). Move the plants on to larger pots as soon as they fill their present pots with roots. Young plants will probably need 5- or 6-in. pots by flowering time the first spring, but older plants may well need larger pots.

Watering and Feeding. Only give sufficient water in winter to keep the soil moist (not sodden) but increase this considerably in spring and summer. As flowering time approaches start feeding once a week with a liquid or soluble fertiliser.

Pruning. After flowering, cut the plants back quite severely as they tend to grow too tall and weak if left unpruned. From this time until September they are best stood in a sunny sheltered place out of doors and, until new growth appears, reduce the water supply. Provide a winter temperature of 7°C. (45°F.).

ZONAL PELARGONIUMS

Although mainly grown as a summer bedding plant, Zonal pelargoniums make fine pot plants for the frost-free greenhouse. The term 'zonal' derives from the

Regal pelargonium

dark zone on the leaves which most varieties carry.

Cuttings. These are usually taken in spring or late summer. Firm shoots are chosen, the lower leaves being removed and each cutting trimmed below a joint at the base. Several cuttings can be placed round the edge of a $3\frac{1}{2}$-in. pot or they may be put singly in small pots of sandy soil. If the pots are stood on the greenhouse staging, rooting soon occurs and the young plants should be moved into $3\frac{1}{2}$-in. pots. Those taken in late summer can be kept in these

Watering a Regal pelargonium. Note how the plant has been stood on an inverted flower pot to raise it closer to the glass

pots for the winter and moved to 5- or 6-in. pots in the spring or summer. To produce plants with a bushy habit the tips of the stems should be nipped out when they are 6 to 8 in. long. Later the sideshoots also need to be stopped.

Winter Flowers. The plants will be in flower the following summer, but if the flower buds are pinched out until September they can be made to flower during the winter. These plants are best stood outside in a sunny spot in summer, and feeding is necessary each week with a liquid or soluble fertiliser. Watering must be done regularly. Before the end of September the plants must be returned to a frost-free greenhouse which should be ventilated freely whenever the weather allows.

Repotting. It is not necessary to raise new plants each year. The stems of old plants can be cut back in spring, some of the old potting soil shaken from the roots and the plants repotted in 5- or 6-in. pots.

Seed Sowing. At one time, zonal pelargoniums raised from seed were very shy to flower and it sometimes took one or two years before the plants produced blooms. Now, with the new F_1 hybrids, particularly the Carefree strain, they can be relied on to flower the first year. They are available in shades of red, pink, salmon and white. The seeds are rather expensive but they germinate reasonably well in a temperature of 13 to 16°C. (55 to 60°F.), and should be sown between January and the end of March, to provide plants which flower from June onwards.

Ivy-leaved pelargonium

For anyone with a new greenhouse this is probably the most economical way of starting a collection.

IVY-LEAVED PELARGONIUMS

The climbing Ivy-leaved pelargoniums are ideal for hanging baskets and for training up the wall of a lean-to greenhouse.

Cultivation. Cuttings are rooted in August

or September and the plants grown on close to the glass in a cool greenhouse with a minimum temperature of 7°C. (45°F.). The plants are moved to 4-in. pots in February or March, using a similar compost to that recommended for Zonal varieties. The tip of the main-shoot is now nipped out. Then, in April or May, they are repotted into 5-in. pots or planted in hanging baskets. The pot-grown plants are trained to canes. Water the plants freely in summer but sparingly at other times, and feed with liquid or soluble fertiliser when in flower.

Pruning. Prune back old plants in February or March. Only the laterals need to be cut back on climbers but plants in hanging baskets should be pruned severely to encourage fresh growth.

FRAGRANT-LEAVED PELARGONIUMS

These are attractive for their sweet fragrance when the leaves are bruised or crushed. Cultivation is as for summer-flowering Zonal pelargoniums, but they do not have a resting period out of doors in summer. Cuttings can be rooted at any time from spring to late summer.

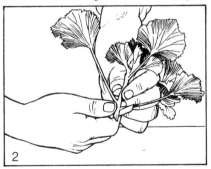

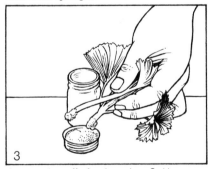

Taking cuttings of a Regal pelargonium. **1.** The cuttings should be prepared after flowering and firm young shoots should be

selected. **2.** Each cutting should be trimmed immediately below a leaf joint and the lower leaves should be removed to prevent

them rotting off after insertion. **3.** Hormone rooting powder will assist the production of roots and the cuttings should be dipped first

in water and then in the powder. **4.** Insert the cuttings in a sandy compost. If they are placed around the edge of the pot this

tends to speed up rooting. **5.** Each batch of cuttings should be labelled clearly with its varietal name. **6.** Finally, the cuttings should

be watered in thoroughly to settle the compost around the stems

The showy bracts of poinsettia, *Euphorbia pulcherrima*, make it a particularly popular plant at Christmas time

Despite the mystery which surrounds orchids there are many, such as these cymbidiums, which are relatively easy to grow

Many varieties of Regal pelargoniums are available, covering a wide colour range. This pretty bicolor is called Stardust

PEPEROMIA

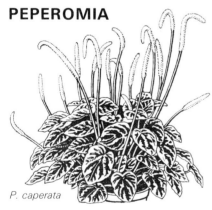

P. caperata

The peperomias all like warm, humid conditions and thrive in a temperature of around 21°C. (70°F.) in summer and 13 to 16°C. (55 to 60°F.) in winter. All are grown primarily for their foliage, always attractive in shape and often variegated as in *Peperomia sandersii*, which has leaves striped silver and green, and *P. magnoliaefolia variegata* with cream and green leaves. *P. caperata* has interesting dark green crinkly leaves.

Peperomias need shade in summer and plenty of water, both at the roots and in the atmosphere. They are ideal plants for placing at the front of the staging or underneath the staging where there is glass to the floor. In winter they need full light and less moisture, but they should never be dry.

Propagation. Most peperomias can be increased by cuttings using either a single leaf or a piece of stem with several leaves attached. (The latter is essential with most variegated types.) *P. sandersii* is an exception and is increased by pieces of

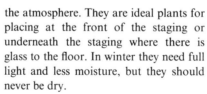

leaf. First, a well-developed leaf is removed from the plant, together with its stalk. The leaf is cut up into about four pieces which are then pressed, with their cut edge downwards, into pots filled with a mixture of sand and peat or with Vermiculite. The leaves are well watered in and the pot is covered with a sheet of glass and placed in a propagating frame with a temperature of 21°C. (70°F.). Roots and shoots will soon form at the base of the cut veins.

P. magnoliaefolia variegata

P. sandersii

PLUMBAGO

P. capensis

The plumbago is a tender shrub with pale blue flowers in summer which is ideal for growing up the wall of a sun lounge, a conservatory or a lean-to greenhouse. The best species for these conditions is *Plumbago capensis*. It is not a true climber but may be treated as one and is excellent for training on canes, on trellis work or a wire 'umbrella'.

Cultivation. Plumbago can be grown in large pots (6-, 7- or 8-in. size), or tubs, using John Innes No. 3 Potting Compost. Alternatively, it can be planted out in a bed of good loamy soil. The shoots should then be trained as I have outlined. With pot-grown specimens I find it is best to push four canes in the sides of each pot, each cane being 4 to 5 ft. long, then as the shoots develop – which they do very vigorously – they can be trained round and round the canes to form a pillar of blue flowers during the summer months.

In the spring, plants growing in large pots or tubs should be topdressed with fresh compost, having first scraped away 2 or 3 in. of the old compost.

Propagation. This plant can be raised from cuttings of soft young shoots, 3 to 6 in. long, taken in May or June, or made from harder wood taken in August, September or October. These cuttings should be rooted in a propagating frame with a temperature of 16 to 18°C. (60 to 65°F.), and potted up in 3-in. pots using John Innes No. 1 Potting Compost. Pot on into larger pots as the plants increase in size, using No. 2 and No. 3 potting composts as necessary.

POINSETTIA

Euphorbia pulcherrima

Poinsettia is the popular name for *Euphorbia pulcherrima*, an ideal plant for the warm greenhouse. Its flowers are quite insignificant but they are surrounded by large leaf-like bracts (scarlet in this species) which are extremely showy. At one time these bracts were only seen around Christmas time – when they are especially welcome – but since the introduction of special light treatment we can have them in flower the year through. There are also pink and white varieties available now, and a dwarf form has been introduced from America.

Cultivation. I prefer to treat the poinsettia as a winter-flowering plant, producing its bright bracts between November and February. In this case the plants are cut back by half their height as soon as the bracts fade, and the soil is then left completely dry for this is the resting period. Watering should start again in early June and this will encourage the plants to produce new shoots.

Cuttings. The sideshoots that are produced when growth restarts are ideal to use as cuttings. The shoots are removed when they are 3 to 4 in. long and each is prepared in the usual way, the cut ends being dipped in sand to prevent 'bleeding'. (Poinsettias have a very milky sap which flows profusely when the tissue is cut.) The cuttings should be inserted round the edge of pots filled with a mixture of loam, sand and peat, and placed in a propagating frame with a temperature of 21°C. (70°F.) or more.

An alternative is to cut up the stems made in the previous year into pieces about 2 in. long. If these are treated like ordinary cuttings they will soon form roots.

Late Cuttings. Plants raised from cut-

tings taken in May and June will grow to a height of about 6 ft. before the end of the year, but if smaller plants, about 12 in. tall, are required, cuttings can be taken in July. Three small plants can be put in a 5- or 6-in. pot.

Potting. When well rooted the cuttings are potted individually, first into 3½-in. pots using John Innes No. 1 Potting Compost and later into 5-in. pots using John Innes No. 2 Potting Compost. I prefer not to use pots above 5-in. size.

At first the plants should be grown in a warm rather humid greenhouse, with shade from the sun during the hot part of the day. As they become well established they can be accustomed to a lower temperature.

During August and early September the plants can be stood in a frame but they must be brought back into the greenhouse before there is any danger of frost, this being heated to 16 to 18°C. (60 to 65°F.) – more if early bracts are required. For the finest development of the bracts the plants should be restricted to one stem each and fed from late September until the bracts form with a soluble or liquid fertiliser.

Pay particular attention to watering as dryness will cause the leaves to turn yellow and drop. Fluctuations in temperature will also cause leaf fall.

After 'flowering' the plants are cut back and rested under the staging until growth starts again.

Pruning a poinsettia after the bracts have faded. This is followed by the resting period and water is withheld till early June

PRIMULA

P. malacoides

Primulas grown in greenhouses are exotic relatives of our native primrose and cowslip. They are mainly winter flowering and are ideal plants for the amateur gardener as they do not require much heat. The three most popular species are *Primula obconica*, *P. malacoides* and *P. sinensis* (including the form *stellata*). An attractive hybrid for the greenhouse is *P. kewensis*.

Primula obconica has the longest season of flowering and often blooms intermittently throughout the year, but it is as a winter- and early spring-flowering plant that it is chiefly valued. Colours available are pink, salmon, red, blue and white. The leaves can cause a rash with some people.

Primula malacoides has smaller, more numerous flowers borne in elegant sprays, one whorl of flowers above another. The colour range of this primula used to be limited to shades of pink, rose and carmine, but more recently other colours such as lilac, violet-blue and salmon-scarlet have been added. This is certainly one of the most valuable winter- and spring-flowering plants for the amateur.

Primula sinensis has larger flowers and a greater range of colour and flower forms, one type with more star-shaped flowers being distinguished as *P. sinensis stellata*. These flowers are borne in winter and early spring. Another form with fringed flowers is sometimes called *P. sinensis fimbriata*. In all its forms, *P. sinensis* is a little more difficult to grow than either *P. obconica* or *P. malacoides*.

Primula kewensis is a hybrid with yellow flowers which appear in spring.

Cultivation. The cultivation of *P. obconica*,

P. malacoides and *P. sinensis* is similar but there are differences in sowing time. Seed of *P. obconica* and *P. sinensis* is best sown in March or early April; *P. malacoides* in late May or June. It is very fine and needs only a light covering of the seed compost in which it is to be germinated. A temperature of 16°C. (60°F.) is needed for quick germination and it must not fall below 13°C. (55°F.) in any case. It is wise to cover the seed pots or pans with both glass and paper until germination takes place but then the seedlings must have full light to keep them sturdy. The compost must also be kept moist throughout.

Primula kewensis is treated similarly with the sowings in this case being made in February or March to give a longer growing season. Once established, this hybrid prefers lower temperatures than the other primulas, and needs only enough heat to keep frost out of the greenhouse.

Seedlings. As soon as the seedlings can be handled they should be pricked out into seed boxes, 3 to 4 in. apart, or potted separately in 3½-in. pots using the John Innes No. 1 Potting Compost. I think possibly the best method is to prick out first into boxes, shading these from strong sunshine for the first few days and then pot up separately into 3½-in. pots as soon as the leaves touch. From these pots they are moved on to 5-in. pots when ready, which should be before the middle of August. Use John Innes No. 2 Potting Compost for this move.

Summer Treatment. From June to the end of September they can be housed in a garden frame – the greenhouse is apt to get too hot and dry – with shading pro-

P. kewensis

vided from the sun during the hottest part of the day. It helps to plunge the pots to their rims in sand, ashes or peat to prevent them drying out too quickly. If they are left in the greenhouse the glass should be permanently shaded and the paths and staging damped down each day to maintain a moist atmosphere.

The early flowers should be picked off to encourage the plants to build up their strength.

Feeding. As soon as the pots are well filled with roots, feeding with liquid or soluble fertiliser should start, and should be repeated every week or 10 days up to and during the time of flowering. This is particularly important with *P. malacoides*.

Housing. By the end of September the plants should be back in the greenhouse again. They require a cool temperature and are best if kept on a shelf near the glass.

Watering. Once back in the greenhouse, very careful watering is needed. Apply the water direct to the soil from the spout of the watering-can. Primulas need plenty of water but not on their leaves in autumn and winter where it is likely to encourage grey mould, a disease to which they are rather subject, especially in a cold, damp atmosphere. Grey mould is less likely to appear at temperatures above 13°C. (55°F.), but perfectly good primulas can be grown at a minimum of 7°C. (45°F.) if care is taken to prevent damp. If trouble should develop, pick off any leaves that show signs of decay. If yellowing of the leaves occurs sprinkle calcined sulphate of iron around the base of the affected plant.

P. sinensis

A beautiful collection of schizanthus, a half-hardy annual which well deserves its common name of Butterfly Flower. This is an invaluable plant for spring display in a cool greenhouse

Several primulas are suitable for cultivation in the cool greenhouse or conservatory. Shown here is *Primula obconica*, a species with a rich variety of shades including blue, red, pink and white

Saintpaulia ionantha, the African Violet, is a favourite plant for the greenhouse or the home

SAINTPAULIA

Double-flowered saintpaulia

Many people find African Violets – *Saintpaulia ionantha* and its varieties – difficult to grow, but this does not prevent them being popular greenhouse and room plants. The flowers, which are borne almost throughout the year, range from rich purple to violet-blue, blue, pink and white in colour. They are extremely attractive, as are the leaves, which are velvety in texture and often pleasantly curled and marked.

Saintpaulias need special shading and watering and higher than average tem-peratures and humidity. They are best grown in the warmest part of the green-house in association with plants like poinsettias which have similar require-ments.

Saintpaulias grow better under arti-ficial light than almost any other plant, hence their popularity for growing in plant cases in living rooms where the miniature greenhouse atmosphere, electric lighting and heating suit them very well.
Cultivation. Potting is best done between February and May, small plants in 3-in. pots, larger ones in 4½-in. I find they grow better in soilless compost than the John Innes mixture. Light potting is needed and careful watering at all times, keeping the water away from the leaves. Shade is needed except in winter, and high humidity during the warmer part of the

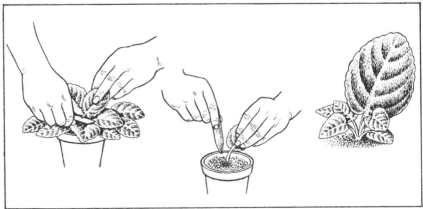

Raising saintpaulias from leaf cuttings. A mature leaf is severed from the plant with about an inch of stalk and inserted in cutting compost. After a few weeks small plants will develop which should be potted singly when large enough to handle

year. In winter the plants need to be kept rather drier.

Propagation. Saintpaulias can be increased by seed or leaf cuttings. Seed sown in spring provides plants for autumn flowering, and August sowings flower the following year. The very small, dust-like seed is quite difficult to germinate. A temperature of at least 18 to 21°C. (65 to 70°F.) is needed and the seed should be sown thinly on the surface of pans filled with soilless seed compost. The resulting seedlings should be pricked out into trays of soilless potting compost and later transferred to 3-in. pots filled with the same mixture.

Leaf cuttings are an easier method of propagation. Mature leaves are removed from the plants in mid-summer with an inch of stalk and inserted in a mixture of peat and sand. After watering in these are rooted – with shade from the sun – in a warm propagating frame, or the pots can be enclosed in an air-tight polythene bag until rooting occurs. Each leaf may produce up to ten plantlets which should then be potted singly.

SANSEVIERIA

S. trifasciata laurentii

The type most commonly cultivated is *Sansevieria trifasciata laurentii*, the Bow-string Hemp, or, less kindly, Mother-in-Law's Tongue. This attractive foliage plant has distinctive, mottled, sword-shaped leaves, with two yellow bands running throughout their length close to the edges. It is popular as a house plant, and is useful for the conservatory, sun lounge or greenhouse. A minimum winter temperature of 7 to 10°C. (45 to 50°F.) is desirable although lower temperatures than this can be withstood if necessary.

Watering. Great care must be taken when watering sansevierias, particularly in the winter, for many plants are lost through overwatering at this time. I like to let the soil become almost dust dry before watering again for if the soil is over wet, rotting is likely to occur. Even in summer, wait until the soil is almost dry before watering.

Division. Sansevierias have a suckering habit and the best method of increase is by division in the spring. Rooted suckers can be detached with a sharp knife and placed in 3-in. pots. A suitable compost is the John Innes No. 1 Potting Compost. After potting, keep the plants in the warmest part of the greenhouse to encourage them to make new roots rapidly. Repot later into 5- or 6-in. pots using a similar compost.

Repotting. Established sansevierias will remain healthy even when completely root-bound. However, it is best to repot the plants before the soil has become completely exhausted.

Dividing a sansevieria. **1.** When a mature plant is taken from its pot, rooted suckers will be visible, which can easily be detached

SCHIZANTHUS

Poor Man's Orchid and Butterfly Flower are two appropriate common names for this lovely half-hardy annual which will provide a delightful display in spring and summer in a frost-free greenhouse. I consider it to be one of the most valuable of all our cool greenhouse plants. It should never be subjected to a temperature of less than 4°C. (40°F.) in winter but I have seen plants frozen solid which have been sprayed over with cold water before the sun got up and have come through unharmed. In fact, this plant is more likely to be ruined by high temperatures than low ones.

There are several fine seed strains in colours from red, pink and crimson to mauve and purple. The large-flowered kinds grown in 6- or 7-in. pots are magnificent but may be too tall for many greenhouses. A splendid large-flowered kind is the Pansy-flowered strain, and the Dwarf Bouquet strain is also excellent. The Bouquets, 12 to 18 in. tall, are sometimes used for bedding but are best treated as cool greenhouse plants.

Seed Sowing. Seed can be sown at different times for different flowering periods. It is usually sown in August or early

with a sharp knife. **2** and **3.** The separate pieces should be potted up individually in the normal way

Pinching out the growing tip of a schizanthus. This encourages side branches to develop, thus producing a well-shaped plant

September to obtain flowers the following April, May and early June, but seed can be sown in February, March or April for flowers in summer. Space the seeds out well to avoid overcrowding and place the August or September sowings in a cold frame, for high temperatures are not needed for germination.

Seedlings. Pot the resulting seedlings individually in 3-in. pots of John Innes No. 1 Potting Compost. To keep them growing sturdily they need cool conditions, and a position on a shelf under the greenhouse roof is excellent.

Potting. A further move to 5-in. pots can be made in November as the plants begin to fill their 3-in. pots with roots. Use John Innes No. 2 Potting Compost which contains sufficient nutrients to keep the plants growing slowly but steadily through the winter. The final move into 6-, 7- or 8-in. pots is made in February, using the No. 2 compost and firming this evenly around the plants with a rammer.

Watering. Water must be given sparingly in winter, for overwatering leads to

damping off in cold weather. When growth accelerates in spring the water supply must be increased.

Ventilation. Although a minimum temperature of 4°C. (40°F.) is needed, the plants will not do well in damp, stuffy conditions and the roof ventilators must be opened a little whenever possible for at least a few hours each day except when the weather is foggy.

Stopping. To give the plants the desired bushy habit the tips of the main stems can be taken out when they are about 6-in. tall. This will encourage sideshoots to form and when the plants are established in their final pots, the tips of these can be removed also.

Staking. Support the growths as they develop. At first a short split cane is sufficient, but once side growths develop, twiggy sticks are needed which are inserted around the edge of each pot. Later, larger canes are necessary. I put three or four canes round the sides of the final pots, 3- to 4-ft. canes being needed for the taller kinds and 2- to 3-ft. canes for the smaller ones. Raffia ties are made around the canes at intervals to keep the growths in place. The new foliage soon covers the ties.

Feeding. From January until the plants begin to flower, the plants need feeding once a fortnight with a liquid or soluble fertiliser. Yellowing foliage is a sign that the plants need extra nourishment.

Pest Control. Greenfly can soon spoil plants, and a careful watch should be kept for this pest. Control with a systemic insecticide watered on the soil or fumigate with a BHC smoke pellet or nicotine shreds.

SMITHIANTHA

One of the things we have to live with in gardening is name changes decided on by the botanists for their own – but not necessarily our – good reasons. Thus what we now have to call smithianthas may still be more familiar to some gardeners under their old name of gesnerias.

The smithianthas are tender, tuberous-rooted perennials and very attractive plants with their spikes of tubular flowers in red, orange, yellow and apricot shades and handsome foliage. Most of the smithianthas that are available are hybrids. They need a temperature of 16 to 21°C. (60 to 70°F.) from March to August, 16°C. (60°F.) in September and October, and 10 to 13°C. (50 to 55°F.) from November to February. The flowers are borne from July to December.

The Growth Cycle. The tubers should be planted singly in March in 5-in. pots filled with John Innes No. 1 Potting Compost, setting them 1 in. deep in the mixture. Provide moderate amounts of water from the time growth begins and water freely after the shoots have reached a height of 3 to 4 in. With flowering completed, gradually reduce the water supply and keep the plants quite dry until March, when potting for the next season is carried out. When the foliage has died down the pots can be stored on their sides under the staging.

Propagation. Smithianthas are usually increased by cuttings of young shoots inserted in pots of sandy soil in spring and for this a temperature of 24°C. (75°F.) is needed. They can also be raised from seed sown in March or April in pots filled with sandy peat. The seeds should be sown on the surface of the compost and germinated at the same temperature recommended for rooting cuttings.

Schizanthuses need staking as they are rather floppy. When young, twiggy sticks inserted in the pot will give adequate support

When schizanthuses reach their final pots firm staking with bamboo canes and raffia is necessary to keep the growths in place

SOLANUM

S. capsicastrum

The Winter Cherry, *Solanum capsicastrum*, is a popular plant with its bright red berries from October to February or March and especially valued at Christmas time. It is not difficult to grow and needs a minimum temperature of only 7°C. (45°F.).

Seed Sowing. Although solanums are shrubby and can be kept from year to year it is best to raise new plants from seed annually. The seed can be bought or it can be collected from the berries by cutting them open with a sharp knife. Sowing should take place in February, March or early April in small pots of seed compost. The seeds can be spread out individually in the pot to prevent overcrowding, and should be covered lightly with fine compost. After a good watering each pot should be labelled and covered with glass. If the pots are stood in a propagating frame heated to 16 to 18°C. (60 to 65°F.) germination will soon take place and the glass must then be removed.

Seedlings. The seedlings should be moved

Spraying solanums lightly with water during the flowering season. This is important if a good crop of berries is to be achieved

Above: The tubular flowers of smithianthas are available in shades of red and orange, as well as the yellow shown here

Below: *Tibouchina semidecandra*, a striking plant for a warm greenhouse. It can be grown as a bush or a climber

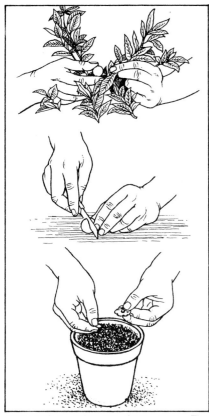

Propagating solanums from seed. The berries are removed and split open with a knife to reveal the seeds. These are then sown in pots of seed compost, spacing them individually to prevent overcrowding

Above: The exotic flowers of *Strelitzia reginae* make it a fascinating plant. Its common name is Bird of Paradise Flower

Below: *Tradescantia* Quick Silver, a fairly recent introduction. Despite a trailing nature, its habit is quite compact

to 3-in. pots filled with John Innes No. 1 Potting Compost when about 1 in. tall. When they have filled the pots with roots they should be potted on into 5- or 6-in. pots using the same mixture.

Stopping. To encourage a bushy habit pinch out the tip of each plant when it is a few inches tall and pinch back the side growths during the summer.

Summer Treatment. From early June to September stand the plants in a frame or plant them in a warm, sunny border.

Pollination. To ensure a good crop of berries, spray the plants with water each day when they are in flower.

Watering and Feeding. Plants kept in pots in summer need feeding once a week with liquid or soluble fertiliser and copious supplies of water in hot weather.

Housing. Move the plants back into the greenhouse in September, repotting into 6-in. pots those which have been grown in a border and keeping them close and warm until they have settled down.

STEPHANOTIS

S. floribunda

A delightful shrub for the greenhouse, provided one can supply the right conditions, is *Stephanotis floribunda*. This tender, evergreen twining plant which bears clusters of fragrant, pure white flowers from May to July – and sometimes carries blooms in the winter as well – needs warm greenhouse conditions and a minimum winter temperature of 13°C. (55°F.). The flowers are borne in the axils of the leaves and as they open fill the greenhouse with their heavy fragrance. This shrub is best trained on wires or canes up one side of a span-roof greenhouse or against the wall of a lean-to.

Stephanotis floribunda will be perfectly happy in a large pot, provided it is given a lime-free soil and is fed regularly with a liquid or soluble fertiliser in spring, summer and autumn, but it is better grown in a border of rich, lime-free loam with good drainage. No pruning is needed beyond the removal of weak shoots in spring.

Propagation. Increase is by cuttings made in spring from shoots of the previous year's growth. These are inserted singly in 2-in. pots filled with a mixture of sand and peat and rooted in a propagating frame with a temperature of 18 to 24°C. (65 to 75°F.).

Pest Control. The two main pests of this plant are mealy bug and scale insects. Spraying the plants with derris or malathion will effectively control mealy bug, and spraying with an oil emulsion or malathion, or fumigation with nicotine will combat scale insects.

STOCK

Beauty of Nice stock

Few gardeners seem to grow stocks in their greenhouses but they are excellent for a cool greenhouse in late winter. The Beauty of Nice type are particularly recommended for cultivation under glass and they are available with rose, pink, violet, salmon and white flowers. There are also varieties which, if one selects only the lighter coloured seedlings, will produce entirely double flowers.

Sowing. The seed is best sown in September or October in pots or boxes filled with seed compost and stood in a shaded cold frame until germination takes place.

Seedlings. When the resulting seedlings can be safely handled they should be pricked out into boxes of John Innes No. 1 Potting Compost and placed in a frame where they will have cool, airy conditions. Before colder weather arrives they should be taken into a greenhouse with a temperature of about 7°C. (45°F.) but if circumstances dictate they can be overwintered in a cold frame, provided they are protected from severe frost. Cool treatment and plenty of light are essential at all times.

Potting. Young plants can be put first into 3-in. pots and later moved into 5-in. pots filled with John Innes No. 2 Potting Compost.

Ventilation. During the winter they must be kept in a light place and the roof ventilators should be opened a little whenever possible to avoid damp and stuffy conditions.

Watering and Feeding. Water must be given sparingly in winter and only when the soil is dry, for if over wet, the plants will damp off. Start feeding the plants once a week at the end of January, using a liquid or soluble fertiliser, and continue this until flowering begins.

STRAWBERRY

I like to have greenhouse-grown strawberry fruits ready for picking by the end of April, which is at least a month before outdoor-grown plants will be fruiting. With a few exceptions – nowadays we can buy ready-made standard soil mixtures and there are plastic pots as well as clay ones – the fruits I grow in my greenhouse are grown in the same way as in my days in the gardens of Windsor Castle, when we had to provide strawberries for the Easter court.

Cultivation. Select your plants in the spring from the strawberries growing in the garden and remove their blossom to prevent fruiting and ensure the production of strong, early runners. Inspect the plants regularly during the spring and summer and if there are any signs of virus or disease discard the affected plants immediately.

The first runners will usually be ready for layering by the beginning of July. The young plantlets should be pegged down in 3½-in. pots filled with a mixture of equal parts of loam, peat and sand. Not more than six runners should be used for propagation purposes from any one plant. The plantlets are secured to the compost with pieces of bent wire.

Keep the plantlets well watered and when they have rooted sufficiently, sever the runners from the parent plant. This stage should have been reached by the first week of August.

By the end of August the plants should be potted on into 6½- or 7-in. pots – I prefer the plastic kind for this purpose –

Removing strawberry flowers to ensure the production of strong, early runners. These are important for pot cultivation

Strawberry plants are brought into the greenhouse for forcing from mid-January onwards. A greenhouse shelf makes an ideal position for them, for they will be close to the glass and receive as much light as possible

using the John Innes No. 3 Potting Compost. They are stood in a cold frame until mid-January when the first batch should be brought into the greenhouse heated to a temperature of at least 4°C. (40°F.). I grow 36 plants in this way in three batches of 12. When the first batch of 12 plants is in flower I bring the second batch of plants into the greenhouse and the same routine is followed with the third batch to provide a succession of fruits.

To return to the first batch of plants, when these are housed in the greenhouse they will slowly begin to produce new leaves and, not long after that, open their first flowers. Eventually, the aim should be to have only 10 flowers on each plant, thinning them out to leave the best, but it may be prudent to delay the final thinning until the fruits have set. The growth should be supported with raffia tied to stakes so that the developing fruits do not come in contact with the pots or compost, as this might damage them.

From the time the plants begin to develop their flower buds they should be fed with liquid or soluble fertiliser once a week.

Varieties. The variety I choose for pot culture is Cambridge Favourite, an early to mid-season variety when grown out of doors. The best flavoured strawberry is undoubtedly Royal Sovereign but, unfortunately, these days it is very susceptible to attack by virus diseases. It is important to always go to a reputable nursery or garden centre when buying strawberries as only virus-free plants should be purchased.

Propagating strawberries from runners. The young plantlets are pegged down into pots of suitable compost at the beginning of July. Strong, healthy parent plants are selected and not more than six runners should be used from any one plant. Sometimes the plantlets are grouped together in a batch, as this will make watering quicker and easier

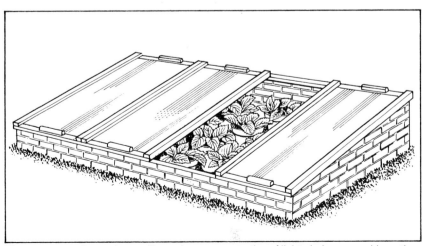

The young strawberry plants will remain out of doors in a cold frame until mid-January. From October onwards they will require the protection of lights during very cold weather, but ventilation should be given freely whenever possible

STRELITZIA

S. reginae

The striking South African *Strelitzia reginae*, the Bird of Paradise Flower, is ideal for a greenhouse, conservatory or sun lounge which can be heated to 10°C. (50°F.) or more in winter. For brief periods, however, the temperature can drop to as low as 4°C. (40°F.) without ill effects. The common name comes, of course, from the remarkable flower which, with its brilliant orange and purple colouring, has an exotic appearance few other plants can rival. The flowers are borne in spring and at other times on stems up to 3 ft. tall.

Cultivation. Potting should be done in spring or autumn, using the John Innes No. 3 Potting Compost and 8- or 9-in. pots. Full sun should be given to the plants in the summer and plentiful supplies of water. Less water must be given in winter. In spring, summer and autumn the plants should be fed once a fortnight with liquid or soluble fertiliser. The plants flower very freely when grown in pots – they like to be pot bound – and they give even better results if planted in a border.

Propagation. Plants can be increased easily by division. Single crowns with roots attached should be potted first into 6-in. pots (the crowns are rather large) and later in 8- or 9-in. pots. A single crown will make a very large plant in a matter of a few years. Seeds, which will set only after hand pollination, will germinate in a temperature of about 21°C. (70°F.), but it will take three, four or perhaps more years for the plants to come into flower.

STREPTOCARPUS

The Cape Primroses, as streptocarpuses are called, are very attractive greenhouse perennials of which fine hybrids have been developed. The flowers, whose colours include purple, blue, violet, red, pink and white, are trumpet shaped and are borne in clusters on 18-in. stems well above the foliage. The main flowering season is summer and autumn, but blooms are borne intermittently for most of the

Propagating a streptocarpus from a leaf cutting. **1.** A mature leaf is selected and cut from the parent plant with as much of the

stalk attached as possible. **2.** Using a dibber, the leaf stalk and lower portion of the leaf are inserted into the cutting compost.

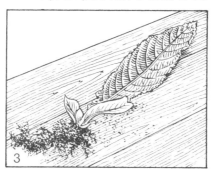

3. Eventually roots and a small plant will develop at the base of the leaf. **4.** When the plant is big enough to handle, it should be

potted up using the John Innes No. 1 Potting Compost

year. Provided one can maintain a minimum temperature in winter of 10°C. (50°F.) these are delightful plants to add to one's collection. Splendid as the mixed hybrids are, I must say that my favourite streptocarpus is the named variety Constant Nymph. This has lovely mauvish-blue flowers and with warm greenhouse treatment it will remain in flower for most of the year.

Seed Sowing. Seeds are sown in January or February in pots or pans filled with seed compost to provide plants for autumn flowering and a July sowing will provide plants for flowering during the early summer of the following year. Sowing in March or early April will mean savings in fuel costs over earlier sowing but the plants will, of course, be later in coming to maturity. A temperature of 18°C. (65°F.) is needed for successful germination.

Seedlings. Prick the resulting seedlings out into boxes of John Innes No. 1 Potting Compost and pot them into 3½-in. pots before they become overcrowded, using a similar compost mixture. Later, move the plants on into 5-in. pots of John Innes No. 2 Potting Compost.

Shading. During the hottest part of the day from May onwards streptocarpuses need some shade from strong sunshine, particularly from about 10 a.m. to 3 to 4 p.m. Airy conditions are also needed at this time of year and frequent spraying overhead with clean water to maintain a moist atmosphere. A temperature of 16 to 21°C. (60 to 70°F.) should be maintained throughout summer.

Watering and Feeding. Water freely and start feeding with weak liquid manure as soon as the plants begin to fill the compost in their final pots with roots.

Resting. During the winter the plants can be allowed to become really dry so that they are almost dormant or resting. By late February or early March they will be starting to make new growth and the water supply should then be increased gradually to meet the full requirements of the plants.

Repotting. When growth restarts, the plants should have some of the soil shaken from their roots and new John Innes No. 2 Potting Compost added in its place.

Propagation. I have already explained about raising streptocarpuses from seed. They can also be increased by dividing mature specimens in February or March into separate crowns with roots attached. These are grown on in exactly the same way as seedlings. New plants can also be raised by leaf cuttings. These should be prepared by removing a complete leaf and inserting the leaf stalk and lower portion of the leaf in a pot of cutting compost in a propagating frame with a temperature of 18°C. (65°F.).

Spraying streptocarpuses with a fine mist of water to create a moist atmosphere is very beneficial during the summer months

STREPTOSOLEN

S. jamesonii

A tender evergreen climbing shrub which can be grown in a greenhouse where a minimum winter temperature of 7°C. (45°F.) can be maintained is the attractive *Streptosolen jamesonii*. This plant bears bright orange flowers from June to September.

Cultivation. Specimens grown in 6- or 7-in. pots in John Innes No. 1 Potting Compost will make a good display as will those planted directly in the greenhouse border in good loamy soil. Potting is best carried out between February and April. Good light and plenty of sunshine are essential requirements. The greenhouse in which this plant is grown need not be heated during the summer.

Streptosolen is a plant which needs plenty of water in spring and summer but much less in autumn and winter, when the compost must be kept just moist and no more, to avoid trouble. An occasional feed with weak liquid or soluble fertiliser during the summer is recommended.

The growths should be trained up wires or on bamboo canes to the rafters and they should be pruned back quite hard when flowering has finished to prevent the plants becoming straggly.

Propagation. Cuttings taken in the usual way in spring or summer can be rooted in a light, sandy compost in a propagating frame. A temperature of 16 to 18°C. (60 to 65°F.) is necessary.

TIBOUCHINA

T. semidecandra

Another beautiful shrub for a greenhouse heated to a temperature of at least 10°C. (50°F.) in winter is *Tibouchina semidecandra*. This evergreen has rich purple blooms, with a velvety appearance, which it bears over a long period in summer. Like the streptosolen (see left), *T. semidecandra* can be grown in pots or tubs or in a border. In this country it is known as the Brazilian Spider Flower, but in some other countries I believe it has the amusing name Yesterday, Today and Tomorrow, an allusion to the fact that as yesterday's flowers are beginning to fade today's flowers are a rich bluish purple and tomorrow's are just beginning to open in an even richer shade of purple.

Cultivation. This plant grows well in John Innes No. 3 Potting Compost and any repotting should be done in February or March. Water the plant freely during summer, but reduce the amount in winter as there must be a definite resting period. Established plants need feeding regularly with liquid or soluble fertiliser in spring, summer and autumn to keep them flowering and in a healthy condition.

The growths can be trained to wires or canes against the side of the house, but I prefer to see it restricted in size to form a bush. Such pruning as is necessary to keep the plants reasonably compact should be done after flowering.

Propagation. Cuttings made from half-ripe shoots can be rooted in a propagating frame with a temperature of 21 to 27°C. (70 to 80°F.) at any time between early spring and autumn.

TOMATO

Most amateur gardeners like to grow a few tomato plants. In so far as one can generalise, I would suggest restricting the number of plants grown to between eight and twelve. Grown well, this number would be sufficient for the average family providing fruits from late June or early July until well into September or October, with green fruit after this to put in a drawer to ripen slowly.

Tomato plants can be grown in large boxes (orange boxes for example) or pots, by the ring culture method in bottomless rings, or in a border. There are numerous varieties from which to choose, including excellent F_1 hybrids. I grow my plants by the ring culture method, which I consider the best, and my main variety is Ailsa Craig which is a good cropper of excellent flavour. However, the variety one grows is very much a matter of personal preference.

Sowing. To be able to germinate tomato seed successfully a temperature of 16 to 18°C. (60 to 65°F.) is needed. Most amateur gardeners sow their seed in

Space sowing tomato seed. This is the best way to prevent overcrowding, which results in weak, spindly seedlings

February or March, and I consider mid-March quite early enough. Tomatoes need lots of sunshine and reasonably high temperatures (more costly to maintain earlier in the year) and they grow better when the days are longer – all good reasons for delaying seed sowing until the time I have suggested. If the necessary temperature required for germination cannot be maintained, buy your plants from a good local nursery.

The seeds must be sown thinly in boxes or seed pans of seed compost. They should be well spaced out and not covered by more than $\frac{1}{8}$ in. of soil. Overcrowded seedlings become drawn and spindly and are prone to damping off. If the compost is watered before sowing takes place there is often no need to water again until the seedlings come through. Cover the container with glass and paper to cut down moisture losses. Germination should take place in just over a week, and the container should then be stood on a shelf close to the glass in good light to keep the seedlings sturdy.

Potting. Pot the seedlings separately into $3\frac{1}{2}$-in. pots of John Innes No. 1 Potting Compost as soon as they are large enough to handle. Treat them gently and never hold them by the stems which are easily bruised and are then very prone to foot rot. A temperature of 16°C. (60°F.) is now needed and watering must be done very carefully.

As soon as the first flower buds can be seen in the tip of each plant pot them on into 9-in. pots or large boxes, or plant in bottomless rings or in a border. For potting use the John Innes No. 3 Potting

Pricking out a tomato seedling. Note how the plant is held by a leaf rather than the stem, which is very easily damaged

Supporting young ring-culture plants with the aid of strings attached to galvanised hooks and overhead wires

Compost and, if planting in the border, make sure the plants have the good loamy soil which is needed. When preparing a border I dig in well-rotted manure or peat and sprinkle bonemeal over the soil mixed together with a well-balanced organic fertiliser at the rate of 2 oz. to the square yard. Space the plants 18 in. apart in rows 3 ft. apart. It is important to remember that tomatoes need a minimum soil temperature of 14°C. (57°F.) to keep the roots active.

Plants grown in pots or boxes need very careful watering in the early stages for by being sparing with the water then the plants will be harder and achieve a better balance between root and top growth.

Ring Culture. This is an excellent way to grow tomatoes. The plants are grown in bottomless pots, or rings as they are called. These are made of plastic, black polythene or bitumised paper and should have a minimum diameter and depth of 9 in. The pots are stood on a base of coarse ashes or sand or $\frac{3}{4}$-in. grade ballast. If ashes are used these must be well weathered to remove the sulphur deposits. A space of at least 18 in. must be left between the rings. They are then partly filled with John Innes No. 3 Potting Compost and the plants must be transferred to these before they have completely filled their $3\frac{1}{2}$-in. pots with roots. With planting completed, the compost surface should be about 1 in. below the rim of the ring.

Before knocking the plants out of the

Twisting the main stem of a tomato around its supporting string. This job must be attended to regularly as the plant grows

Planting out young tomato plants in the special bottomless pots used for ring culture. After an initial watering to settle the plants in their new containers, all subsequent water is given to the aggregate base on which they stand

Sideshoots must be removed as soon as they can be handled. They should be snapped off cleanly without tearing the main stem

$3\frac{1}{2}$-in. pots, make sure that they are well watered. Two root systems are encouraged to develop with ring culture – fine feeding roots in the rings and coarse roots in the aggregate. To make the plants send down roots into the aggregate as quickly as possible, the compost in the rings should only be watered once to settle the soil around the roots. After this, all further waterings should be given to the aggregate, however dry the compost in the rings may appear.

Feeding. As soon as the first fruits form, feeding with a liquid or soluble fertiliser specially recommended for tomato ring culture is carried out. This should be applied to the compost in the rings at intervals of a week.

Plants grown in the conventional man-ner in borders or boxes also need feeding. I like to begin when the fruits on the first truss are about the size of marbles. Several excellent proprietary tomato ferti-lisers are available through garden stores or centres.

Support. Whether tomatoes are grown in borders of soil or rings they need adequate support. One method is to insert a hooked galvanized wire close to each plant. Lengths of soft string are tied, not too tightly, from the wires to overhead sup-ports on the greenhouse roof. As the plants develop the main stem is wound round the string, taking care not to snap the stem.

Plants grown in large pots or boxes on the staging can be supported with stout bamboo canes and the main stems tied loosely to the canes.

Sideshoots. Tomatoes are grown as cor-dons with one main stem and the side-shoots that form in the joints of the leaves must be removed as soon as they can be handled. Bend the shoot over with finger and thumbs and it will break away cleanly at its base.

Temperature and Ventilation. To grow tomatoes well they must have a mini-mum temperature of 16°C. (60°F.) at night rising higher by day. In lower temperatures growth is made slowly and there is not a good set of fruit. During the summer the roof ventilators must be opened gradually as the temperature rises and in hot weather it may be neces-sary to give light shade to prevent over hot conditions inside the greenhouse.

Pollination. To ensure that the flowers set fruit satisfactorily it pays to spray over the plants each day with water. This is best done in the middle of the day and the ventilators should be closed for half an hour so that the air becomes really humid around the plants. Afterwards, the ventilators should be reopened gradually as tomatoes must have a good buoyant atmosphere. In a poorly ventilated green-house fungus diseases are likely to develop.

Fruiting. Average plants in a greenhouse should carry from eight to ten trusses of fruit if grown in the border or by the ring culture method. Plants grown in pots and boxes, however, should only be allowed to carry six trusses.

Disorders. A great many of the troubles that affect tomatoes arise because of cultural faults. Blossom end rot, which causes black sunken areas at the base of the fruit, occurs if the plants have been allowed to dry out at some stage. Leaf-mould is a disease that is common in poorly ventilated greenhouses and apart from improving ventilation, spraying with a copper fungicide is necessary as soon as the first signs of the disease are noticed. White fly may appear despite good culti-vation but the insects can be destroyed as soon as they are noticed with one or two fumigations with BHC smoke pellets. Tomato fruits which have a hard green skin around the stem (green back) may be suffering from lack of potash or have been exposed to direct sunshine through the glass.

TRADESCANTIA

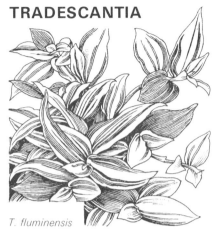

T. fluminensis

Tradescantias, which have such common names as Spiderwort, Wandering Sailor and Wandering Jew, are very popular plants. They are grown for their attractive variegated or silvery foliage. A very popular species is *Tradescantia fluminensis* which is available in white, cream, gold and pink-variegated forms. Others are *T. blossfeldiana* and *T. purpurea* which have larger leaves. An especially attractive recent introduction is the white-and-green variegated Quick Silver. All are ideal for placing near the front of the staging so that their shoots can hang down. They are good plants for the sun lounge, the conservatory or a window-sill in the home, and they are ideal for use in hanging baskets.

A closely related plant needing similar conditions is *Zebrina pendula*. Indeed, it used to be called *Tradescantia zebrina*. This has larger more regularly marked leaves – in silver and green – than the tradescantias. There is a variety *quadricolor* which has leaves prominently striped

in shades of cream, green, grey and red.
Cultivation. Routine potting should be done in March or April using John Innes No. 1 Potting Compost. From March to September these plants are happy with temperatures up to 24°C. (75°F.) and for the rest of the year 7 to 10°C. (45 to 50°F.) is satisfactory. They are equally happy in sunshine or light shade but heavy shade can reduce the leaf colour of the variegated forms. These should also be given a stronger feed than the green ones as otherwise there is a tendency for them to lose their colour. Plain leaves which appear on variegated plants should be removed to prevent the whole of the

Zebrina pendula

plant eventually reverting to this form.
Cuttings. Tradescantias are very easily rooted from cuttings at almost any time of year. I prefer to put three cuttings round the edge of a 3-in. pot of John Innes No. 1 Potting Compost. It is not necessary to root them in sand and peat first, and a 'group' plant is made very quickly. When well rooted, pot on into 4-in. pots using a similar mixture.

T. Quick Silver

VALLOTA

V. speciosa

The Scarborough Lily, *Vallota speciosa*, is a splendid bulbous plant for late summer and early autumn colour in the cool greenhouse or the home provided it is given a light, sunny position. The bold scarlet trumpet flowers have a superficial resemblance to the flowers of lilies. The leaves are strap shaped. A winter temperature of 4 to 10°C. (40 to 50°F.) is required.

Cultivation. The best month to pot the bulbs is March, one being accommodated in a 5-in. pot and grown in John Innes No. 1 Potting Compost. Annual repotting is not required; indeed this plant benefits from being slightly pot bound. This attention should only be necessary about once every three or four years. However, vallotas should not be undernourished and mature plants may well need 9- or 10-in. pots. Established plants should be repotted in March or April.

Vallotas need watering freely in spring and summer but more moderately in autumn and winter; they are not bulbs which need a resting period. Some gardeners like to stand them out in a sunny frame from early summer until the flowers arrive.

From spring until early summer the plants benefit from a weekly feed with liquid or soluble fertiliser.

Offsets. Propagation is by offsets, which are detached and potted separately when the plants are repotted.

The Practice of Greenhouse Gardening

Forms of Heating

Although a great deal of interest can be obtained from an unheated greenhouse, it is impossible to exclude frost from it at all times of year. It cannot, therefore, be considered as a permanent home for tender plants.

The range of plants is greatly increased if frost can be kept out even in the coldest weather and is still further increased if a minimum temperature of 7°C. (45°F.) can be maintained. There are many tropical plants which require even higher temperatures but the cost of heating a house can increase disproportionately as these much higher figures are reached.

There are five main ways in which a greenhouse can be heated: by solid fuel, electricity, gas- or oil-fired boilers or by paraffin. The most convenient of all is undoubtedly electricity but, of course, all the different methods have their advantages and disadvantages. I will now discuss these in more detail.

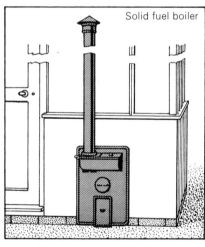
Solid fuel boiler

Solid Fuel Boilers. Solid fuel boilers heating water and circulating this through a system of pipes are a good form of heating. They are probably the cheapest to operate, burning anthracite, coke or special fuels, but they require the most attention. In small greenhouses the boiler is normally installed in the end wall, often alongside the flue. Unfortunately in such a position they are exposed to changes of wind which may affect the rate of burning. This effect can be reduced by erecting a shelter around the boiler and building a tool or potting shed onto the end of the greenhouse to contain the boiler. Water from the boiler is usually circulated by thermosyphon action through 4-in. dia-

Oil-fired boiler

meter metal pipes which must have a steady rise of about 1 in. in 10 ft. to their furthest point from the boiler and an equally steady fall back to it.

Oil-fired Boilers. Oil-burning adaptors for solid fuel boilers are available and may be thermostatically controlled, thus reducing the amount of attention they require to the minimum. For larger installations special oil-fired boilers are manufactured and have a very high degree of efficiency and automation.

Gas-fired Boilers. These are as easy to operate as those burning oil and are equally adaptable for full automatic control by a thermostat. Some care should be taken to site the boiler and its flue where there is no danger of gas fumes being carried into the greenhouse for they are, if anything, even more damaging to plants than fumes from an ill-adjusted or dirty oil burner. This kind of heating can, however, be almost as expensive as electricity.

'Natural Gas' Heater. A new heater making use of natural gas was introduced in

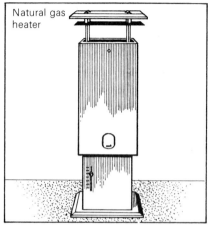
Natural gas heater

the summer of 1971 which promises to alter many ideas about greenhouse heating. Thermostatically controlled and completely automatic it is claimed to be cheaper to run than paraffin and to cost only half as much as electricity. In addition, the greenhouse atmosphere is enriched with carbon dioxide, so encouraging plant growth. Thus, the established commercial glasshouse practice of atmospheric enrichment has been brought within the amateur gardener's sphere. The heater has a safety valve which prevents the main supply from being turned on unless the pilot flame is alight.

Paraffin Heaters. No form of heating is simpler or cheaper to install than a portable paraffin heater. It is advisable to choose one specially designed for greenhouse heating rather than to use a stove made for household use as paraffin fumes can be deadly to some plants. The greenhouse heaters are designed to reduce to a mimimum the risk of fumes and are

Gas-fired boiler

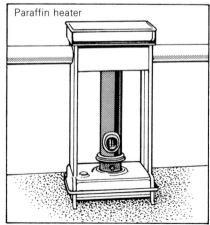
Paraffin heater

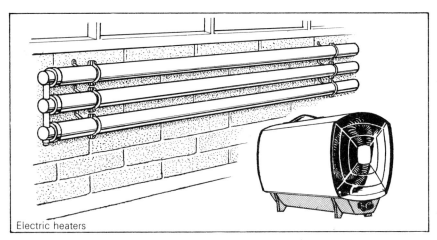
Electric heaters

often fitted with tubes or other devices to distribute their heat as evenly as possible.

It is sometimes thought that paraffin heaters dry the atmosphere but precisely the opposite is actually the case, for as paraffin burns, water vapour is produced and the atmosphere remains humid. Paraffin heaters should be kept spotlessly clean and should never be turned too high nor stood in draughts.

Electrical Heating. Electrical heating may prove more costly than solid fuel, oil, paraffin or gas heating but it has the compensating advantage of ease of control, cleanliness and safety from the point of view of plant health. It must be installed by a competent electrician for exposed or ill-made electrical connections can be lethal in the damp atmosphere of a greenhouse.

Many different types of electrical heating apparatus have been developed for greenhouses. Tubular heaters, positioned along the side of the house, have much the same capacity for even distribution of heat as hot water pipes. They may be installed in single lines or banks according to the degree of heat required. The normal loading is 60 watts per ft. of tube.

A more compact heater is the fan-assisted type. Such heaters are readily moved about, and will push hot air to all parts of the greenhouse. A quite typical small unit would have a loading of 3,000 watts, i.e. equivalent to 50 ft. of tubular heating. When heat is not needed, such heaters can be used to circulate cool air.

During recent years, under-floor heating has been tried with some success, two methods being adopted: warming cables below a concrete floor and night-storage heaters. The trouble is that when morning comes the heat has built up in the storage unit or the concrete whether it is wanted or not and there is no means of getting rid of it except through the house. So although it can be economical because off-peak electricity is used it can also be very wasteful.

Thermostats. All forms of electrical heating may be controlled thermostatically and special thermostats are available for greenhouse use. The most sensitive is the rod-type thermostat and it should be mounted as near as possible to the centre of the house where it will register the mean temperature. It is an advantage to shield the rod from direct sunlight by silver foil as this will enable the thermostat to give a more accurate reading.

Soil Warming by Electricity. Warming the soil from below by means of electricity offers numerous advantages to the gardener, like growing earlier-than-normal crops of tomatoes and lettuces, and easier rooting of cuttings and germination of seeds.

There are two main methods of soil warming by electricity: low voltage current, reduced from the mains voltage by a transformer, which is passed through bare wires, or the full mains voltage passed through insulated soil-warming cable. In either case wire or cable should be buried 4 to 6 in. in the soil.

When laying wire the soil is first excavated to the required depth and a good layer of sand scattered over the bottom. This is then raked level. Next, the required length of cable, to be ascertained from the maker's recommendations, is spread evenly over the whole surface in lines as nearly parallel and equi-distant as possible. Small, hairpin-like pegs of bent galvanised wire will be found useful to hold the cable in position.

With low voltage wire there is no need to take any special precautions to protect the wire, but mains cable can be dangerous if it is accidentally severed by a spade, trowel or other tool. To guard against this it is an excellent plan to lay a length of galvanised wire netting right over the cable. More sand is thrown over this and then the soil is replaced. The cable should be plugged into a waterproof switch socket provided for it in a convenient place, preferably well above soil level where it is unlikely to be accidentally splashed with water.

It is possible to obtain soil-warming cables complete with built-in thermostats so that the current is switched off automatically when the soil temperature rises above a certain point. This is useful and economical but not essential as the loading of these cables is never very high – usually enough to provide a temperature of about 16°C. (60°F.).

Rod thermostat

Soil-warming cables

Plant Propagation

There are few more satisfying pastimes for the keen amateur gardener than the various forms of plant propagation. Whether raising plants from seed, rooting cuttings, layering plants or increasing them from offsets there is much to interest the enthusiast. Let us examine each of the various methods in detail.

PLANTS FROM SEED

Seed sowing is, for the amateur gardener, the most popular form of plant increase. Most sowing is done between February and May and warmth, moisture and air are essential ingredients of success. This presupposes the use of a suitable compost such as the John Innes Seed Compost, one of the soilless seed mixtures, or, in special cases, a mixture made up to meet the particular needs of an individual plant. (Soil mixtures are fully discussed on pp. 120 and 121). Most plants, however, are perfectly happy with standardised composts and this is an appropriate place to acknowledge what a boon these are to the present-day gardener. They have made plant cultivation much easier by simplifying one of the most important working procedures.

Temperatures. Some seeds need much higher temperatures than others to germinate successfully. For example, begonias need a temperature of 18 to 21°C. (65 to 70°F.) and tomatoes 16 to 18°C. (60 to 65°F.) while some other plants, including many annuals grown under glass require a temperature as low as 4°C. (40°F.).

For seed sowing within the greenhouse a propagating frame which can be kept at a higher temperature than the rest of the house is, I consider, essential. It is also very efficient for such a frame, heated electrically and thermostatically controlled, can provide regulated conditions within very fine limits and there is a big saving on the fuel bill if only a small area of the house is heated to the required temperature. It is often important for another reason, for high temperatures may be damaging to other plants which one may wish to grow.

Seed Sowing. Seeds can be sown in wooden seed boxes, clay flower pots, half-pots or seed pans and plastic pots or seed trays. Whichever container is used it must be scrupulously clean if trouble from diseases is to be avoided. If clay pots or seed pans

Preparing a seed box for seed sowing. **1.** The slit in the bottom of the box should be covered with crocks to prevent the compost from being washed away and to aid drainage. **2** and **3.** The compost is carefully firmed, first using the fingers and then a wooden presser. Particular attention should be paid to the corners and edges. **4.** After levelling and firming the compost should be watered. It is best to do this an hour or two before sowing to allow the surplus moisture to drain away

Watering seeds by partially immersing the pots in a bowl of water. They should be left until the surface soil appears moist

are used, pieces of broken flower pot or crocks, as they are called, should be placed in the bottom to ensure good drainage, and boxes should have an open slit along the bottom to allow surplus water to drain away freely. This slit, like the holes in the flower pot, should be covered with pieces of crock to prevent the soil washing through. Plastic containers – and more and more of these lightweight, easily cleaned and easily stored receptacles are being used nowadays – are well supplied with small drainage holes and it is not necessary to use crocks to help drainage.

The container will now be filled with compost, and if a soilless mixture is chosen this should not be made quite so firm as if the John Innes mixture is used. Do the firming with a wooden 'presser', a flat piece of wood to which a handle is attached. This useful tool can easily be made at home. The surface of the compost should not be too fine or it may form an unwelcome 'pan'. A compost passed through a $\frac{3}{8}$-in. sieve would be ideal, even in the case of very small seeds.

It is always best to water the compost an hour or so before seed sowing so that any surplus moisture has time to drain away, leaving the compost in an ideal condition. This watering may be done by immersing the receptacle almost to the rim in clean water until the moisture is seen to seep through to the surface. Alternatively, the compost can be watered carefully from overhead, using a watering-can fitted with a fine rose.

It is a cardinal rule when sowing seed to spread it out as thinly and evenly as possible. Small seeds should be sprinkled

Raising plants from seed. **1.** If the seeds are large enough to handle, they can be spaced out individually. Smaller seeds should be sprinkled from their packets, taking care to spread them thinly and evenly. **2** and **3.** After sowing, the seeds are lightly covered with a layer of sifted compost, and labelled with the name of the plant and the date. **4.** Finally, a sheet of glass is placed over the container together with a piece of paper. These coverings help to prevent loss of water from the compost

over the surface and large seeds positioned with the fingers. In the case of small seeds like those of begonias and lobelias, no covering of compost is needed. Instead, a small sprinkling of fine sand gives sufficient cover. Some gardeners like to just press the seeds into the compost with a wooden presser such as I have already referred to. Slightly larger seeds should be little more than hidden under a layer of compost (tomato seed, for instance, needs a covering of about $\frac{1}{8}$ in.) and larger seeds should be about $\frac{1}{4}$ in. under the surface. There is rarely any need to sow more deeply than this.

Label each pot or box immediately with the name of the plant, and, for good measure, the date of sowing. Then place a sheet of glass or polythene over the container, cover this in turn with paper and place in the required temperature.

The coverings will cut down the loss of moisture from the soil and in many cases watering will not be necessary until the seeds have germinated. As soon as germination takes place the coverings must be removed and the seedlings exposed to full light, but not hot sunshine. If this uncovering is left too long the seedlings will become weak and drawn and more open to attack by disease.

Damping off disease is a constant hazard to seedlings, causing decay at the base of the stem and the collapse of the plants. The use of partially sterilised loam when preparing the seed compost and the avoidance of damp, stuffy conditions will go a long way towards ensuring freedom from this disease.

Pricking Out Seedlings. Seedlings of plants like begonias, gloxinias, streptocarpus and lobelia, which inevitably must be very close together, should be pricked off as soon as they can be handled safely. Such seedlings are too small to separate with the fingers alone without damage and a pointed stick or small label with a V cut in the end is a valuable aid in this respect as it can be used as a lever to ease the seedlings from the compost.

PLANTS FROM CUTTINGS

Cuttings fall into several categories – hard-wood, half-ripe, soft-wood, leaf and root cuttings, leaf bud cuttings, stem cuttings and vine eyes – and these allow the gardener to obtain exact replicas of

Damping off disease is the reason for many seedling losses. It is often caused by sowing the seeds too thickly

existing stock of an enormous range of valuable garden and greenhouse plants. Popular greenhouse plants raised in this way include Zonal and Regal pelargoniums, chrysanthemums, carnations, winter-flowering and double begonias, poinsettias, dieffenbachias and such shrubs as fuchsias, camellias and *Plumbago capensis.*

Success with half-ripe and soft-wood cuttings depends, to a large extent, on keeping the atmosphere suitably moist and close to prevent flagging. (Hard-wood cuttings are much tougher and are usually rooted in the open or in a cold frame, except in the case of tender woody subjects.) Shading from the sun, the use of an open, sandy rooting medium to encourage root formation (pure sand can also be used if the cuttings are provided with a growing compost as soon as roots form) and the use, whenever this is considered necessary, of hormone rooting powder are other ingredients of success with this form of propagation.

Cutting Composts and Containers. Good rooting mediums consist of equal parts loam, peat and sand; equal parts sand and peat; Vermiculite; and seed sowing compost. Pots or boxes can be used as receptacles. If pots are used it will be found that the cuttings will root more readily if they are inserted around the edge of the pots. The number which can be accommodated in one pot will depend on the size of the cuttings and the pots used; these are usually of 3- or $3\frac{1}{2}$-in. size. Always make sure that the cutting rests firmly on the bottom of the hole made for it; if an air space is left below the cutting

any roots which form will wither and die.
Hard-wood Cuttings. Cuttings of this type are made in autumn from the firm, well-ripened current year's wood of trees and shrubs. I usually do this job in November. These cuttings are often rooted in the open garden but some are rooted in cold frames from which the lights are removed. This gives slightly tender subjects the little protection they need.

Some are best taken with a heel of older wood attached and these are referred to as heel-cuttings. A small sideshoot is pulled away from the parent plant for this purpose. It can be up to $\frac{1}{4}$ in. thick but all weak, spindly shoots should be rejected. The bark which forms the heel of the shoot is trimmed smooth with a sharp knife and the other end is tipped just above a bed to leave a cutting 9 to 10 in. in length. The lower leaves are removed at this time. If the cuttings are taken without a heel, cut them through cleanly at the lower end just below a leaf joint.

The base of each cutting should now be dipped in water and then in hormone rooting powder before planting in the frame. Plant the cuttings in rows 2 in. apart with 2 in. between the cuttings in the rows. About one third of the cutting should be below soil level after planting with a wooden dibber and the rooting medium should be light and well drained.

Rooting with this type of cutting is slow and little can be expected to start happening until the following spring. The rooted cuttings should not be moved to a nursery bed until the following autumn.
Half-ripe Cuttings. A wide range of shrubs, including those splendid greenhouse plants camellias, fuchsias and pelargoniums, as well as many other popular plants like nepeta (catmint), potentilla and spiraea are raised from half-ripe cuttings taken in July, August or September from shoots made during the current season which have not fully hardened. Wood which is too immature or soft must be avoided. Neither too hard nor too soft should be the rule.

Where possible I advise taking such cuttings with a heel of the older wood attached. Most will be quite small, not much more than 4 to 6 in. and some, like

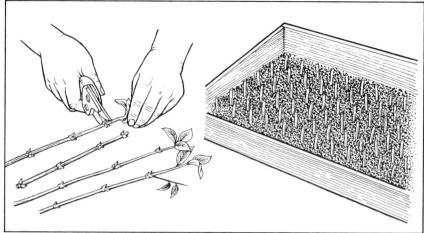

Hardwood cuttings are prepared in the autumn from firm shoots of the current year's growth. They are trimmed to a length

the heathers, only 1 to 2 in. long. If the tip of the shoot is soft this is best removed and cuttings taken without a heel are cut off cleanly with a sharp knife just below a node. The leaves should be removed from the lower part of the cuttings, otherwise they are likely to rot off in the rooting medium and cause infection.

The prepared cuttings can be rooted in a cold frame, or under a cloche with its ends sealed with glass panes. Alternatively, they can be placed in a propagating frame in the greenhouse. This will give the quickest results, especially if bottom heat is provided. Another good method with small numbers of such cuttings is to root them in pots – with the cuttings placed

of about 9 in. by cutting just above a bud at the top and just below a bud at the base, and rooted in a cold frame or the garden

round the edge as recommended earlier – these being individually enclosed in polythene bags. They are then placed on the greenhouse staging to root. Again, dipping the base of the cuttings in water and then in hormone rooting powder before insertion much increases the chances of rapid rooting.

Set the cuttings 2 in. apart and make the planting holes with a wooden dibber. Make quite sure that the cutting sits firmly on the base of the hole, as I have already described. Suitable cutting composts are suggested on p. 115.

Water immediately after planting and keep the atmosphere moist and close. Shading should be provided against strong

Half-ripe cuttings are often taken with a heel of more mature wood attached, for this encourages rooting to take place

Many plants can be propagated from softwood cuttings. Here, a young dahlia shoot is removed from the tuber for this purpose

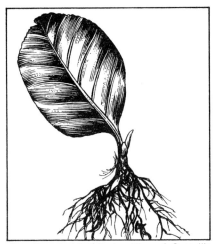

A well-rooted leaf bud cutting of *Camellia japonica*. Further details of this method of propagation are given on p.46

sunshine. If the cuttings are being rooted in a cold frame they should be kept closed for three to four weeks with the cuttings being given a daily syringing for the first week or so. The frame light should be lifted for a very short time each morning (a few minutes) to allow the condensation to run off the inside of the glass. After a month, rooting should be well under way and ventilation should be gradually increased. The young plants which result will stay where they are during the winter – with protection from a frame light during severe weather – and be planted out in nursery rows the following spring. By the autumn they will be ready for permanent planting.

Preparing leaf cuttings of *Begonia rex*. Mature leaves are cut up into pieces about an inch square and rooted on the surface of

Greenhouse-raised half-ripe cuttings which have been assisted to root by the provision of heat will have to be hardened off gradually, the resulting plants going through acclimatisation stages in a cool greenhouse and cold frame before being subjected to normal outdoor conditions.

Soft-wood Cuttings. These are cuttings made from young shoots of the current season's growth and they are usually rooted in spring in a temperature of 13°C. (55°F.) or more. A large number of plants are raised in this way from chrysanthemums and dahlias to begonias, violas and salvias, to mention but a few.

Shoots of 2 to 3 in. in length are chosen for this purpose and they are trimmed off cleanly below a leaf joint with a sharp knife or razor blade. The lower leaves should be removed. When necessary, the cutting can be dipped in hormone rooting powder before insertion to make successful root formation more likely. The cuttings can be rooted in pots or boxes filled with sand or Vermiculite or a mixture of loam, peat and sand, afterwards being placed in a warm propagating frame on the greenhouse bench. Alternatively, the cuttings can be inserted directly in the compost of a propagating frame. (The cuttings which are rooted in pure sand or Vermiculite must be moved into a good growing medium as soon as they have formed useful root systems.) As with other cuttings, shade must be provided against strong sunshine and all must be potted on

cutting compost. This fascinating method of plant increase will intrigue many people

without undue delay whatever the mixture is in which they are rooted.

Leaf Bud Cuttings. Some plants, including those popular greenhouse shrubs the varieties of *Camellia japonica*, can be raised from leaf bud cuttings made from half-ripe wood. The cuttings consist of a small piece of stem, together with a leaf and the growth bud which is found in the axil of the leaf. They are inserted like ordinary stem cuttings in a propagating frame.

Leaf Cuttings. Many greenhouse plants can be grown from leaf cuttings, including streptocarpus, *Begonia rex*, gloxinias, saintpaulias, peperomias and sansevierias. Mature leaves must always be chosen for this form of propagation. In the case of *Begonia rex* it is only necessary to cut through the larger veins on the under-surface of the leaf with a sharp knife. The leaf is then laid flat on the compost (a mixture of peat and sand) in a well-drained pan or box. Small stones or pebbles placed on the leaf will keep it in close contact with the compost. The container is then placed in a warm propagating frame. Young plants will develop at each point where the veins were cut. One leaf could produce as many as twenty plants.

An alternative is to cut up the leaves of *Begonia rex* into small squares, each piece with a main vein running through it, and root these in the same way as already described for the other method.

In the case of peperomias, gloxinias, streptocarpus and saintpaulias the leaves are pressed into the compost, stem end first, and the veins are not cut. The sansevieria, with long, strap-like leaves, can be rooted from pieces of leaf cut up into 3-in. long strips and inserted in the compost of a warm propagating frame. But take note that many variegated plants, including sansevierias and peperomias (with the exception of *P. sandersii*) will not come true to type from leaf cuttings. The sansevieria, for example, loses the yellow band along its leaves and the peperomias, with the exception of the one I have just mentioned, lose the variegation on their leaves.

Propagation from leaf cuttings is, in my opinion, fascinating and it is a form of plant increase I am sure many gardeners find especially enjoyable.

Stem Cuttings. Another method of propagation, useful with a few plants like dieffenbachias and draceanas, is by stem cuttings. Using a sharp knife, the stem is cut up into short sections, 1 to 3 in. long and including at least one dormant bud. They are rooted by placing them horizontally in sand in a warm, moist propagating frame. When rooting is well under way, they should be potted up separately in John Innes No. 1 Potting Compost. This can be anticipated when signs of sprouting from the previously dormant bud are evident.

Root Cuttings. Many plants can be increased from root cuttings, the majority of them perennials with thick roots like anchusa, oriental poppies and verbascums, but also others with fibrous roots like gaillardias and the border phlox which has thin, wiry roots. Dracaena is a greenhouse plant which can be propagated in this way. Small portions of root, an inch or so long, are prepared by cutting their top ends straight across and their bottom ends on the slant, this to avoid the possibility of their being planted upside-down. The prepared cuttings are inserted upright in the growing medium, using a blunt-ended dibber. A few types of root cuttings, such as phlox, are laid flat on the compost and in such cases it is not necessary to distinguish between the top and the bottom.

The cuttings are raised in seed boxes filled with a seed sowing compost or a mixture such as is used for rooting stem cuttings. The cuttings should be just covered with compost and be placed in an unheated frame or greenhouse for rooting

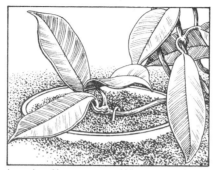

Layering *Hoya carnosa*. When a good root system has developed, the new plant can be detached from the parent

and growing on. The compost should be kept just moist at this stage. When the cuttings – or young plants as they now are – start to make growth they should be potted individually into small pots or replanted in boxes, using a suitable compost.

OTHER METHODS

Offsets. Numerous plants, particularly bulbs and corms, but also other plants which produce several crowns, can easily be divided to make new plants. These are exact replicas of the parent. They are removed with their roots intact and are potted up separately to develop as individual plants. Cryptanthuses and gloriosas are examples of greenhouse plants which can be readily increased in this manner.

Layering. Ordinary layering, when growths are pegged down in a free-draining, light compost mixture to root at leaf joints and form new plants, is not a common method of increase in the greenhouse. But it is used to increase plants such

as the lovely greenhouse climbers *Hoya carnosa* and *Lapageria rosea*. Selected strong growths are pegged down at a leaf joint into small pots filled with John Innes No. 1 Potting Compost to root and form new plants. Sometimes, one or two leaves are removed to make it easier to secure the stem in the compost. Layering is done in spring or summer and when rooting has taken place the new plants are severed from the parent plant and potted on as necessary.

Air Layering. This useful technique has been fully described on p. 68 in connection with ficus and reference is also made to it in the description of codiaeum cultivation on p. 57, so there is no need to repeat the details here. It is another quiver in the bow of the greenhouse propagator which should be made good use of when opportunities arise.

Runners. A variation on ordinary layering is propagation from runners which some ornamental plants like *Saxifraga sarmentosa* (Mother of Thousands) form in the same way as strawberries. The plantlets which form on the runners are pegged down singly in 3-in. pots of loam, peat and sand, or John Innes No. 1 Potting Compost, and severed from the parent plant when they have rooted.

Scales. A method of propagation used in connection with lilies is increase from scales, which are removed from the bulbs. This is done in early autumn. They are inserted upright in a seed box filled with a mixture of peat and sand and covered to a depth of $\frac{1}{2}$ in. with a similar mixture. They are then moved to a cold frame and by the following autumn bulblets will have

Stem cuttings are taken of plants with bare, woody stems, such as dieffenbachias. Previously dormant buds give rise to new shoots

Many plants with thick fleshy roots can be propagated from root cuttings. When preparing the cuttings, the top end of the root

should be cut straight across and the lower end at a slant. This will ensure that they are planted the correct way up

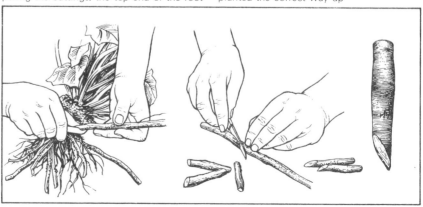

Inserting lily scales in a box of sandy compost. Many new plants can be raised from one bulb in this way

formed at the base of the scales. These are removed and potted up or planted out in a nursery bed.

Division. Simple division of mature plants which have become too large or are losing vitality is a form of increase adopted with numerous greenhouse plants including arums, ferns, marantas and orchids. The plants are taken from their pots and the old compost removed before dividing each one with a sharp knife or separating it carefully with the fingers. The separate pieces are then repotted in good compost and grown on as usual. This is a job best done in spring when growth is getting under way. Re-establishment is quickest at this time and the plants have everything in their favour.

Tuberous begonias bear buds on their tubers and these can be divided to make new plants after growth has started. Dahlias, which can be started into growth in a greenhouse with a temperature of 16°C. (60°F.), do not have buds on the tubers themselves but at the base of the old stems. If these are to be divided

it is essential that each division includes a piece of the old stem with at least one bud attached. By starting the tubers into growth in this way it is possible to be certain that each division has one or more buds attached. The tubers are boxed during April in a mixture of peat and sand or peat alone. They are divided immediately before planting them in the garden at the end of May or early June when there is no longer any danger of frost occurring. Dahlias can be increased in this way if one does not have a greenhouse but with this facility success is more assured.

Vine Eyes. Grape vines are increased by means of 'eyes' which are the dormant growth buds removed from well-ripened sideshoots in autumn with a small portion of stem attached. These bud cuttings will be about 1½ in. long when prepared, with the bud in the middle. They are placed horizontally and bud uppermost on the surface of a sandy compost, either one to a small pot or several to a larger one. They are given little or no covering, but some gardeners like to peg them down with pieces of bent wire to obtain really firm contact with the compost. The pots are then placed in a propagating frame with a temperature of 18°C. (65°F.) for the eyes to root and form new plants. When this occurs, they should be potted up in the normal way, using John Innes No. 1 Potting Compost.

MIST PROPAGATION
The technique of mist propagation is now very widely used and has certainly lightened the load of the propagator in

addition to making the increase from cuttings of some notoriously difficult shrubs very much easier.

Like so many successful items of equipment, a mist propagation unit is basically very simple. It consists of a spray unit, or units, which are automatically operated and have the function of keeping the leaves of cuttings inserted underneath their coverage permanently moist. This is achieved in various ways, but the one most often adopted is by using what is called an 'electronic leaf' which is set amongst the cuttings. When it becomes dry an electrical relay is set in motion which operates the water supply and the spray nozzle ejects a fine mist until the electronic leaf's surface is again saturated. The cuttings are, therefore, never left dry and flagging will not occur. It is, of course, heavy moisture losses through the leaf surfaces which are in normal circumstances difficult for the home gardener to counteract. In sunny weather the cuttings would need repeated syringing, which is not generally a practical proposition.

The cuttings, prepared in the normal way, are inserted in a bed of sand heated by soil-warming cables. Half-ripe cuttings will normally have formed roots within three weeks of insertion. Also, large-leaved evergreen shrubs which are difficult to propagate in other ways present no difficulties when raised under mist.

Once rooted, the cuttings are potted singly in a suitable growing medium and are put back under the mist for ten days or so to become gradually acclimatised to ordinary greenhouse conditions.

One of the simplest methods of propagation is by division. Here, the rootstock of a pteris fern is being gently pulled apart

A cross section of an electric mist propagator, showing its component parts. As with all electrical equipment it should be installed

by a competent electrician, for in the damp atmosphere of a greenhouse, poor connections are especially dangerous

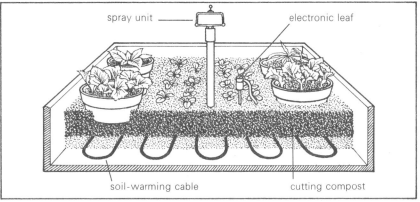
spray unit — electronic leaf

soil-warming cable   cutting compost

Seed and Potting Composts

I can well remember the time when it was necessary to mix up different composts for almost every kind of greenhouse plant. But this has not been necessary for many years now for in the 1930s The John Innes Horticultural Institute, after long research, gave the gardening world the standardised seed and potting compost formulae for which they are renowned. Instead of a multitude of composts a single seed compost and a few variations on a potting compost suffice for the vast majority of pot-grown plants, and these are readily available at gardening shops and centres. A word of caution is, however, necessary for not all dealers in these composts are scrupulous in keeping strictly to the formulae, so be sure to go to a reputable supplier.

More recently, there have been the introduction of the soilless composts, the development and introduction of which was triggered off by the increasing difficulty of obtaining loam, one of the ingredients of the John Innes composts, of the desired quality. These certainly have their place in the scheme of things and I shall have more to say about them later. For the moment I want to explain in some detail the composition of the John Innes composts.

JOHN INNES COMPOSTS

There are, as I have already noted, two basic formulae, one for seeds, the other for potting. Both make use of loam, a term rather loosely used for soil that contains some clay, sand and humus. The definition of the loam needed for John Innes compost is medium, neither too heavy (clay) nor too light (sand), with a pH of 6·5 or thereabouts. One way of providing loam is to obtain turves cut thickly with two or three inches of soil from a good meadow or building site. This should be stacked, grass side downwards,

Various stages in the preparation of John Innes compost. **Top:** Good fibrous loam is obtained by stacking turves grass side downwards and leaving them for several months to rot down. **Centre:** Peat is often very dry when purchased. If this is so, it should be spread out before use and thoroughly moistened. **Right:** When the turves have rotted down the resulting loam should be passed through a ⅜-in. sieve before it is used to remove unwanted stones and debris and left for some months (as much as a year if possible) so that grass and root fibres decay.

The second bulk ingredient of the John Innes composts is horticultural grade peat which should be granular and reasonably free from dust. When purchased this is often very dry, and dry peat resists moisture. As it is essential to get the peat moist before use it should be spread out and liberally watered. It may be necessary to repeat this several times, turning the peat after each watering and then spreading it out again.

The third bulk ingredient is sand, defined for this purpose as coarse and damp, with particles grading up to $\frac{1}{8}$ in. in size. Cornish river sand is ideal.

Mixing Composts. If one wishes to mix up one's own composts at home this is not particularly difficult. The loam should first be sterilised by standing it over boiling water in a saucepan or copper or in one of the special sterilisers which can be purchased for the purpose. The idea is to raise all the soil to a temperature of 93°C. (200°F.) and maintain it at that for 20 minutes.

The John Innes Seed Compost consists of 2 parts loam, 1 part peat and 1 part sand, all parts by loose bulk. To each bushel of these combined ingredients is added $1\frac{1}{2}$ oz. superphosphate of lime and $\frac{3}{4}$ oz. of either finely ground chalk or limestone. First the loam is passed through a $\frac{3}{8}$-in. mesh sieve to remove stones. Then the peat and sand are added and finally the chemicals, carefully measured out, are scattered over the top. The heap must then be turned several times so that all the ingredients are thoroughly mixed together.

The preparation of the John Innes Potting Compost is similar but the proportions are different – 7 parts loam, 3 parts peat and 2 parts sand. A base fertiliser is added to this mixture. This can be purchased ready mixed or it can be made with 2 parts of hoof and horn meal, 2 parts superphosphate of lime and 1 part sulphate of potash, all parts by weight. This is added to the other ingredients at the rate of 4 oz. per bushel for No. 1 Compost, 8 oz. per bushel for No. 2 and 12 oz. per bushel for No. 3. To No. 1 add $\frac{3}{4}$ oz. of finely ground chalk or limestone per bushel of mixture; double and treble this

amount is needed for No. 2 and No. 3 respectively.

Compost Uses. As a basic guide the No. 1 Compost is used for all initial pottings, No. 2 Compost for older plants in pots over 4 in. in diameter and No. 3 Compost for very strong growing plants in large pots and tubs.

SOILLESS COMPOSTS

The soilless composts, sold under proprietary names and consisting of peat, or peat and sand, with fertilisers added, are very useful, I find, for pots up to $3\frac{1}{2}$-in. in diameter, but I do not like them for

larger ones than this as there is little weight in the compost and large plants tend to tip over. Seed and potting mixtures are available, and I use them for propagation purposes and for growing smaller plants. Saintpaulias, for instance, grow particularly well in such mixtures.

Soilless composts need much more careful watering than ordinary compost, for with their heavy peat content they are naturally absorbent and hold water for much longer than the traditional kinds. One soon gets used to this, however, and they are a valuable addition to the range of growing mediums.

The amounts of fertilisers used in the John Innes composts have been scientifically worked out, and it is important that they

should be adhered to when mixing one's own compost. For the most accurate results, a pair of scales should be used

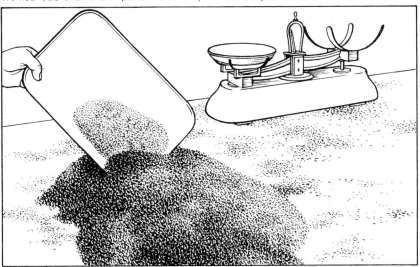

Thorough mixing of the ingredients when preparing compost is just as important as correct proportions. Turning the heap several times will ensure that the ingredients are evenly distributed and that each plant receives the right amount of fertiliser

Pricking Out, Potting and Hardening Off

The germination of seeds has been fully described on pp. 114 and 115, and the next stage is pricking out, the transfer of the seedlings into more spacious growing conditions where they can develop fully in a suitably nutritious compost.

After germination the seeds should be given as much light as possible to keep them sturdy. As soon as they can be handled conveniently, which is usually just as they are about to produce their first true leaves as distinct from their seed leaves, they must be transplanted into other boxes.

The boxes used are the standard seed trays. They are prepared exactly as for seed sowing and as a rule the same seed compost is used but, occasionally, for strong growing plants, a richer compost is used such as the John Innes No. 1 Potting Compost.

Transplanting Seedlings. The seedlings should be very carefully lifted, one at a time, from the seed box. A wooden label makes a good tool for this and it is important that the compost in which the seedlings have been growing is in the right condition, nicely moist right through, neither too wet nor too dry, otherwise the roots will be damaged. Hold each seedling by one leaf and transfer it immediately to the box in which it is to be pricked out. Make a small hole for it with a wooden dibber, drop the roots straight down into this and press the soil gently around them with the dibber. The seedlings should be spaced approximately 2 in. apart in straight rows, except for those which are to remain in the boxes until planting out time which should be set 3 to 4 in. apart.

Aftercare. When the box has been filled with seedlings it should be watered to settle the soil around the roots. The watering-can must have a fine rose to prevent the soil being washed away and the roots disturbed. Give enough water to soak right through the container.

It is important to remember that the plants at this stage are unable to take up all the moisture they require and shading from the sun is necessary for the first few days after pricking out until they have made fresh roots. Sheets of newspaper placed above the seedlings will provide shade and spraying overhead on warm days will help to prevent flagging. The shading must be removed as soon as the plants have re-established themselves for they now need the maximum amount of light, except in the case of begonias and other plants which scorch easily and need shade during the hottest part of the day.

Bedding plants can be moved out to a frame once they have become established, but those which are to be moved on into pots should receive this attention before they become overcrowded – in fact as soon as the leaves of adjoining plants are touching. Pricking out is the half-way stage between the development of seedlings and potting or planting out.

POTTING

This is an operation that can be mastered very quickly. One should always aim to grow a large plant in a small pot rather than the reverse. This is why the moves to larger pots are usually only modest increases: the progression is in easy stages. Plants from boxes or trays are normally potted into 3- or 3½-in. pots. When established in these they are moved on to 4- or 5-in. pots and, if it is necessary to pot them on again, use the 6- or 7-in. size. Large plants such as chrysanthe-

mums or tomatoes will eventually need 8- or 9-in. pots.

The reason why only modest increases in pot size are made is that where large amounts of compost are involved it is liable to become wet and sour before the plant can fill the pot with a network of roots. This results in sickly plants which never develop satisfactorily. It is usual for John Innes No. 1 Potting Compost to be used when potting plants in small pots and John Innes No. 2 and No. 3 Composts for the larger sizes.

Plants must never be removed from pots or boxes when the soil is dry. It is always advisable to give them a thorough soaking an hour or two before such moves. When removing the plants care must be taken to keep the root ball intact.

Plastic pots, which have more drainage holes in the base than the traditional clay pots, need not be provided with a layer of broken crock before filling with compost, but clay pots need crocks to prevent the drainage holes from becoming blocked. Place a little soil in the bottom and press moderately firmly with the finger tips. The plant is then centred in the pot and the space between the root ball and the side of the pot filled in with compost trickled from the hand. This is lightly pushed down and then firmed with the fingers. This process is repeated until the firmed compost is within 1 to ½ in. from the pot's rim (depending on the size of the pot). This

Pricking out seedlings. **1.** When they are large enough to handle, the seedlings are gently levered from their box. **2.** The seedlings are dropped individually into small dibber holes made in the compost, and lightly firmed. **3.** Careful watering from a can fitted with a fine rose settles the compost around the roots

space is left for the purpose of watering.

A potting stick or rammer is often necessary when potting on plants into 7-, 8-, 9- or 10-in. pots. This can be made from a broom handle by cutting a piece about 12 in. long and shaping a wedge at one end. The firming done with the fingers in the case of smaller pots is done much more effectively with the wedge end of this simple tool, and potting is completed by firming the surface with the blunt end of the rammer. The soil must be really firm when potting into such large containers.

On the whole it is difficult to generalise about the firmness of the soil, but plants which need light potting include calceolarias, double-flowered and winter-flowering begonias, gloxinias and streptocarpus. Plants like pelargoniums, fuchsias, impatiens and hydrangeas can be firmed adequately with the fingers. Strawberries, chrysanthemums, carnations and tomatoes in their final pots, and the majority of woody plants need firm potting with a rammer.

If the soil used for potting is reasonably moist, as it should be, and the plants are watered an hour or two before potting, then there is no need to water the plant immediately after this operation is completed. The plants can be left unwatered for two days in summer and three to four days in the wetter, duller months. A rose should be used on the can for the first

watering to avoid soil disturbance.

Soilless Composts. The remarks I have just made refer to conventional composts and not the soilless kinds, which need different treatment. A rammer should never be used with these for they do not need to be made so firm, and as I have already mentioned, they are not really suitable for large plants because they do not provide sufficient weight to keep the pots upright.

Pot Hygiene. All pots must be thoroughly cleaned before used. Clay pots need soaking and scrubbing. Plastic pots are easily cleaned with a damp cloth. Remember, too, that new clay pots must be thoroughly soaked in a tank of water for an hour or so before use otherwise they will draw moisture from the soil to the plant's disadvantage. In addition, it becomes very difficult to remove plants from pots which have not been soaked.

HARDENING OFF

The term hardening off refers to the gradual acclimatisation of plants grown in heated structures to outdoor conditions. In this instance 'gradual' is the operative word for this is a process which must not be rushed. A too rapid transfer from warm to much cooler conditions would give plants a very severe check or indeed kill them outright.

Let us consider seedlings and cuttings raised in a warm propagating frame first. When these are ready for hardening off it is best if the frame can be left open for a day or so before moving the young plants into the greenhouse proper. This cannot be done, however, if the propagating frame also includes seedlings or cuttings which are not sufficiently advanced to be subjected to such treatment. Once out

Hardening off young plants before bedding out. A cold frame is the best place for this essential stage

on the staging it will be necessary to move the plants gradually to the coolest part of the house.

Those plants intended eventually for outdoor cultivation will be moved on to a garden frame where, over a period of ten days or so, the ventilation will be progressively advanced from nil on the first day or so to the complete removal of the frame light. During this time watch the plants carefully to make sure they are not suffering from too much exposure. This will be shown by markings forming on the foliage and a general blueing and cessation of growth. If cold winds develop during the hardening off process, the frame light should be so propped open that the wind does not reach the plants. All plants abhor draughts and none more so than those at this delicate stage of their development.

If space is at a premium, the plants can often be removed from the frame rather earlier (say, after about a week) and stood under a sheltered wall of the greenhouse, garage or home.

Potting on a young plant. **1.** A little compost is placed in the bottom of the new, larger pot. **2.** A sharp knock on the side of the staging will remove the plant from its outgrown pot. **3.** After centring the plant in its new pot, fresh compost is trickled in around the root ball and firmed gently with the finger tips

Watering and Damping Down

I have said many times that a good plantsman is one who knows how and when to use a watering-can. The watering-can itself is an important piece of equipment and is something well worth paying quite a lot for. Good balance is all-important, and the fine and coarse roses with which the can is fitted must be efficient, for any dribbling from the end of a rose can do considerable damage to seedlings.

Roses are only needed when watering seeds, cuttings and very young plants. Also newly potted plants, or the surface compost will be disturbed. Established plants should always be watered direct from the spout of the can, but this should be held close to the soil so that the water does not wash it out of the pot. Sufficient water should be given at each application to soak right through the compost and no more should be given until it begins to dry out.

When to Water. One way of checking the amount of moisture in a clay flower pot is to tap it with something hard such as a cotton reel on the end of a cane. If the pot gives out a clear ring the compost within is dry; if it sounds dull and heavy the compost is wet. With a little practice considerable accuracy can be attained in assessing the plants' needs.

With plastic pots is is not so easy, as plastic does not give the same results as clay when tapped. One must therefore resort to lifting the pots and judging by their weight if the compost is wet or dry. Alternatively, an assessment can be made of the position by feel or by the colour of the surface compost. This is a more hit and miss method as the surface compost may not truly represent what is underneath.

The moisture needs of plants varies tremendously and individual plants will need more or less water according to the season and the stage of their development. With higher temperatures and sun heat the summer is a time when the greenhouse gardener must be particularly alert, for moisture losses on hot, sunny days can be extremely rapid. Spring and autumn are the intermediate seasons in this respect and winter, the time when least watering needs to be done, calls for attention of a different kind. Over-damp conditions then can lead to all kinds of complications with many plants.

Often the simplest gadgets are the most useful. Here, a cotton reel on a cane is used to check whether a plant needs water

It is a sobering thought that more plants are killed by over-watering than under-watering, particularly during the winter months. Certain plants, like fuchsias, poinsettias and gloxinias either need very little or none at all during the winter. On the other hand, if chrysanthemums are allowed to become too dry when the buds are forming this will cause a hard centre to form in the flowers, while if tomatoes on which the fruits are developing become too dry and are then watered, fruit splitting will result. Vigilance is always necessary and the water requirements of all plants must be checked individually as often as experience proves necessary.

One point which should be specially emphasised is the need to water plants thoroughly a short time before repotting. A dry root ball is extremely difficult to soak after potting has been completed, and inability to correct this condition can have serious consequences.

Automatic Watering. This is the age of automation and one way in which the greenhouse gardener benefits is through automatic watering. This can be a boon to the busy gardener away from home for many hours each day, and for longer periods on occasions. The capillary bench, as it is called, makes use of the ability of plants to take up the moisture they need through capillary action. The pots are stood on a sand-covered bench which is kept permanently wet by means of perforated piping laid in the sand and connected to a header tank. As the plants

only take up water to meet their needs they are in fact watered much more precisely than could ever be possible by use of a watering-can and personal judgement. An important point to note, though, is that plants in clay pots must have wicks through their drainage holes to connect the compost in the pots with the sand base. Plants in plastic pots will take up water without this aid.

DAMPING DOWN

Moisture is needed in the air as well as in the soil, but the amount required varies with different plants. Succulents like a much drier atmosphere, for example, than ferns or foliage plants. Atmospheric moisture can be supplied from evaporating trays, by watering paths and under staging and by syringing between the pots or even over the leaves of plants that like a lot of moisture. This so-called damping down creates in the artificial conditions of the greenhouse the growing atmosphere which is so essential. In summer it is often done in the early morning, at midday and towards evening, when closing down the greenhouse. In late spring and early summer I like to damp down and close the ventilators at the end of the afternoon and the combination of a rising temperature and atmospheric moisture creates just the kind of growing conditions I have referred to. This is especially necessary after pollinating peach trees and spraying tomatoes to help set the fruit. Damping down also keeps red spider at bay, another important factor.

Damping down the path of a greenhouse to keep the atmosphere humid. This is particularly important during the summer

Shading and Ventilation

During the summer most greenhouse plants, with the exception of cacti and other succulents, will require some shading from direct sunlight. Plants which 'scorch' easily include the begonias, especially the large double-flowered and winter-flowering types, gloxinias, streptocarpus, fuchsias, ferns, orchids, African Violets, young poinsettias, seedlings of many plants, unrooted cuttings and newly potted plants. Sunshine beating through clear glass can raise temperatures to unacceptable heights very quickly and this is something the greenhouse gardener has to reckon with during the warmer months of the year. Fortunately there are numerous ways and means of coping with this problem, some more sophisticated and therefore more expensive – and by the same token more efficient and allowing greater control – than others.

The most simple way to provide shade in a greenhouse is to paint the glass with whitewash. Plain whitewash made with lime and water will wash off fairly quickly but if just a little size is added it will adhere much better. An alternative is to make use of one of the proprietary shading compounds, available from any garden sundries store or garden centre.

Shading can be stippled on the glass with a brush, but this should only be applied lightly so that it breaks the rays of the sun without excluding too much light.

The drawback to coating the glass in this way is that the shading is permanent, and cannot be altered to suit changing conditions. This is where blinds that can be lowered or raised at will have an advantage. Fabric or polythene blinds are excellent for internal use, but if blinds are to be fitted outside the house, it is better to choose those made of wooden laths – preferably cedar wood – or split cane. These are really ideal for they provide a mottled shading which gives a barrier against the sun but again lets a lot of light through. Another way to provide shade, in the absence of blinds is by means of very fine nylon netting.

Of course, the ultimate is to have automatic blinds. Wooden lath blinds are available for exterior fitting which will roll and unroll automatically by electric motor, the electric current being activated by a thermostat or photo-electric cell. For the busy greenhouse owner who is away from home for long periods of time during the day the advantages are obvious. In combination with automatic heat control and watering it can indeed be a real boon.

One other use for blinds should be mentioned here – their use to keep heat in the greenhouse on really cold winter nights as opposed to keeping heat out on sunny summer days. This can be important, not least in saving fuel where the temperature is maintained at a set level by thermostatic control.

Frames can also be treated with whitewash or proprietary shading compounds. A more temporary expedient, which may be preferable where the need for shading is short term, is to cover the lights with

A simple method of shading a greenhouse is with whitewash. This may be applied with a brush, or it can also be sprayed on

Roller blinds fitted inside the greenhouse are very popular. They can be made of fabric or polythene

A capillary bench watering system is a boon for the busy gardener. Water is supplied automatically, in this case from an inverted bottle, to the sand beds on which the pots stand, and the plants obtain their water by capillary action

Slatted wooden blinds which cut the glare of the sun but allow light to reach the plants are an excellent proposition

A typical ridge ventilator. In some greenhouses these may form a continuous opening along the roof

Side ventilators allow cool air into the house. With all ventilators, only those facing away from the wind should be used

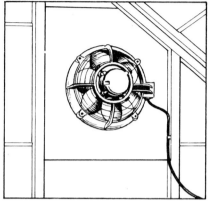

An electric extractor fan fitted at one end of the house will change the air automatically by thermostatic control

green polythene, hessian or newspaper kept in place by bricks or other suitable objects.

VENTILATION

I never consider that the average greenhouse has sufficient ventilation. No greenhouse, of whatever size, should be without top and bottom ventilation (on both sides in the case of a span-roof house) and there should be at least one top and bottom ventilator for every 10 ft. of greenhouse length. For obvious reasons, the number provided by the makers is commensurate with the cost of the product.

Ventilation is required to change the air in the house and keep the temperature from rising too high. If hinged ventilators are used these should be mounted high up near the ridge to let hot air out and in the sides of the house, to let cool air in, especially when the weather is warm. The aim should always be to maintain a fairly steady temperature, but higher by day than by night.

The intelligent use of ventilators allows the experienced greenhouse owner to maintain the buoyant atmosphere which plants like so much. With ventilators fitted of the type I have described it should be possible to keep the air in gentle circulation at all times which is very much to the advantage of the plants. Night condensation can be much reduced for instance, by leaving the ridge ventilators open a little whenever weather conditions permit. As in all aspects of gardening, one soon learns to master ventilation problems in the greenhouse and profit by experience.

Side ventilators are only used when the outside conditions are warm or relatively warm for a cold flow of air over plants can have a very adverse effect on their health. It goes without saying that draughts must be avoided for there are few plants which will put up with such conditions without protest.

In moderately heated or unheated greenhouses the conservation of sun heat to boost up house temperatures in the night hours is a number one priority during the cooler months of the year. Much can be achieved in this respect by closing all the ventilators well before the sun goes down and opening them up in the morning after the early morning chill has disappeared.

An electric extractor fan with thermostatic control can be fitted high up at the end of the greenhouse to give frequent changes of air which will be of great benefit to the plants. These fans have louvres which are kept open by a stream of air being sucked through the house. When the electric motor cuts out, the louvres automatically close by gravity.

An excellent way of circulating warm air in greenhouses is by electric fan heaters and if these are controlled by a thermostat they can be completely automatic in operation. Some will blow cool air when the thermostat cuts out the heating elements and so provide the gentle circulation of air which I have already said is desirable.

As far as I am concerned automatic ventilation is a 'must' for I am away from home so much during the daytime. The best automatic ventilation is provided by

the non-electric type in which a cylinder of fluid expands and contracts to operate a rod attached to the ventilators, opening and closing them as the temperature rises and falls. This type, which does not have any source of external power, is absolutely trouble free and can be relied on.

Ventilation is necessary, of course, in garden frames, for the plants here require the same buoyant atmosphere as those in a greenhouse. In a propagating frame, too, ventilation is essential to gradually accustom seedlings and newly rooted cuttings to more airy conditions. Such ventilation can be provided by sliding the frame light up or down to allow the necessary amount of outside air in. Alternatively, it can be propped up at the end or on its side, whichever way avoids excessive breeze on the plants.

Frames are very easily ventilated by propping the lights open with a block of wood or a brick, or by removing them altogether

Pest and Disease Control

If hygiene is important in the garden, as it undoubtedly is, it is doubly so in the confined quarters of a greenhouse where even the smallest outbreak of trouble from pests or diseases can spread rapidly unless it is checked immediately. Cleanliness, which is so relevant to plant health, is dealt with later (see p. 132) and I am now more immediately concerned with the chemical means of pest and disease control.

Fumigation. Many pests and diseases can be killed by fumigation which is much easier to carry out than spraying. Some plants, though, will not tolerate this treatment and spraying must then be resorted to in any case.

The simplest method of fumigation is by means of special smoke generators which are rather like small fireworks. These come in varying sizes and shapes, including cones, pellets and shreds. One of suitable size (or more than one if necessary) is placed low down in the house in a central position and ignited. It emits dense clouds of smoke which carry the particular chemical contained in the generator to all parts of the house. Electrically operated ones are also avilable which are very efficient.

Generators are available for houses of all sizes and it is necessary to work out the cubic capacity of your greenhouse to know which is the right one in your case. This is simply a matter of multiplying the length of the house by the breadth by the height to half way up the roof. The generators are made to contain most of the well-known insecticides and there are also fungicidal ones for use against diseases. The amount of air space for which each generator is effective will be printed on it or on the container in which it is purchased.

Fumigation is best done towards evening. The atmosphere in the greenhouse should be dry and ventilation must be given beforehand to ensure this. Plants to be fumigated must be moist at the roots. All ventilators should be closed and, most important, the house vacated immediately and not re-entered for several hours. It is imperative to make sure that the chemicals used are not harmful to any of the plants in the greenhouse. Read the manufacturer's instructions carefully and follow them implicitly.

Smoke generators of various types including nicotine shreds. Many pests and diseases can be controlled by their use

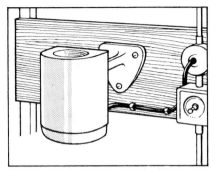

For the greenhouse owner who likes automatic equipment, an electrically operated fumigator would be an asset

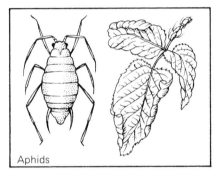

Aphids

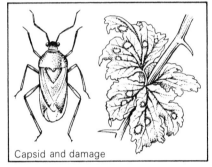

Capsid and damage

Spraying and Dusting. When applying insecticides and fungicides in the form of sprays, dusts and aerosols, it is advisable to have the ventilators and doors open so that there will be no heavy concentration of the chemicals in the atmosphere. Again, before making such applications note particularly if the manufacturer warns that certain plants will be damaged or killed by the chemicals in question and take such plants out of the house if they are present. For example, ferns will be damaged by malathion.

It cannot be said too often that having vigorous, healthy plants is one of the best defences against pests and diseases. It is unfortunately true that plants in indifferent health succumb most easily to attacks of this kind. In the plant world, too, it is the survival of the fittest. So, by growing one's plants well one is giving them a head start, which can often make all the difference.

One final reminder about garden chemicals: keep these locked away when not in use, especially if there are children or pets in the family.

GREENHOUSE PESTS

Ants. Ants are not thought of, perhaps, as typical greenhouse pests but they can be troublesome by invading the compost in which pot plants are growing, upsetting its porosity and structure. They can be controlled by sprinkling BHC dust on the soil, or by using a proprietary ant killer.

Aphids. The two main types of aphid are the greenfly and the blackfly which attack many greenhouse plants, including chrysanthemums and bulbous flowers. These insects suck the sap from leaves and stems, checking and distorting growth. They can be combated by spraying with BHC, malathion or derris, or by fumigating with BHC smokes or nicotine shreds.

Root aphids are small greyish insects which suck the sap from the roots of plants and ultimately cause their collapse if action is not taken against them. Lettuces and auriculas are particularly affected. Pot plants should be removed from their pots and the compost sprayed with BHC, and plants in borders can be watered with BHC solution.

Capsid Bugs. The sap-sucking capsid bugs, which attack chrysanthemums and fuchsias, are green in colour and about $\frac{1}{4}$ in. long. They pierce the stems, young leaves and flower buds and cause distortion of the growth and general weakness. Spraying or fumigating with BHC is advised.

Caterpillars. Caterpillars are the larvae of butterflies and moths and they can be removed by hand picking or by spraying with BHC, malathion, derris or pyrethrum.

Earwigs. These insects can be troublesome in the greenhouse, chrysanthemums in particular being prone to attack. A BHC smoke will give control under glass or this chemical can be applied as a dust or spray to affected plants.

Eelworms. This minute insect is a very serious pest of chrysanthemums and its many other victims include narcissi, hyacinths, lettuces, tomatoes and cucumbers. All affected plants should be destroyed by burning. The colourless slender worms live within the tissues, in the leaves in the case of chrysanthemums, and in the stems and roots of other plants. They cause the plants to become swollen and deformed and to stop growing. Chrysanthemums

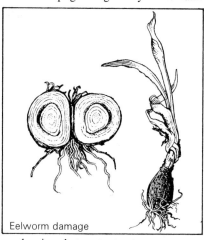
Eelworm damage

can be given hot water treatment to overcome this pest, as can other plants, but it must be said that it is not easy for the home gardener to carry out this operation to the fine limits necessary for success and the avoidance of damage to the plants. The stools of chrysanthemums which will be used as a source of cuttings for new stock should be totally immersed in water heated to 43°C. (110°F.) for 20 to 30 minutes, followed immediately by immersion in cold water. Some bulbous plants can be similarly treated, the temperature of the water and the period of immersion varying from plant to plant. Thus narcissi need 3 hours immersion in water heated to 43°C. (110°F.) and irises require only 1 hour. Again, it must be emphasised that all bulbs known to be affected must be burnt and only apparently healthy bulbs

should be given hot water treatment.

Leaf Hoppers. Many soft-wooded greenhouse plants are attacked by leaf hoppers, or frog flies as they are called, among them pelargoniums, primulas, fuchsias, chrysanthemums, tomatoes and cucumbers. The larvae of this pest suck the sap from the leaves with the expected weakening

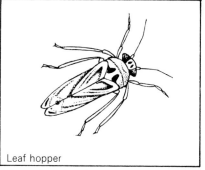
Leaf hopper

effect. The winged adult leaf hoppers are pale yellow in colour, the larvae are similar, but smaller and without wings. Spray with BHC, malathion or derris, or fumigate with BHC.

Leaf Miner. This again is a major pest of chrysanthemums, the adult fly laying its eggs in the leaves and the resulting grubs later tunnelling and eating the tissues. Silvery, wavy lines will be noticed on attacked leaves. The larvae of several kinds of fly are called leaf-miners but all attack the plants in the same way. Other affected plants are cinerarias, carnations and tomatoes. Badly attacked leaves should be removed and burnt. On less badly damaged leaves feel for the insect by running the leaf between the fingers and

Leaf miner damage

squash them. Alternatively, spray with BHC or malathion or use a BHC aerosol or smoke.

Mealy Bug. This destructive and serious greenhouse pest is a member of the scale insect family and is related to the aphids. It resembles a woodlouse but is much

smaller and has a covering of white, waxy, wool-like material which gives it protection against water and makes it a formidable pest to control, since it multiplies rapidly. Once fully grown this insect moves very little and it attacks the plants by sucking the leaves and stems. Grape vines are a major sufferer from this pest, and other plants include cacti, codiaeums and hippeastrums. The root mealy bug, which is very similar in appearance, is often found on cacti.

If the infestation is caught at an early stage it can be nipped in the bud by painting the insects with a paint brush dipped in an insecticide such as derris, malathion or white oil emulsion. Alternatively, these can all be used as sprays, repeated applications being necessary to deal with the insects as they hatch out from eggs which have escaped treatment. The difficulty is the protective covering which I have already referred to. To be effective all sprays must contain what is

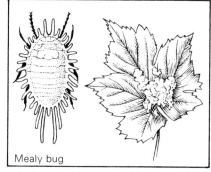
Mealy bug

called a wetting agent which enables the chemical to adhere to the body of the pest more easily.

Root mealy bug presents a different problem. Once identified, the soil must be shaken out from the roots of pot plants, the worst affected roots being cut away and the remaining roots being dipped in insecticide before repotting in fresh compost.

All the loose bark should be removed from grape vines during the winter, the rods and spurs being painted with white oil emulsion. The surrounding woodwork of the greenhouse should also be thoroughly scrubbed with hot, soapy water.

Narcissus Flies. Both the large narcissus fly and the small narcissus fly are pests which concern the greenhouse owner. The large narcissus fly looks rather like a small bee and is a major pest of narcissi as well as attacking numerous other bulbous plants – hippeastrums, hyacinths, lilies, scillas and vallotas. The larvae penetrate the bulbs through their basal plates and any plant with distorted foliage and in a generally poor condition should be suspect. All badly attacked plants should be burnt immediately, and less badly affected ones can be given hot water treatment while dormant – this means total immersion in water heated to 43°C. (110°F.) for one hour. As I have pointed out in connection with eelworms, though, such treatment is not easy for the amateur gardener to complete satisfactorily. An alternative is to immerse the dormant bulbs in a solution of BHC, to which a wetting agent has been added, for 3 hours. The small narcissus fly, which is especially troublesome with hyacinths as well as narcissi, can be dealt with in a similar manner.

Red Spider Mite. This minute pest – it

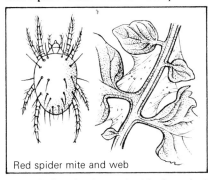
Red spider mite and web

can only just be detected with the naked eye – attacks a great many greenhouse plants, including carnations, arums, vines, peaches, melons and cucumbers. It is most troublesome in hot, dry conditions and frequent syringing with clear water is the most effective way of keeping it under control. The mites congregate on the undersides of the leaves which become mottled and yellowish in appearance, and a very fine web can be seen. This pest can be combated by fumigating with azobenzene, which can also be applied by aerosol, or by spraying with white oil emulsion or malathion.

Scale Insects. Ferns, orchids, peaches, camellias, *Nerium oleander* (Oleander), citrus fruits and aspidistras are greenhouse plants which are particularly affected by scale insects. These small insects attach themselves firmly to the leaves and

stems and suck the sap, so causing the general decline of the plant. There are numerous species of which the grey mussel scale is the most common. Another fairly frequent intruder is the brown scale. The adult insect is covered with a hard protective shell making it difficult for insecticides to penetrate. Often leaves and

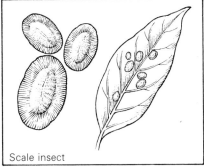
Scale insect

stems become coated with a sticky substance, and sooty mould grows on this, giving the plants a blackened appearance. Attacked plants should be sprayed with malathion, diazinon or white oil emulsion. In small numbers the insects can be removed with a knife or finger nail. Fumigation with nicotine shreds is also possible.

Slugs. Perhaps slugs are not thought of as normal greenhouse pests but these find their way into the greenhouse by various means to make a meal of young growth, seedlings and bulbs. The answer is to leave small heaps of metaldehyde and bran or proprietary slug pellets on the greenhouse staging when slugs are known to be present.

Springtails. Bulbs and orchids, seedlings and young plants generally are susceptible to attack by springtails. These small white insects seem to hop when disturbed, hence their common name. They like to congregate on dead or decaying plant vegetation – a good reason for keeping the greenhouse scrupulously clean! Also, if the drainage of pot plants is poor there is a greater risk of damage by this pest. The soil should be watered with a solution of BHC, or alternatively, dust or fumigate with BHC.

Tortrix Moth. The larvae of the tortrix moth are a pest of carnations, and they attack the leaves, spinning these together as a means of protection. This characteristic should, therefore, be watched for as well as any signs of damage to the

foliage and shoot tips. The larvae can be removed by hand, or derris dust or spray can be applied as soon as this pest is noticed in the spring.

Thrips. These minute insects, varying from yellow to black in colour, are a major pest of greenhouse plants and are especially damaging to carnations. Cyclamen, clivias and codiaeums are other plants frequently affected. The buds and flowers are particularly susceptible in the case of carnations and cyclamen. Attacked leaves and stems become distorted and covered with small brown spots.

Thrips move very rapidly and are not easy to find and destroy. Like red spider mites these insects thrive in a hot, dry atmosphere and they are likely to be troublesome in such conditions. Syringing attacked plants with clean water is very helpful. Alternatively, spray with BHC or malathion, or fumigate with BHC.

Vine Weevil. The off-white, rotund, legless, grubs of the vine weevil, which are about ½ in. in length, are not only a pest of the grape vine but of such popular ornamental pot plants as cyclamen, primulas and tuberous begonias. Peaches are also attacked. While the grubs attack the roots, bulbs and corms, the adult weevils damage the leaves, so this is a pest to watch for at both stages of its life cycle. The adults can be destroyed with a BHC

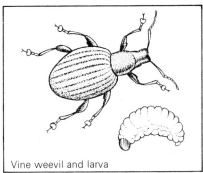
Vine weevil and larva

smoke, and BHC powder can be forked into the soil around grape vines to destroy the grubs. In the case of pot plants, the larvae can be removed by hand if the plants are removed from their pots; the soil can be watered with BHC or, most desirable of all, they can have their old compost removed and be repotted in new compost.

White Fly. This can be a serious pest of greenhouse plants, especially tomatoes, and when present in large numbers they will arise in a white cloud when disturbed. Individually the insects are very small with white wings – the characteristic which gives them their name. They suck the sap from the leaves and as control is not easy and reproduction is rapid it will be understood that this is a pest which should not be treated lightly. Fumigation with BHC is one method of control and spraying with malathion at least twice with a 14-day interval in between is another.

Woodlice. These nocturnal pests eat leaves, young shoots and seedlings. They can be trapped in inverted flower pots filled with paper or chopped hay. The soil can also be dusted with BHC.

GREENHOUSE DISEASES

Blossom End Rot. This is a physiological

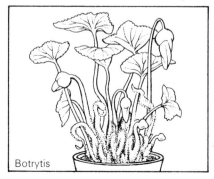
Blossom end rot

disorder of tomatoes which causes the fruits to turn black at the opposite end to the stalk. This trouble is primarily due to incorrect watering – too little usually at the wrong intervals. Affected fruits should be removed.

Botrytis. This is the fungus disease known as blackleg or grey mould, both very descriptive of two marked characteristics of this trouble. It attacks an extremely wide range of plants from tomatoes, vines and lettuces to lilies, chrysanthemums and cyclamen. It thrives when the atmosphere

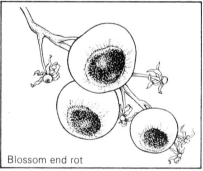
Botrytis

is cool and damp, and if the greenhouse is heated to a temperature of 13°C. (55°F.) or more, with free ventilation being given whenever suitable, this disease should not cause trouble. Spacing the pots out as much as possible also helps, for this allows air to circulate more freely around the plants.

The disease attacks the stems and leaves of the plants and the fruits where applicable. These turn black and rot and a grey mould then develops – hence the common names already referred to. Badly affected plants should be destroyed. Plants can be dusted with flowers of sulphur, sprayed with captan or thiram or the greenhouse can be fumigated with tecnazene (TCNB) or by vaporising copper.

Damping Off. This scourge of seedlings raised under glass is a fungus disease which attacks the stems at or just above soil level bringing about the collapse of the tiny plants. Overcrowding and damp, warm, badly ventilated conditions are its natural allies. To combat this serious trouble, then, water carefully, maintain a suitable temperature by correct ventilation, use sterilised soil, sow thinly and prick the seedlings out as soon as possible. The seeds can be treated before sowing with captan or thiram, and if an attack develops after the seedlings have appeared, water with Cheshunt Compound or thiram.

Foot Rot. This disease resembles damping off and attacks melons, tomatoes and cucumbers. It usually occurs at a later stage than damping off, however, the base of the stem being attacked which brings about the plant's collapse. The aim should be to keep the base of the stems as dry as possible. When an attack has developed, water around the stem with Cheshunt Compound, thiram or captan.

Leafmould. This is a disease which affects tomatoes, causing light coloured patches or spots on the upper surface of the leaves, and a khaki felt on the lower surface. Eventually the leaves wilt completely. The disease flourishes under stuffy conditions, so good ventilation is important, and spraying with a copper fungicide should give adequate control.

Mildew. A group of fungus diseases goes under this name, several of them the enemies of greenhouse plants. It is most likely to cause trouble when the air is

dank and stagnant. Heat should be given to warm the air and keep it circulating with as much ventilation being provided as possible, depending on the prevailing weather conditions. Spacing the plants is also very helpful.

Mildew is identified by the white or greyish patches which form on the leaves and stems of affected plants. When an

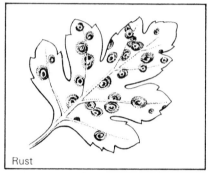
Rust

attack is noticed, dust the leaves of the plants with flowers of sulphur, spray with colloidal copper or dinocap, or fumigate with dinocap.

Rust. There are various kinds of rust and the two most likely to affect the greenhouse gardener are carnation rust and chrysanthemum rust. Both form small, raised orange-brown spots on the leaves and affected leaves should be removed and burnt. Badly affected plants should be destroyed. Spray with zineb or thiram.

Virus Diseases. The term virus is used to describe a very wide range of disease organisms, very much smaller than fungi or bacteria, which cause yellowish mottling, streaking, blotching, distortion and stunting and generally weaken the plants. The viruses increase rapidly in the sap of the plants and are transferred from one plant to another by sap sucking insects as well as by knives and other tools used to take cuttings and for pruning. In a few instances viruses are seed- or soil-borne. Chrysanthemums and tomatoes are two greenhouse plants which suffer attacks by virus diseases.

There are no known cures and all affected plants should be removed and burnt as soon as the trouble is identified. Controlling the insect pests such as aphids, capsid bugs and thrips which spread these diseases is an obvious counter measure. Do not take cuttings or otherwise propagate vegetatively from affected plants.

Routine Tasks

Routine tasks, unspectacular in themselves, are a vital part of the successful cultivation of greenhouse plants. Some, like watering and damping down, shading and ventilation, pricking out, potting and hardening-off I have already dealt with separately under their own headings. But there are other jobs which are just as important in their way as those I have just referred to.

Labelling. I suppose that most of us tend to think that our memories are better than they are in reality. In fact, it is always wise to make a record of sowing dates and other cultural functions when such information is likely to be needed in the future. Immediate and clear labelling is a must as far as I am concerned. Where seed boxes are used there is a method of recording details which makes the use of labels unnecessary. Part of one end of the top edge of the box is pared smooth with a knife and is smeared with white paint so that particulars can be written on the still-moist surface with a lead pencil. This recording technique can be used for seed sowing and also, of course, for pricked-out seedlings.

Carnations and chrysanthemums, both plants with many named varieties, are examples of plants which need careful labelling if confusion is to be avoided. With chrysanthemums, too, stopping dates should be recorded. All plants which are being rested, such as lifted dahlia tubers, should be labelled, and if for some reason the varietal name is not known, then record the flower colour, the plant's height and type and any other relevant information so that when the time comes

Labels can be attached directly to the plant, or inserted in the compost. They are invaluable when dealing with plants such as

to take cuttings all the available information will be to hand immediately.

Labels are available in many forms nowadays, in wood, metal and plastic. One can even punch out one's own in plastic or metal with a small hand machine. There are, too, those labels which can be attached to the stems of plants or to branches as well as the traditional kind for insertion in the growing compost.

Stopping. The term stopping refers to the operation whereby the growing tip of a plant is removed to check further upward development and encourage instead the development of side growths. Stopping is essential in the case of chrysanthemums, particularly the exhibition type, for this operation determines the flowering date. The same applies to perpetual-flowering carnations. Fuchsias need stopping so that they develop the desired bushy habit, and the same applies to schizanthuses.

Stopping is carried out for different reasons in the case of such plants as grape vines and melons. The fruiting laterals of both of these plants are stopped at a leaf or so beyond the fruit and the sub-laterals are also stopped at the first or second leaf to prevent excessive leaf formation.

The tips of shoots to be stopped are invariably pinched between the finger and thumb or are removed with a sharp knife. In both cases the amputation should be clean and workmanlike.

Staking. Many ornamental greenhouse plants need support in some shape or form and since the plants are grown as much for their visual appeal as for the satisfaction of growing them well, it is

fuchsias and chrysanthemums, which have numerous varieties

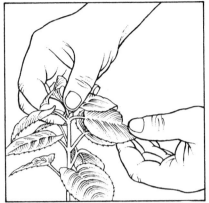

Stopping a fuchsia plant by pinching out the growing tip. A clean break should be made so that infection does not occur

important that the supports used should be unobtrusive as well as strong. Thin bamboo canes painted green are suitable for small flowering plants, bulbs such as daffodils and hyacinths, young carnations, small fuchsias and some pelargoniums, while taller-growing plants, like schizanthuses and chrysanthemums need larger canes up to 4 or 5 ft. tall. When inserting canes to support large, bushy pot plants such as chrysanthemums, they must be positioned as far away from the plant's stem as possible, and they should slope outwards to allow the plant plenty of room to develop. Other plants, though, such as standard fuchsias and rubber plants, should have the cane close to the stem to make it as inconspicuous as possible. When staking bulbous plants, care must be taken not to damage the bulb when inserting the cane. Wire supports can be used for flowering bulbs, perpetual-flowering carnations and begonias.

Staking hyacinth flower buds with a piece of wire. This is bent in a crook shape to support the heavy head

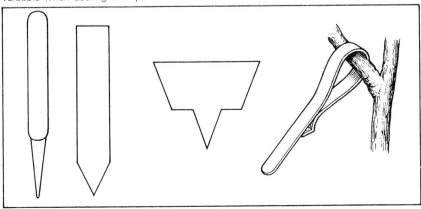

Tying. Again, as with the supports, the ties which are made should be as inconspicuous as possible. Raffia should be split and moistened before use, and this material will be found suitable for tying in the shoots of such plants as schizanthuses, begonias, carnations and chrysanthemums. Large plants will need to be tied in with green twine. Always make the ties in such a way that the growths take up a natural positon. To ensure that they hold the stems firmly but do not cause constriction, twist and knot the tying material between the support and the stem, allowing plenty of space for growth where this will be considerable.

Soil Sterilisation. When mixing one's own composts to the John Innes' formulae, soil sterilisation is a necessity to dispose of pests, diseases and weed seeds. This is done before the other ingredients are added. Soil sterilisation can be done in various ways but the simplest method is to use a small electric steriliser. However, small amounts can be sterilised if they are suspended in a cloth bag just above the surface of a copper of boiling water. The soil will thoroughly absorb the steam in this way and afterwards should be placed on a raised, slatted surface to drain off the surplus moisture.

Of the chemicals used for soil sterilisation the most widely used and probably the most satisfactory is formaldehyde which is purchased as formalin (40 per cent. formaldehyde) and is mixed with 49 times its own bulk of water. Two gallons of the dilute solution will treat about 1

A small, electrically operated soil steriliser for partially sterilising loam. An alternative design is illustrated on p. 18

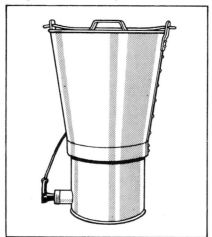

A strip of thin metal, bent at an angle, makes the perfect tool for dislodging dirt caught between the panes of glass

bushel of soil. The soil to be treated should be stood on a hard surface and the solution is then poured over it as evenly as possible. The soil is immediately turned and heaped up and then covered with polythene for at least 48 hours to trap the fumes. After this the covering is removed but the soil is not used until all trace of the smell of formaldehyde has disappeared which may mean a wait of more than a month.

Cleaning the Greenhouse. It would be difficult to over-emphasise the importance of cleanliness in greenhouse management. So many pest and disease troubles arise through neglect of this basic chore and dirty glass will affect the light factor as well.

In winter most plants require all the light they can get and if limewash or other 'permanent' shading has been put on the glass it should be removed. In any event it is wise to wash down all the

Limewashing the inside walls of a greenhouse increases the light intensity and also helps to kill pests and diseases

Removing dirt and rust from the heating pipes with a wire brush. This is important if they are to function efficiently

greenhouse glass both inside and out to remove dirt and grime. A long-handled broom is useful for this and warm water containing a little detergent will soon loosen the dirt.

A most difficult place from which to remove dirt is in the overlaps between the panes of glass. A special tool may have to be made for this purpose from a strip of thin metal slightly bent so that it can be slipped in between the panes and drawn from side to side.

Woodwork and Walls. These also should be scrubbed to get rid of dirt and lurking insects. A little disinfectant added to the water will help. This work can be done more easily and safely if the plants can be removed temporarily. One advantage of doing this work in winter, generally immediately after the last chrysanthemums have flowered and been cut down, is that it is usually the time when the greenhouse is least crowded. If the walls are of concrete or brick it will help to limewash them after they have been scrubbed down. Freshly made limewash will help to destroy pests and fungus spores and, by reflecting light, will improve the illumination of the house. The staging should also be cleaned and if ash or gravel is used as a base on which to stand plant pots this should be washed through with water from a hose-pipe.

Should the greenhouse be heated by hot water pipes these will need annual attention. Remove any rust or scale with a wire brush and then paint with old sump oil. This is not simply a matter of appearance or of preserving the pipes from rust. Heat will be more efficiently radiated from pipes that are clean and black than from those that are scaly and rusty, and one will save on fuel.

Hanging Baskets

Although hanging baskets of summer-flowering plants are usually seen out of doors they can also be used for a display inside a greenhouse where they can be a highly decorative feature if well prepared and given good aftercare.

Plants that are most suited to cultivation in baskets are those with a pendulous habit. Fuchsias, so popular nowadays, are ideal, but, of course, some varieties are better than others. A few good ones are the crimson-scarlet Marinka, the white and deep crimson Cascade, the cerise and white Swingtime, the creamy-white and pink Mrs Marshall and the pink and purple Lena. Pendulous begonias look delightful in hanging baskets as does the popular Busy Lizzie (*Impatiens sultanii*), Plants that are used for baskets outside in the summer are Ivy-leaved pelargoniums, trailing lobelia, *Campanula isophylla*, *Asparagus sprengeri* and petunias.

Hanging baskets are made in various sizes but those of 14 to 16 in. in diameter are likely to look more impressive when the plants are in full flower than those of smaller size. They are obtainable in galvanised wire, plastic-coated wire or polythene, and there are some designs which have the added advantage of a built-in tray underneath to catch the drips after watering.

Preparing A Basket. The time to prepare

Preparing a hanging basket. **1.** The sides of the basket are lined with moss to hold the compost and plants in position. **2.** Compost is added, and small plants are inserted through the sides as work progresses. **3.** Finally, the top is planted up, leaving a slight depression in the compost to allow for watering

Fuchsias, and other plants with pendulous flowers or a trailing habit, are particularly attractive in a hanging basket

hanging baskets is in early spring. To keep the basket steady while it is being made up it is a good plan to stand it on a large flower pot. The basket should be lined thickly with moss to hold the potting compost in position. John Innes No. 1 Potting Compost is a suitable choice, and it should be added a little at a time as the moss lining is built up. Small plants, such as variegated nepeta and lobelias, can be pushed through the wires in the sides of the basket as the potting compost is added so that the whole basket is well clothed with foliage and flowers. When the basket has been completely lined with moss and the compost has been firmed with the fingers, the top of the basket can be planted. Ivy-leaved pelargoniums can be placed at an angle so that the new growth will hang over the sides of the basket.

To allow space for watering it is a good idea to leave a saucer-like depression in the surface of the compost, and also to build up the sides of the basket with extra moss and soil.

Baskets are intended to hang from a beam or other support so that the flowers can be enjoyed at eye level or above, but it may not always be possible to display them in this way. If necessary, they can be left standing on pots on the greenhouse staging – but this should be looked on as a second-best solution.

Aftercare. To encourage a compact, bushy habit the tips of fuchsias stems should be nipped out frequently. Premature flowers should also be removed for the same reason. The plants soon fill the baskets with roots and watering must be attended to carefully as the soil tends to dry out rapidly, particularly when the weather is hot and dry.

I am sure that many gardeners fail to get the best from basket-grown plants because they neglect to feed them at regular intervals. Liquid or soluble fertilisers can be given every seven to ten days in the summer and they will help the plants to go on flowering well into the autumn.

Propagation of Plants for Baskets. To have well-rooted specimens ready for planting in baskets in the spring, cuttings of fuchsias and Ivy-leaved pelargoniums should be taken in July and August, the rooted cuttings being overwintered in 3-in. pots.

Pendulous begonias are started into growth in the same way as the large-flowered tuberous begonias, details of which are given on p. 36. Lobelias are best raised from seed each year.

A Quick Guide to Decorative Plants

Name	Decorative Features	Approximate Time of Display	Conditions Needed
Abutilon	Evergreen shrubs with attractive funnel-shaped flowers	All seasons, but best in spring and summer	Cool greenhouse, sun lounge or conservatory
Achimenes	Pink, purple, scarlet and white flowers. Used as pot plant or for hanging baskets	Summer and autumn	Cool greenhouse
Allamanda	Evergreen climber with trumpet flowers in different shades of yellow	Summer from June onwards	Warm greenhouse
Annuals	Many, in a wide variety of forms and colours	April to July or August	Cool or unheated greenhouse, sun lounge or conservatory
Anthurium	Best known ones have striking spathes in white, pink, red and orange. Others have decorative foliage	All seasons, but best in spring and summer	Warm greenhouse
Aphelandra	Bright yellow bracts and dark green, white-veined leaves	Mainly summer and autumn	Warm greenhouse
Arum	Pure white or yellow spathes	Spring and early summer	Warm greenhouse
Asparagus	Handsome foliage plants	All seasons	Cool greenhouse, sun lounge or conservatory
Azalea	Flowers in red, pink or white, borne profusely	Winter and early spring	Cool greenhouse
Begonia	Various kinds with decorative flowers and foliage	All seasons	Cool or warm greenhouse, sun lounge or conservatory
Beloperone	Salmon-red bracts and white flowers	All seasons	Cool greenhouse, sun lounge or conservatory if heated
Bromeliads	A group of plants with striking foliage, some with handsome flowers	All seasons	Warm greenhouse
Browallia	Blue or white flowers	Early summer until autumn	Cool greenhouse
Brunfelsia	Evergreen flowering shrub with lavender-purple flowers	Late winter and spring	Cool greenhouse, sun lounge or conservatory
Bulbs	Many lovely and familiar bulbous flowers	Winter and spring	Cool greenhouse, sun lounge or conservatory
Cacti and Succulents	A very wide range of plants with decorative flowers and/or interesting shapes	All seasons	Cool greenhouse
Calceolaria	Bright, gay, curiously pouched flowers	Spring and early summer	Cool greenhouse
Camellia	Superb evergreen flowering shrubs with blooms ranging in colour from red to pink and white	Late winter and spring	Cool greenhouse
Campanula	The delightful Bell Flower with white or blue flowers, one kind trailing the other making a plant 4 ft. tall	Spring and summer	Cool greenhouse
Carnation	Perpetual-flowering kind in wide range of beautiful colours	All seasons, but best in spring and early summer	Cool greenhouse
Chlorophytum	Handsome green-and-cream striped foliage	All seasons	Cool greenhouse
Chrysanthemum	Flowers in many colours	Autumn and early winter	Cool greenhouse
Cineraria	Massed flower heads in gay colours	Late winter and early spring	Cool greenhouse
Citrus Fruits	These have novelty value and make decorative plants even when not in fruit	All seasons	Cool greenhouse, sun lounge or conservatory

Name	Decorative Features	Approximate Time of Display	Conditions Needed
Clivia	Lily-like flowers in yellow, red or orange	March to June	Warm greenhouse
Codiaeum	Colourful foliage	All seasons	Warm greenhouse
Coleus	Beautiful, multi-coloured foliage	All seasons	Warm greenhouse in winter, sun lounge or conservatory in summer
Columnea	Red and yellow flowers	Winter	Warm greenhouse
Cyclamen	Superb pot plants with pink, red, white, violet and crimson flowers, including some with frilled petals	Autumn until spring	Warm greenhouse
Dieffenbachia	Attractive large-leaved foliage plant. Leaves spotted with white	All seasons	Warm greenhouse
Dizygotheca	Decorative foliage plants	All seasons	Warm greenhouse
Dracaena	Handsome, colourful foliage	All seasons	Warm greenhouse
Ferns	Foliage effects	All seasons	Cool or warm greenhouse, sun lounge or conservatory
Ficus	Bold, attractive foliage	All seasons	Warm greenhouse
Freesia	Beautiful flowers in delightful soft colourings	Winter	Cool greenhouse
Fuchsia	Handsome shrubs for pots or hanging baskets with flowers of purple, pink, red and white colouring	Spring and summer	Cool greenhouse, sun lounge or conservatory
Gardenia	Evergreen shrub with heavily fragrant white flowers	Spring, summer and autumn	Warm greenhouse
Gloriosa	Climbing plant. Very distinctive crimson or orange and red flowers with narrow, wavy, recurved petals	Summer	Warm greenhouse
Gloxinia	Velvet-like blooms in red, purple, rose and white. Handsome foliage	Summer	Cool greenhouse
Grevillea	Attractive foliage plants	All seasons	Cool greenhouse, sun lounge or conservatory
Hedera	Ornamental foliage	All seasons	Cool greenhouse, sun lounge or conservatory
Hippeastrum	Huge trumpet flowers in scarlet, crimson, pink and white	Late winter and spring	Cool or warm greenhouse
Hoya	Includes a climbing species and one of bushy habit suitable for hanging baskets or for growing in pots. Attractive flowers	Mainly summer and autumn	Warm greenhouse
Hydrangea	Splendid pot plants with large flower heads in pink, red, white or blue	Spring and summer	Cool greenhouse
Impatiens	The popular Busy Lizzie with colourful flowers of various shades	Summer, continuing into autumn and winter	Cool greenhouse, sun lounge or conservatory
Ipomoea	The well-known climbing Morning Glory. A splendid pot plant with flowers in blue, white or dark red	Summer	Cool greenhouse
Jasminum	The popular species with white or bright yellow flowers	Winter and spring	Cool greenhouse

Name	Decorative Features	Approximate Time of Display	Conditions Needed
Lachenalia	Beautiful South African plants with many species and varieties in a good range of colours	February to May	Cool greenhouse
Lapageria	Evergreen shrub with pink, bell-shaped flowers. There is also a white variety	Summer and autumn	Cool greenhouse
Lily	Various kinds with a good colour range	Spring, summer and early autumn	Cool or unheated greenhouse, sun lounge or conservatory
Maranta	Attractive plants with beautifully marked leaves	All seasons	Warm greenhouse
Nerine	Umbels of distinctive flowers in colours which include pink, salmon, orange, red or white	August until autumn	Cool greenhouse
Nerium	Evergreen shrubs with terminal clusters of flowers in colours from white to deep pink	June to October	Cool greenhouse
Orchids	Wide range of species and varieties with beautiful flowers	Winter, spring and summer	Cool or warm greenhouse, depending on type grown
Pelargonium	Three types grown for their flowers, the other for its fragrant foliage	Spring and summer. Foliage type all seasons	Cool or warm greenhouses, sun lounge or conservatory
Peperomia	Handsome foliage, often variegated	All seasons	Warm greenhouse
Plumbago	Shrub with pale blue flowers	Summer	Cool greenhouse, sun lounge or conservatory
Poinsettia	Showy bracts in scarlet, pink and white	All seasons, but especially Christmas	Warm greenhouse
Primula	Various kinds with attractive flowers in wide colour range	Winter, spring and early summer	Cool greenhouse
Saintpaulia	The well-known African Violet with flowers in such colours as purple, violet-blue, pink or white	All seasons	Warm greenhouse
Sansevieria	Distinctive sword-like leaves	All seasons	Cool or warm greenhouse
Schizanthus	Lovely half-hardy annual with flowers in such colours as red, pink, crimson, mauve or purple	Spring and summer	Cool greenhouse
Smithiantha	Tubular flowers in red, orange, yellow and apricot shades. Handsome foliage	July to December	Warm greenhouse
Solanum	Bright red berries	October to February	Cool greenhouse
Stephanotis	Evergreen twining shrub with fragrant pure white flowers	May to July, sometimes also winter	Warm greenhouse
Stock	Flowers in such colours as rose, pink, violet, salmon and white	Late winter and early spring	Cool greenhouse
Strelitzia	The spectacular Bird of Paradise Flower with brilliant orange and purple colouring	Spring	Warm greenhouse or well heated sun lounge
Streptocarpus	Attractive greenhouse perennials with trumpet flowers in purple, blue, red, pink and white	Mid-summer until autumn	Warm greenhouse
Streptosolen	Evergreen climbing shrub with orange flowers	June to September	Cool greenhouse
Tibouchina	Beautiful shrub with rich purple flowers	Summer	Warm greenhouse
Tradescantia	Attractive variegated foliage	All seasons	Cool greenhouse
Vallota	Scarlet flowers	Early autumn	Cool greenhouse

Monthly Reminders

JANUARY

This is the month when there is possibly more space in the greenhouse than at any other time of year and the opportunity should be taken to thoroughly wash down the house, inside and out, as described on p. 132. This includes cleaning the gravel on the staging, cleaning the heating pipes and treating them with sump oil, and cleaning pots and boxes in preparation for the busy seed-sowing season which lies ahead.

Cuttings of chrysanthemums should be taken at this time and fuchsias and pelargoniums potted on. Sow seeds of begonias, gloxinias and streptocarpus and germinate in a propagating frame with a temperature of about 18°C. (65°F.). Towards the end of the month, start to bring pots of narcissi, daffodils and hyacinths into the greenhouse from their plunge beds.

If strawberries are grown in pots then bring these into the greenhouse from the middle of the month onwards, and continue to do so at regular intervals.

FEBRUARY

With the days starting to get longer and the sun having more power it is time to root pelargonium cuttings, at the same time cutting back the old stock plants and repotting them. Trim back fuchsias, shake the soil from the roots and repot them in fresh soil. Calceolarias should be ready to go into their 6-in. pots, and schizanthuses will be ready for their move into 6-, 7- or 8-in. pots. Continue to sow seeds of begonias, gloxinias and streptocarpus as in January. This is also the time to sow freesias, coleus and *Primula kewensis*. More chrysanthemum cuttings can be inserted, both of indoor and outdoor kinds. Pot bulbs of gloriosas. Take cuttings of Lorraine begonias.

Continue to bring narcissi, daffodils and hyacinths into the house, a few at a time, to provide a continuity of colour. As tulips begin to show their flower buds, they may also be brought into the house.

Start planting up hanging baskets if fuchsias are being used, putting these in now. Add Ivy-leaved pelargoniums, verbena and trailing lobelia in March and pendulous begonias in April.

MARCH

March brings much longer days and spring begins in the greenhouse long before it does out of doors. Many plants are now making active growth. This is the time to pot Regal pelargoniums, and to stop pelargoniums generally to encourage them to make bushy growth.

Seeds of many summer-flowering plants for the garden should be sown this month. Sow tomato seed about the middle of the month. Start tubers of begonias and gloxinias into growth by putting them into boxes filled with moist peat. Continue to pot the bulbs of gloriosas if this was not completed last month. Also, if freesia seed was not sown last month do this now.

If you have a peach tree on the wall of your greenhouse it will be in flower now and pollination must be attended to.

Perpetual-flowering carnations should be ready for potting on into 5-in. pots, and as poinsettias finish their display they should be cut down to half their present height and kept dry until the end of June when they should be started into growth again to produce material from which cuttings can be made.

As hippeastrums finish flowering the flower stems should be cut down to just above the bulbs. The leaves are now beginning to grow and it is time for regular watering and for feeding once a week with liquid or soluble fertiliser. Cyclamen should be ready for potting into 3- or possibly 4-in. pots.

Sow seeds of *Primula obconica, P. sinensis, P. kewensis,* impatiens, *Solanun capsicastrum, Asparagus sprengeri* and *A. plumosus.* Start watering cacti and succulents again after keeping them dry in the winter. Chrysanthemums raised from cuttings in January will be ready for stopping. Repot cymbidiums when they have finished flowering if they have been in the same pots for a number of years. The same applies to paphiopedilums.

Strawberries in pots will need feeding as they come into flower, and the flowers need thinning to reduce them to not more than 10 on each plant.

APRIL

This is yet another busy month in the greenhouse when the plants are growing rapidly. Many of the bedding plants are ready for moving out into the garden frame. Sow seed of cucumber and melon for greenhouse or frame cultivation.

Cuttings of fuchsias and pelargoniums root and grow on readily at this time of year. Many plants such as chrysanthemums will now be filling their pots with roots and need moving on into larger pots. Over-wintered hydrangeas can be brought into the warmth to start them into growth. Non-flowering shoots from these can be used as cuttings. These will make good plants for twelve months hence.

Cut back Maidenhair Ferns now and divide and repot them. Pot on other ferns and generally clean them up. Make sowings of *Asparagus sprengeri* and *A. plumosus* if this was not done last month. Plant out tomatoes in the greenhouse, as soon as the first flower buds appear.

MAY

Again, this is a busy month. Plant tomatoes in the greenhouse if this was not done in April. Also, plant cucumbers and melons in the greenhouse or garden frame.

Many more plants that have been raised for use in the garden will now be ready for gradually hardening off, these being moved first to the garden frame and then to a sheltered place out of doors before planting in beds or borders.

Seeds to sow this month include those of cinerarias, calceolarias and *Primula malacoides*; and *Asparagus sprengeri* and *A. plumosus* if this was not done earlier. Thin out the fruits on peaches and tie in the growths. More hydrangea cuttings can be taken and those rooted in April can be potted in 3½-in. pots.

Spray and fumigate regularly to keep all plants free of pests and diseases.

JUNE

Jobs this month include the final potting of chrysanthemums and cyclamen. Pot on many other plants before they become starved in their present pots. Begin to feed plants, particularly those growing in hanging baskets, using liquid or soluble fertiliser added to the normal water supply. Many plants will need the support of stakes now, and this should be attended to.

On warm days both the top and side ventilators should be kept open as well as the door, and shading should be provided for such plants as begonias, gloxinias and streptocarpus.

Sow cyclamen seed now. I like to allow at least 15 to 18 months between seed sowing and the production of flowering plants. Calceolaria and cineraria seedlings will need pricking out into boxes.

Plants such as *Azalea indica*, primulas and camellias should be stood outside. These will need regular watering and feeding to ensure that they develop into good flowering plants for the following season. Arum Lilies should be dried off and rested by laying the pots on their sides in a sheltered spot outside.

JULY

This is the time when the well stocked greenhouse is filled with many exotic flowers. Chrysanthemums, which are now outside for the summer, need staking and tying and later in the month a programme of feeding should be started.

The later-flowering chrysanthemums are now ready for their final stopping. Pot perpetual-flowering carnations into their final pots. Continue to water and feed hippeastrums to build up strong bulbs for flowering next winter and spring. Prick out cyclamen seedlings as necessary. Some seed may take a long time to germinate, so do not discard the seed pan until enough seedlings for one's requirements have appeared.

Cucumbers and melons need regular stopping and tying and some of the melons will be ready for pollinating. Tomatoes need feeding and watering, side-shooting and spraying over with water on bright days to assist pollination and the setting of fruit.

Specimens of *Solanum capsicastrum* should be ready by now for potting into 5- or 6-in. pots. If these plants are then plunged out of doors they will set berries much better than if kept inside. Start cyclamen corms into growth again by watering carefully and spraying lightly overhead to encourage the development of new shoots.

Now is the time to begin taking cuttings of Regal and Zonal pelargoniums, fuchsias, coleus and other plants which are to be kept through the winter:

AUGUST

It is now time to sow seeds of schizanthus and mignonette, and there is still time to sow seed of cyclamen. Make sure that hanging baskets are well supplied with water and that the plants are fed regularly to keep them growing and flowering well on into the autumn.

Climbing plants along the walls and sides of the greenhouse need regular tying in and some cutting back to prevent them keeping the light off other plants.

Cinerarias are ready for potting into $3\frac{1}{2}$-in. pots, these being placed in the garden frame with shade from the sun. Calceolarias, too, should be ready for potting up in 3-in. pots.

SEPTEMBER

Out of doors we now begin to see signs of autumn and it is time to start planting bulbs of specially prepared hyacinths and Paper White and Grand Soleil d'Or narcissi for flowering in time for Christmas and early in the new year.

More cuttings of pelargoniums can be taken now if they are needed. If it is intended to sow annuals such as clarkia, annual carnations, larkspur, salpiglossis and Sweet Scabious for flowering in the greenhouse in spring this is the time that seeds should go in. Pot schizanthus seedlings into $3\frac{1}{2}$-in. pots.

As the buds form on chrysanthemums they must be brought inside, and this must be done before the first autumn frosts arrive. These plants will also need disbudding.

Plants such as *Azalea indica, Solanum capsicastrum,* cyclamen, primulas, cinerarias and freesias which have been stood outside for the summer will also need bringing in. Do not forget to feed these plants at regular intervals. Cyclamen and primulas should have the first flower buds removed to build up the strength of the plants. I like to have my first cyclamen blooms towards the end of October.

OCTOBER

The greenhouse will probably now be packed to capacity with chrysanthemums and other plants which have been brought inside. Keep a careful watch on the temperature and turn some heat on at night if there are forecasts of frost. This will keep the air circulating, which is good for the plants, as well as keep out the frost. Fumigate to keep the plants free from pests and diseases and use the ventilators with care.

During the early part of the month pot the remainder of the pre-cooled daffodils which will be in flower before Christmas. Hydrangeas will need potting into 7-in. pots and calceolarias and cinerarias can be moved to 5-in. pots.

Reduce the supplies of water to hippeastrums, begonias, gloxinias and streptocarpus which will soon be resting for the winter. From now on all watering must be done much more carefully for a dryish atmosphere is necessary if trouble from botrytis is to be avoided.

NOVEMBER

Late-flowering chrysanthemums will now be at their best. This is the time to insert cuttings of perpetual-flowering carnations. Rooted cuttings of fuchsias and pelargoniums need potting into 3- or $3\frac{1}{2}$-in. pots, and plants at a more advanced stage into 5- or 6-in. pots.

Large fuchsias should have their water supplies reduced because they will be resting during the winter. Reduce, too, the amount of water given to cacti and succulents.

Make a sowing of lettuce seed to provide plants to grow on when the chrysanthemums no longer need greenhouse space, or for planting in the garden frame. Pot on schizanthuses as necessary into their 5-in. pots.

DECEMBER

The darkest month of the year, and it is necessary to be even more careful with the watering and doubly so with the ventilation. The bulbous flowers must be brought into the greenhouse to encourage more rapid growth and get them into flower for Christmas. This applies to pre-cooled daffodils, specially prepared hyacinths, Roman hyacinths and Paper White and Grand Soleil d'Or narcissi. Lorraine begonias will now be needing canes to support their stems and flowers.

As the chrysanthemums finish flowering cut the stems down to within 9 in. of soil level. I find it best to shake the soil from the roots and put them close together in boxes where they take up much less room. These are kept to provide material for cuttings in January and February.

Freesias will be coming into flower and twiggy sticks should be pushed in between the plants to support them.

Index

Abbreviation: p = photograph or line drawing